UNEASY PARTNERS

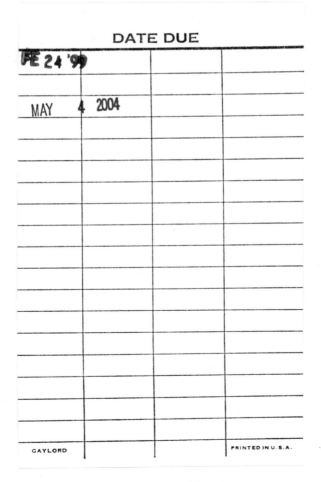

THE AMERICAN MOMENT
Stanley I. Kutler, Series Editor

Uneasy Partners

BIG BUSINESS IN AMERICAN POLITICS, 1945–1990

Kim McQuaid

The Johns Hopkins University Press
Baltimore and London

© 1994 The Johns Hopkins University Press
All rights reserved
Printed in the United States of America on acid-free paper

The Johns Hopkins University Press
2715 North Charles Street
Baltimore, Maryland 21218-4319
The Johns Hopkins Press Ltd., London

Library of Congress Cataloging-in-Publication Data will be found at the end of this book.

A catalog record for this book is available from the British Library.

*For the quietly capable people with whom I've trekked
the High Arctic wilderness of Canada and the United States*

CONTENTS

FOREWORD

The partnership between government and business lies at the heart of the history of political economy in the United States. Yet it is little known and widely misunderstood. The tight entanglement between government and business usually is portrayed as a development of relatively recent history and is traced to the Depression, World War II, and the Cold War. The modern state of affairs is juxtaposed as a rejection of an idyllic day of laissez-faire, when businessmen made their decisions without the intervention of government, which essentially provided for the common defense and sold postage stamps.

Laissez-faire is the most tenacious, yet the most tenuous, of myths. In fact, the mutually beneficial and dependent relationship between government and business has pervaded American history since the colonial founding. It is exemplified by Alexander Hamilton's state policy of increasing "the ligaments" between government and business, a policy predicated on the belief that a meaningful "pursuit of a common interest" for prosperity required effective government. We readily narrate and analyze our political and social history, yet we largely neglect economic relationships and their effects on the nation's political and social structure.

The popular imagery simplistically projects government and business as ideological combatants locked in ceaseless struggle; in reality large doses of cooperation and the recognition of mutual need dominate conflict in the relationship. As Kim McQuaid notes in this fascinating account of that relationship, "It is by the interaction of these two dominant forces in our society that much of the economic and political present has come to exist."

Yet political rhetoric and manipulation of symbols clash with that reality. Businessman H. Ross Perot, for example, amassed his fortune in the 1960s through government contracts that seeded, nourished, and expanded his "private enterprise." Ironically, Perot later grounded his political ambitions in assaults on an excessive, inefficient, interventionist government, which he promised to shrink to some manageable proportions. But Perot never advanced any programmatic scheme to diminish the governmental role in stimulating and supporting private enterprise.

The relationship of government and business is mired in myths that largely reinforce the notion of mutual hostility. McQuaid effectively dissolves the picture of relentless conflict. He also usefully describes a symbiotic relationship that varies and sometimes overlaps with such characteristics as parasitic, mutually beneficial, or commensual. Varied and complex, indeed, is the story; what is more, it is a story that is vital for understanding the dominant forces in our lives.

Stanley I Kutler
The University of Wisconsin

PREFACE

"It ain't what a man don't know that makes him a fool," humorist Josh Billings observed over a century ago, "but what he knows that ain't so." John F. Kennedy cast the same concept in presidential idiom in 1962: "The great enemy of truth is very often not the lie—deliberate, contrived, and dishonest—but the myth—persistent, persuasive, and unrealistic."

This book sets out to inform myths, myths about the interactions between big business and the federal government in modern America. It is a book about the ecology of power, about the varied relations between the two most important political and economic actors in our society today. I argue that ideology and reality in the United States often are not well integrated and that ideology too often blinds us to what reality is.

Big business and the federal government in modern America are like two people who have been living together much longer than either cares to admit. They are not married, and they never will be, but they maintain a close, symbiotic relation because they need each other. Government needs business to make and to implement investment, output, employment, trade, and lending decisions, both domestically and internationally, that government is ill equipped to make and implement given America's traditions of federalism, delegated powers, and state minimalism. Business, for its part, needs government to organize, referee, underwrite, and subsidize trade to trade's advantage, particularly in periods when corporate selfregulation means little regulation at all. There is, necessarily, a politics of business in this country and, likewise, a business of politics.

Politicians are businessmen, and businessmen politicians—not because of abstract desires but because of concrete requirements. Corporations of various kinds, for instance, regularly desire Washington to be a financier, investor, subsidizer, financial guarantor, lawgiver, regulator, and international trade promoter of last resort. A tour through the pages of any major American newspaper of 1991 makes the point. Varied financial interest groups hotly disputed precisely how the federal government should continue with a gargantuan government bailout of half the savings and loan associations and more than a few of the banks in the country, an unprecedented exercise in economic salvation that would cost taxpayers $500 billion over the next thirty years. Political discussion regarding what, precisely, America should or shouldn't do to forward peace in the Middle East after the successful conclusion of the Gulf War against Iraq in 1990–91 was conditioned, throughout, by the fact of growing American dependence upon imported petroleum and the perceived need to protect U.S. and Allied access to strategic petroleum producers, including Saudi Arabia and Kuwait. Over half a million U.S. soldiers made these debates very much more than academic.

Also among the headlines were foreign trade negotiations with Japan, the European Community, Canada, and Mexico. Then there were defense industry reorganizations mandated by the purchasing and technology requirements of the Department of Defense and the military services. Continued airline deregulation to assist market competition and lower fares between major cities versus reregulation to forward passenger safety and the interests of smaller population centers was another hardy issue. As economists squabbled furiously about what economic indicators meant in terms of how long or severe the recession might be, many an economic eye strayed to ponder the import of Federal Reserve monetary policies and their probable effects on interest rates and economic growth. Even peanut farmers put in an appearance, as Congress debated continuing production licensing and tariff protections first instituted on behalf of this segment of U.S. agriculture fifty years before.

Examples of a mixed system of public and private power in contemporary America are legion. In policy arenas as diverse as health insurance standards for working-age Americans and drilling by private oil companies on the Arctic National Wildlife Reserve in northern Alaska, "private" and "public" sectors are intimately related. Business—in particular, big business—and government in America are not separate universes; they can't be, any more than two blades of a pair of scissors can. It is by the interaction of these two dominant forces in our society that much of the economic and political present has come to exist. Corporations are more independent of central state control in the United States than they are in almost all other major developed capitalist economies, and they shall remain so. But relative independence is not separation, nor has it been throughout the twentieth century.

Scholars know this. They know, too, that most major political issues in modern America have enduring economic dimensions and that resolving these issues have put businessmen and politicians in contact, in conflict, or in cooperation with one another on a regular and continuing basis. The question for these analysts has not been whether big business and big government are connected but how and why.

The concept of symbiosis can clarify political phenomena and the varied theories with which thinkers from many disciplines have tried to explain them. *Symbiosis*, simply put, is a biologist's way of talking about the intimate living together of two dissimilar organisms. Such interdependence comes in different forms. One type is *parasitic*, in which one life form benefits at another's expense; a tapeworm in an animal's digestive system is a common example. A politic analogue to parasitism is the capture of part of the public sector by a component of the private sector, for instance, an industry dominating a regulatory agency either to protect itself from laws it doesn't like or to profit from government controls it has called into being.

Symbiosis need not be parasitic, however. It can also be what biologists call *mutualism*, or mutually beneficial to both parties. Birds, for instance, clean ticks off the hides of grazing animals, and ants protect aphids in return for their milk. Political examples of mutualism are a recycling company benefiting from environmental laws and a solar energy firm receiving government support for R&D, both of which will help the United States become either less wasteful of resources or less dependent upon nuclear power or petroleum imports.

A third form of symbiosis is *commensualism*. Here, one organism obtains benefits from another without damaging it. Think of the remora and its relation to the shark. The remora dines on leftovers from the shark's kills, then hitches a ride to the next meal. Political examples of commensualism include operation standards that federal agencies like the National Transportation Safety Board assist private companies with. Whenever large commercial airliners crash, Safety Board inspectors arrive to sift through debris, locate the government-mandated cockpit voice recorders, and reconstruct what went wrong, so that private firms can avoid repeating such accidents. Government is not penalized by providing this public service; and airlines, airplane manufacturers, and air travelers all benefit from reduced risks.

All three types of symbiosis occur in the biological world, and all have political analogues. Relations between corporations and the state can be parasitic, mutually beneficial, or commensual. Used carefully, the concept of symbiosis can clarify the mixed system of public and private power in which we live. Precise definitions, however, very often depend upon precise circumstances and upon who is doing the defining. Military contracting, for example, can be lauded as mutually beneficial or derided as parasitism. Tariffs, public utility pricing, affirmative action regulations, worker health and safety rules, and hosts of other connections between public and private sectors regularly elicit as much heat as light in academic debates. Analysts have plenty of theories about what they believe the right relation between business and government should be. And theories, especially if applied universally, have a very nasty habit of hardening into the realities those models were designed to help explain.

In few other historical areas is this problem more acute than in analyses of corporate and political power in modern America. Marxists, New Leftists, and some power elite thinkers make claims for parasitism, pluralist political scientists see this power as mutualism and commensualism, while New Right and libertarian scholars reverse the parasitic emphasis favored by the left, and instead of big business exploiting the people, it is government exploiting entrepreneurs and popular majorities.

Marxists, New Leftists, power elitists, pluralists, neopluralists, conservatives, neoconservatives, neoliberals, libertarians, and others, then, hardly lack for models, many of which will have influenced the assumptions or habits of mind of teachers and students using this volume. This book, however, has a historical purpose. It aims not to apply one model to everything but to test various models in historic circumstances—all to enlighten theory and to restrain it from turning into a morality play featuring heartless plutocrats, a monster state, or libertarian laissez-faire.

Throughout this volume, the often elastic terms *big*, *medium*, and *small* business are defined in relation to the total number of workers employed in a business. A "small" business, therefore, is any firm employing fewer than 500 people; a "medium-sized" business employs between 500 and 10,000 workers; a "big" business employs more than 10,000 people. These definitions apply to all years after 1920.

What follows surveys patterns of continuity and change in big business–government relations in the United States during the past half century. The book aims to analyze data without the myths. To assist the reader to make a wider investigation, a bibliographical essay follows the text.

UNEASY PARTNERS

PROLOGUE: AUGUST 1945

It is August 14, 1945. The end of the mightiest and most brutal war in human history has come at last. A mysterious atomic bomb has just compelled Japan, the last aggressor nation, to surrender. As night falls on crowds celebrating on the streets of New York City, a sixty-year-old president of a major U.S. corporation sits quietly at his desk pondering the history he has seen. The America he was born into in 1885 flickers like a dimly remembered dream. It was the country of Mark Twain's *Huckleberry Finn*, published only the year before his birth—a nation of horses and wagons and of a vivid new technology called the telephone, just put into service between the cities of Boston and New York. Electric lighting had only recently been invented. The "new immigration" from southern and eastern Europe had only just begun in its strange and earnest millions. And the Washington Monument in the nation's capital had just been completed after half a century of effort.

The 1880s and 1890s, however, were fine years to be young. Newly invented or newly standardized sports were everywhere: baseball, football, basketball, golf, bowling, all with their nationally known athletes to hero-worship. There were cheap, safe, modern bicycles to ride, some made out of a novel metal called aluminum. Teddy bears, ice cream parlors, and newspaper comic strips had all come into being by the time our businessman entered puberty—along with Franklin Delano Roosevelt, Harry S Truman, and Dwight David Eisenhower. Streetcars hummed and clattered to new "sub-urban" communities, powered by new electric motors. It had, nevertheless, seemed a simpler, less driven, world then—before skyscrapers and Freudian psychology, automobiles and airplanes. He vividly remembers his first glimpses of a Model T and a Curtiss biplane, for Henry Ford had built his first commercial motorcar and the Wright brothers had flown at Kitty Hawk in 1903, the year of the first World Series and the year the businessman had graduated from high school at age eighteen.

Not, of course, that many of his peers had put on academic caps and gowns to march to Sir Edward Elgar's just-composed "Pomp and Circumstance." Few stayed in school that long: only 6.5 percent of seventeen-year-old Americans had finished high school in 1903, in fact. But the businessman was one of the fortunate ones. His parents had seen to that. They'd subscribed to new mass-circulation magazines and made sure he used the new free public libraries that philanthropists like steel maker Andrew Carnegie were building throughout the land and that helped him to dream dreams of bigger, wider worlds.

Achieving dreams required education. Again, hopes and fortunes had coincided. He'd left home for Boston to attend the Massachusetts Institute of Technology. MIT was only forty years old then, a new sort of school for a new sort of age: an engineering school in an era of new "scientific management" doctrines. Scientific management provided gospels of efficiency by which manufacturing processes could be measured, gauged, modified, and understood and by which labor and managerial productivity could be improved, further advanced, and then improved again. Informal, artisanal, factory folkways were replaced. The reign of rules succeeded the reign of people.

Single-owner industrial capitalism began to be superseded by multiple-owner managerial capitalism and functionally specialized corporate hierarchies. Time and motion study was central to the scientific, technological, and administrative evolution, as were innovations as seemingly mundane as the routing slip, the organization chart, and the punch card. The new breed of national and international corporations were vertically and horizontally integrated: high-technology giants like General Electric and US Steel were both created during a turn-of-the-century merger wave that occurred just as the young engineer made his decision to hitch his star to the technical future of his age.

Four years at MIT paid off handsomely. The relation between engineering and business became obvious as new machines and production processes cascaded into the factories, farms, offices, and emerging mass-distribution outlets of the nation. New science-based industries made scientific and technological training an increasingly necessary requirement for the effective administration of anything: to mass produce automobiles on assembly lines like those pioneered by Ford Motor Company in 1914, to design, build, and market airplanes, to refine the petrochemicals needed to keep airplanes and automobiles running, or to complete the Panama Canal, the largest construction project America's federal government had ever undertaken. Engineers were so essential that two-thirds of all engineering school graduates from 1884 to 1924 became corporate managers within fifteen years. In the 1920s, the heads of four of the largest corporations in America and the world—General Motors, General Electric, DuPont, and

Goodyear Rubber—had been classmates at MIT a quarter of a century before.

Our businessman had been part of that shift in the basis of power and authority in the new scientific and technical age. He had risen in the ranks of corporate management, as had most of his MIT classmates—men like Alfred P. Sloan of General Motors, Gerard Swope of General Electric, and Pierre S. DuPont of DuPont. He was fifteen years old as the new century began and only sixteen when Theodore Roosevelt used his "bully pulpit" for an activist presidency after the assassination of William McKinley, the last Civil War veteran to occupy the White House. By the time Woodrow Wilson led America into World War I a decade and a half later, however, our engineer was thirty-two, romanced and married and settled into the affairs of family and career. He was helping change the nature of the industrial world, whose largest two or three hundred firms were accumulating nearly half the total manufacturing assets of the nation.

There were dark sides to this industrial world and to the burst of scientific, technological, and administrative innovation that combined to turn the United States into the premier economic power on earth in the half century between the end of the Civil War and 1917. Machine guns, flame throwers, submarines, tanks, and poison gases were only some of them: 25 million human lives were snuffed out during World War I. But the United States was spared the worst of it; its territory remained inviolate, and its combat casualties totaled only 116,000 dead and 204,000 wounded in a nation of just over 100 million people.

What was general and unrestricted were the possibilities of ever widening affluence. And what possibilities they were—the golden era of the 1920s, or so it later seemed. It seemed nothing very important could ever go wrong with American capitalism: modern business enterprise had come of age, manufacturing output and productivity set impressive standards, and the leaders of the largest and most innovative corporations were accorded regal status. "The man who builds a factory builds a temple," Republican President Calvin Coolidge said, and "the man who works there worships there." He'd meant every tersely adulatory word. Just as the Democrats had meant business when they nominated John W. Davis, a prominent Wall Street lawyer with House of Morgan connections, as their unsuccessful candidate against Coolidge in 1924.

For our businessman, to be in his thirties and ascending the corporate ladder in the 1920s was very heaven. He'd succeeded better than he realized—well enough, anyway, to survive the desperate decade following the stock market crash of 1929. Thinking about those Great Depression years was cheerless: 40 percent of U.S. banks went bankrupt in only four years; 30 percent of savings deposits disappeared. A quarter and more of the labor force was unemployed. Manufacturing output halved in three years. Bread lines, homeless wanderers, and cardboard slums proliferated. Prime interest rates eventually fell to one-tenth their 1920s peak. It was an encyclopedia of disaster.

Labor unions added infuriating variations on dismal Depression era themes. A minor chord in American corporate life swelled into an angry symphony. Only one year after the businessman's birth in 1885, modern unions were born when locally based craft alliances began a loose-knit national cooperation via the American Federation of Labor (AFL)—because the firms that craftsmen more and more worked for were becoming nationwide in their economic operations. The AFL began with only 400,000 members, but its member unions' members increased ten times by the end of World War I.

Thirty years of advance, however, was followed by twenty years of stasis and decay. As the 1930s began, only seven of every hundred workers were union members. Powerful craft unions existed in relatively decentralized trades like construction, where firms remained local and where artisanal skills were high. But craft-based organizing proved far less successful in the new technology-intensive mass production industries, where highly skilled workers were rare and where semiskilled workers laboring in scientifically managed factories were a norm. A skilled-only approach to labor organizing had reached the end of the line. Since artisans were a progressively smaller percentage of the labor force, craft unions could rarely wage successful strikes against huge agglomerations of corporate power. Accordingly, managers of large and technologically innovative firms making new goods via novel production techniques did not worry much about unions.

All that changed in 1935. Fifty years after the AFL's birth, a fundamental principle of union organization was transformed: a new breed of union leader began enrolling *all* the workers in a mass production industry into an industrial union, which represented everybody from janitors to craftsmen. Unionism was redefined. The Congress of Industrial Organizations (CIO) was created in November 1935 to champion the new unionism, despite feral opposition from the standpat hierarchy of the AFL.

The new industrial unions became dangerous organizational opponents to capital. Hard-fought CIO organizing drives in nonunion industries like automobiles, steel, rubber, petroleum refining, and electrical manufacturing were bad enough, but things got worse for it in 1935 with the passage of the National Labor Relations (or Wagner) Act, which put federal enforcement power behind industrial workers' rights to organize and bargain collectively via representatives of their own choosing. Through this act, Washington set minimum labor standards for high-technology industry: independent industrial unions had a legal right to exist and a mandate to grow, and the National Labor Relations Board (NLRB) made Wagner Act guarantees real. The NLRB conducted representation elections based on formulas of majority rule and winner take all. Employer intimidation, delay, and union busting were often declared illegal. Employer-dominated "company unions" representing all workers in a plant could no longer be substituted for AFL or CIO unions without workers' consent.

It had been a frustrating time, the businessman recalls. Unions weren't part of the Depression you could ignore. You didn't glimpse them briefly through train windows on your way to work. Unions were there in your plant when you got to your office every day, and they weren't going away. "Communism and revolution," plenty of businessmen had called it. And even when managerial attitudes toward unions and labor legislation were less horrified, strike numbers said it all: 640 in 1930, 4,750 seven years later. AFL and CIO leaders and organizers were at each other's throats. Businessmen—and especially big businessmen—were blamed for every protracted economic catastrophe. Union numbers more than doubled, to 8 million (14.5 percent of the labor force), in only eight years. Almost 10 percent of all workers first joined unions in the single decade of the 1930s.

All the major industries that had successfully avoided unions now had to deal with them. It was infuriating, sometimes, particularly when genuine radicals, who hated you as a capitalist to begin with, got involved. Sit-down strikes and communists got headlines; high-technology industry was equated with ruthless class exploitation; occasional speeches about "economic royalists" even emanated from the New Deal administration in Washington. The heroes of the 1920s became the villains of the 1930s. Electoral disasters occurred for the national Republican party: only 89 Republican congressmen and a pitiful 16 GOP senators were left after the 1936 elections to face 331 Democrats in the House and 76 Democrats in the Senate. Alfred M. Landon lost the presidential race to Franklin D. Roosevelt that same year by over 10 million votes. There was concern that America was abandoning the party that had made it great and that free enterprise and political liberty were both at risk.

Meanwhile, federal power proliferated. Time was when Washington did little for anybody—our businessman well remembers that time. Most of the United States west of Kansas hadn't even been organized into states when he was born in 1885, not North or South Dakota, Montana, Washington, Oklahoma; not Idaho, Wyoming, or Utah; certainly not Arizona, New Mexico, or Nevada. At that time, Washington basically delivered the mails, gave away public lands, and fought the occasional Indian war on the plains. It also paid pensions to war veterans and their survivors, if they hadn't fought for the Confederacy. That was about all it did. States, localities, and private groups—including business corporations—did the rest, just as they always had. Washington hadn't even created laws regulating modern corporations until 1887 and 1890 with the Interstate Commerce Act and Sherman Antitrust Act.

When our businessman was six years old, in 1891, federal civilian employees in a land of 63 million totaled 157,000: one for every 4,000 inhabitants, and 60 percent of these bureaucrats worked for a single agency, the U.S. Post Office, and were scattered in 64,000 localities. In the same year, one large American corporation, the Pennsylvania Railroad, employed 110,000 nationally. As late as 1929, all the federal civilian employees located in Washington did not add up to the total work forces of major U.S. firms such as General Motors, US Steel, or Standard Oil of New Jersey. In that same year, 96 percent of all federal welfare expenditures went to war veterans. Washington was spending 25 cents per person for all civilian social welfare—up from 9 cents per person in 1919. It was not until 1935, 160 years after the Declaration of Independence, that the U.S. government created Social Security cards, the first place of distinctly federal identification gradually required of all adult citizens. As late as 1940, America's army, although bigger than Bulgaria's, was smaller than Portugal's. Only American naval power enrolled it among the military great and mighty of the earth.

Not until the Great Depression and the New Deal did traditions of federal minimalism finally begin to change. In 1930, 600,000 federal civilians spent $3 billion. But then fear, want, and panic following economic catastrophe pushed Washington to become the peacetime guarantor of last resort for powerful political groups in ways it had never attempted before. By 1940, a million federal employees were spending $10 billion a year: triple the 1930 level. Farmers, the elderly, the unemployed, businessmen, industrial workers, and financiers all demanded ad hoc intervention. Washington taxed more, spent more, purchased more, regulated more, guaranteed more, subsidized more, loaned more, and required more in the way of minimum economic standards. It became a primary national economic coordinating center in hitherto unknown ways. All this transformed business-government relations.

Supply (or investment) changes came first. Almost the first official act of the New Deal was to temporarily close all the banks. Shortly thereafter, the national treasury underwrote bank savings deposits to stop financial panic, rescue capital markets, lower interest rates, and encourage greater private investment. In the process, Washington also guaranteed the debts of the owners of firms throughout the commercial banking industry in the event their firms went bankrupt. It did this via new emergency institutions such as the Federal Deposit Insurance Corporation (FDIC). In return for such unique federal protection, most commercial bankers had to accept unwelcome federal regulations on how they organized and conducted their business and on how they made loans. Investment banks, for instance, could no longer engage in commercial banking.

Bankers' ability to make profitable loans, however, depended upon the overall health and profitability of the economy, and during the Depression there were often few profits to be had. Private financial institutions hesitated to invest. The federal government, therefore, entered financial markets as investor of last resort for firms that couldn't get loans on any but pariah terms from private banks. Key, here, were the operations of the Reconstruction Finance Corporation (or RFC), an emergency agency created by President Herbert Hoover in 1931 and vastly expanded under Roosevelt. The RFC made tens of billions of dollars worth of long-term loans and other investments during Roosevelt's presidency, and it made them cheap. In the process, it rescued many hard-hit companies in important high-fixed-cost industries, including banking, railroading, and electricity generation.

Washington made investments in still another way: it built public works. Here, it did not seek to prop up the private sector; it replaced it. Federal officials did things that private companies weren't going to do themselves because they couldn't make private profits on the exercise. Post office construction was traditional; so was road building and the improvement of national parks. City and state governments got federal money for buildings, roads, sewers, water supplies, and parks. Immense belts of trees were planted to halt desertification in the semiarid West. Slums were cleared and housing rehabilitated. Mammoth federal projects to improve river navigation and harbors were begun; hundreds of dams were built. The scope and scale of this building dwarfed anything the country had ever seen in peacetime since the Panama Canal. For instance the Tennessee Valley Authority, or TVA, a huge flood control and electricity generation system spanning half a dozen states, put a federal agency in economic competition (actual or potential) with many of the same southern public utilities that benefited from RFC's loans.

Scope and scale were important in other ways. To build huge public projects like the TVA, Washington became an employer of last resort. It paid millions of people to plant trees, build dams, install electric generators, pave streets, and construct post offices. In the process of doing all this and more besides, it also entered the demand-side (or consumption side) of the economy in hitherto unknown ways. Washington had always paid people to build or do things in wartime; that's what central governments, soldiering, and war contracting are traditionally all about. But wars had been few, small, and short since 1865. Peacetime had always been different.

No longer. Throughout the domestic phase of the New Deal, Washington together with the states paid the wages of as much as 10 percent of the civilian work force, and 20 percent of all New Deal spending went for employment. People were paid to do many untraditional things. Students received money to stay in school and out of the unemployment-ridden labor force. People raked leaves in public parks. Artists painted murals in public buildings. Writers wrote travel guides to all the states and territories of the nation. Actors, actresses, and playwrights were even paid to participate in the short-lived Federal Theatre Project. Democratic politicians did well by doing good, sometimes favoring their political friends with jobs which Republicans equated with flagrant vote buying.

It was all a bit much, recalls the businessman: there were new federal programs for new political constituencies, groups FDR and the Democrats were molding into a diverse political alliance of southern whites, northern blacks, urban ethnics, unionized workers, and others of a kind never before seen. Worse, Democratic strategy worked at the polls, realigning political power in Depression America. Meanwhile, still other policy changes affected the sickly U.S. economy, changes that alienated and confused businessmen ideologically unprepared for them. There were more federal minimum standards laws, unprecedented federal social insurance laws, new federal-state welfare programs, and new federal price support programs, variously established to improve the economic conditions of needy or powerful groups demanding protections from the risks of free enterprise.

Economic interventions occurred quickest in agriculture, since the constitution's two-senators-per-state rule gave rural states disproportionate congressional clout. Farmers and farmers' organizations had sought Washington's help in avoiding boom-bust cycles in agriculture for forty years. Agrarians most particularly concerned were larger wheat, cotton, corn, dairy, and tobacco producers specializing in one often-used (or staple) commodity for distant markets, both national and international. These very commercial agrarians wanted a New Deal in agriculture that transformed the federal government into the buyer of last resort for their crops whenever market conditions didn't allow them to recover their costs of production. They also wanted Washington to pay for storing those crops, and to allow farmers to buy them back later and sell them themselves when prices rose.

Organized agriculture was amenable to Washington indirectly limiting output of key staples via acreage allotments as a means of boosting prices. They accepted a trade-off between production restraints and price supports. They wanted Washington to further decrease farm output and boost prices by paying farmers to take marginal land out of cultivation entirely by creating tree farms and soil bank conservation programs. They wanted the federal government to become a lender of last resort to financially failing farmers via a system of RFC-style farmers' banks, which would refinance massive numbers of rural mortgages at below market rates. They wanted a multitude of federal subsidies for as many as half the farmers in the country. And they got them all—first, and temporarily, in 1933 and again, and permanently, in 1935. It helped that food, like money, was not just another industry. Agriculture, like banking and finance, was a precondition of all other industries.

The same logic applied to energy. Oil and coal producers, moreover, were uncomfortably like boom-bust farmers mass producing one commodity. They couldn't successfully limit their total output, boost prices, and avoid bankruptcy without government help. Oil and coal producers, therefore, did precisely what powerful agricultural interests did. They deluged Washington and state capitals with demands that government help them increase prices by enforcing cutbacks in overall output and by creating output quotas for individual producers. Both types of energy producers succeeded—coal only temporarily but oil far more permanently. By 1935, for instance, governments of all major oil-producing states set and enforced production quotas for their producers. The federal government, via the Connally "Hot Oil" Act, prohibited interstate transportation of any petroleum produced in violation of state quotas. Here was business-government symbiosis with a vengeance.

State-orchestrated cartels, however, didn't work as well for other businessmen as they did for oilmen. Energy was the staple of an industrial economy; without it, business would die, just as without wheat and cotton most people would starve or freeze. The political logic of economically underwriting oil and key segments of agriculture by supply cutbacks and price supports, therefore, was inescapable. Industries outside of energy and agriculture were less essential, less familiar to voters, less united, less damaged by economic circumstances, and more suspect as major causes of or profiteers from the Depression. Business generally, therefore, was much less successful than farmers and oilmen at convincing politicians and the public to support (or tolerate) its efforts to restrict output, apportion production, and set prices.

The short unhappy life of the National Industrial Recovery Act (NIRA) from 1933 to 1935 illustrated the problem. What the New Deal did for farmers and oil producers NIRA also tried to do for all American industry. Businessmen were told that it was acceptable to form cartels to avoid economic destruction. Hundreds of national trade associations were to do the job for their industries, and the federal government was to guarantee and enforce their agreements and plans. Business had pressed FDR's predecessor, Herbert Hoover, since 1930 for quotas, output limits, and price-fixing, but most individual industries were far less politically powerful than big oil or commercial agriculture. Industries also often couldn't agree: small manufacturers fought large ones, competing and overlapping trades feuded, suppliers fought with their customers, producers with shippers. Price increases for some meant higher costs for others. Business, therefore, often spoke in a babble of tongues during the formative period of the NIRA. The political and economic costs of federal support for economywide cartelization were also much higher than those for farmers and oil producers.

To get the NIRA for a two-year trial, business was supposed to accept package deals: it was to allow employees to join trade unions, to accept federal public works jobs programs, and to abide by emergency national minimum wage, maximum hour, and anti-child-labor regulations. Big firms were not supposed to exploit smaller firms. The list of quid pro quos went on, the point being that the price for the NIRA for industry generally was relatively steep, much steeper than regulation was for oil producers and farming interests. Business paid the price, temporarily. But for the vast majority of smaller businesses, the package deals cost more than they did larger firms. The dissatisfaction of all businesses killed NIRA within two years.

Collective bargaining struggles show why NIRA died. NIRA's labor regulations hit industry much harder than they did favored Democratic constituencies like southern agriculture. Agriculture protected itself from unions by exempting agricultural laborers from NIRA's collective bargaining provisions. Wherever farm labor unions popped up, commercial farmers ruthlessly crushed them. Even the Wagner Act became law only after agricultural workers were exempted from its protections. NIRA's industrial minimum wage, maximum hour, and anti-child-labor provisions again carefully exempted farmers. Business, accordingly, felt exploited. It wanted cartels; it just didn't want to pay for the privilege of having them by allowing the unionization of its workers.

It wasn't only unions, of course. The whole failed package deal named the NIRA took place during a period in which Washington assumed its modern role as regulator and guarantor of last resort. Symbiosis replaced laissez-faire in key segments of the economy. Business primacy was contested, and few businessmen liked it. The year 1934 saw the first corporate revolts against the New Deal, but 1935 was the watershed. In this year the Wagner Act, the CIO, the TVA, and the Social Security Act were born. In 1935, the NIRA died, mostly unmourned. And in 1935, the Democrats tried (unsuccessfully), to levy higher tax rates on larger firms than on smaller firms and to increase taxes on inheritances and upper-income individuals.

Corporate reactions to Social Security, as to unions and wage and hour regulations, mixed ideology and economics. Social welfare cost money, tax money—new taxes that all big and medium-sized (though not very small) businesses had to pay. Farmers, like many very small businessmen, were exempt from the Social Security program. Conservative Democrats again wrote their favorite economic constituencies out of the expensive symbiotic reforms that liberal Democrats wanted, before helping liberals pass the legislation. Larger businessmen, mostly Republican, ended up paying most of the political and (especially) economic bills. Partisan irony was ferocious and expensive.

And Social Security was expensive. Most Americans saw Social Security as a simple piggy bank: they dropped money into the bank during their working lives, and they gradually got back the benefits of their mandatory prudence after they retired. Big business, however, knew that Social Security was much more than this. Employers, for instance, had to match employees' contributions to their retirement pension accounts: workers paid in 50 percent, companies paid the other 50 percent. This wasn't cheap for many firms strapped by the Depression. Employers, moreover, paid *all* the new taxes that funded unemployment insurance and unemployment benefits, another component of the political package of the Social Security legislation. Corporations also paid state and federal taxes to finance the benefits Social Security required states to pay to the jobless and to the already retired. Finally, more social charity was mandated for blind Americans and single mothers in other public welfare programs.

Social Security, then, was hardly a retirement annuity piggy bank. It was not private insurance, it was *social* insurance—it redistributed income.

Federal and state monies paid to the jobless or to the elderly ineligible for employment or old age insurance programs were not earned-right pensions, though many saw them as that. They were alms, social charity, that Washington and the states distributed on a never-before-seen scale.

Social Security's redeeming feature, however (the businessman shrugs), was that it had proved far better than the truly horrendous alternative— the 1930s Townsend Plan, by which $200 per month would be paid to every American over the age of sixty; financed by higher income or sales taxes. The cost of Social Security paled before the Townsend Plan and other universal dole proposals like it. Social insurance for retirement and unemployment was manageable for some firms, for his firm. But others were less fortunate. Their labor became more expensive to employ, on social insurance grounds, just as unions struggled to increase wages.

And there were more and more new federal economic rules to contend with, minimum standards laws, for example. These cost Washington nothing but cost business plenty. Such standards had supposedly died with the NIRA, but liberals counterattacked by passing the Fair Labor Standards Act (FLSA) in 1938. Now America had a nationwide minimum wage program, again conveniently exempting farmers and their conservative Democratic allies. Federal courts hadn't allowed state governments to enforce such mandates on business before the New Deal. Yet now Washington was to do so.

Economists were mostly appalled by minimum wage laws. So was the store owner from whom our businessman would buy his copies of the *Wall Street Journal* and the *New York Herald Tribune*. His corporation could afford to pay at least 40 cents an hour to all workers over sixteen years, but other firms couldn't. There were, after all, 9 million jobless and at least 12 million employed people earning less than 40 cents an hour in 1938, when the FLSA was passed. The barely literate fifteen-year-old who worked at the drugstore for 20 cents an hour to support his abandoned mother, the executive recalls, had lost his job by 1939. It was complicated, he admits. He'd sometimes been lucky to keep his company alive and not strikebound in the Depression. But so much had changed from the traditional days of church collections for the deserving poor, state hospitals for the retarded and mentally ill, and county poor farms.

War, when it came to America again in 1941, only made things more complicated. Now Washington *really* began to tax more, spend more, buy more, regulate more, guarantee more, subsidize more, and require more in the way of minimum standards. The peacetime New Deal had almost doubled the number of bureaucrats and nearly tripled Washington's annual budget. By August 1945 federal civilian employees had quadrupled over 1940, and Washington spent ten times as much. Four million wartime federal bureaucrats spent $100 billion a year on everything from paper clips to aircraft carriers to atomic bombs. On top of that, 12 million of 140 million Americans were in the military. One of every nine Americans worked in various ways for Uncle Sam, thirty times the 1930 number. Washington spent thirty-three times as much money in 1945 as it had in 1930. The mind reeled at changes like this, sometimes; it took getting used to.

Washington's physical growth illustrates the torrent of change. Before World War II, the city's only airport was Hoover Field, a single runway crossed by a county road with a traffic light on it to ensure that vehicles weren't on the landing strip when planes arrived or took off. Pilots kept their eyes sharp and used the only navigational aid then available, a wind sock nailed atop a nearby roller coaster. But Hoover Field is gone now. Washington National Airport, one of the largest, most up to date, and most used airports in the world, has replaced it. Where Hoover Field stood is now the site of the Pentagon, military headquarters of a global power and the largest office building on earth. It was completed in 1943.

Wartime Washington also buzzed with swarms of new civilian agencies. Modern war was a gigantic managerial job: Washington generated more official records during 1941–45 than it had in its previous 165-year history. The wartime inflation control agency alone consumed more paper annually than the whole federal government had before the war. Emergency authorities by the hundreds produced acronyms as fast as they consumed paper. Peacetime New Dealers had been called "alphabet soup" addicts, but World War II produced more new federal agencies than the 1930s ever had. The economic and technical requirements of war were immense—complicated, balkanized, and contentious.

Through the alphabet maze of wartime mobilization agencies, however, ran enduring threads of corporate expertise. War improved business's status after eleven lean years of the Depression. Patriotism meant production, and business understood production. War also accustomed business to expanded federal power, as the domestic economic reforms of the 1930s never had. During World War II corporate and political leaders undeniably needed one another—it was a matter of mutual survival; war was a struggle with an external enemy. Wartime industrial debates very often concerned dividing the gains of wartime prosperity, not apportioning the losses of the peacetime Depression. Corporate popularity rose, as over 17 million jobs were created during the war. Washington bought massive economic recovery by purchasing $2 billion a month in military goods just before the Pearl

Harbor attack. It placed a whopping $100 billion in war orders in the first six months after that. The federal government eventually spent $245 billion in five years: more than it spent between 1789 and 1940. By the end of the war, 60 percent of all manufacturing output went to the military: Washington had become the biggest customer American industry ever had.

Moreover, the customer was much better behaved now. The mammoth public works project called World War II was organized and administered in ways that convinced most skeptical business leaders that reform was dead as long as enemies were at the gates. FDR muzzled liberals and approved policies favoring big business producing desperately needed war goods. Corporate profits were guaranteed by cost-plus contracting. Profit margins on defense work weren't limited. Federal war managers renegotiated contracts to entice companies to produce more and faster. Efforts by liberal Democrats in Congress to end such deal making got nowhere. By 1943, corporate profits in America exceeded those of 1929, the affluent peak of the pre-Depression years.

Just as profits swelled with war, so did corporate investments. Private bankers finally got optimistic again. Financiers, too, combined profit and patriotism. One-third of the $25 billion invested in new defense production during wartime, in addition, came from Washington's lender of last resort, the RFC. About 85 percent of the $8.3 billion RFC provided to industry in five years was spent by an RFC affiliate, the Defense Plant Corporation, which paid private companies to build war plants and later leased these government-owned facilities to private firms at cut-rate prices for the duration of the war. During World War I, the private sector alone financed war plants; not so during World War II, especially in key industries such as aircraft, chemicals, steel, copper, aluminum, and shipbuilding. Critics grumbled. But the fact was that you didn't get companies to build new factories to create goods there were no clear postwar markets for without paying them up front to do so.

Symbiotic war capitalism like this added an impressive 10 percent to total wartime productive capacity without threatening large high-technology corporations. One hundred such big firms operated three-quarters of federally owned plants. Antitrust laws were suspended. Only in aluminum did RFC money finance the creation of a competitor to break a production monopoly enjoyed by the Aluminum Corporation of America (ALCOA). Chemicals also ran into trouble because DuPont and others had been involved before the war in international cartel arrangements with German companies, which affected frighteningly scarce war goods like synthetic rubber. War orders therefore went overwhelmingly to big firms. In 1939, firms with fewer than 500 employees had employed 52 percent of all manufacturing workers; five years later, they employed only 38 percent. Firms employing more than 10,000 people accounted for 13 percent of the manufacturing labor force in 1939, but 31 percent by 1944. Efforts to give smaller manufacturers a larger share of war contracts achieved little.

Some in Congress had muttered "conspiracy," the businessman recalls. But there was no conspiracy. Big businesses grew during war emergency because of their comparative economic, technological, and organizational advantages. They had most of the production stock. It was easier and faster for government officials to deal with one prime contractor for a product instead of many. Big firms were much more likely to have corporate research laboratories to develop new technologies quickly. They had large numbers of engineers and managers with experience in handling large and complicated projects. They had lines of credit with banks and thus could borrow large amounts of money relatively quickly and cheaply. And they had employees in Washington who heard about what government contracts were available before smaller businessmen did.

Nor was big business representation in Washington during the war a conspiracy. Again, necessity ruled. The production miracle that turned the United States into the "arsenal of democracy" and made it the source of half the total manufacturing output of the planet by 1945 was impossible without big business. Big business didn't seize this power, it was given it. Washington simply couldn't do the job without it.

Prewar federal bureaucrats had very rarely regulated the basic operations of any industry. Although the New Deal had intervened on the labor standards front often enough, except for the TVA it hadn't touched the central allocation and production powers that transformed a ton of iron ore into a locomotive or a tank or segments of an oil pipeline. The public sector simply didn't have the expertise to handle the enormous and complex jobs of administering transportation systems, steel mills, mines, chemical plants, aviation companies, auto factories, and banks. They had enough difficulty with the Manhattan Project and the atomic bomb, the businessman had heard. They had to drag university professors of physics and engineering into that effort wholesale. And though professors had designed the atomic bomb, hundreds of corporations turned these academic designs into terrible realities.

So big business was essential to national survival, so essential that he and other executives like him had been in Washington a lot during the war, running varied agencies that the peacetime federal bureaucracy often knew nothing about. A corporate government had, in effect, been erected on top of the political one. All this to get weapons built, people trained to use them, and vast economic and technical battles fought and won. This effort involved everything from building the first large cross-country oil pipelines, to denying global strategic commodities to enemy nations, to launching merchant ships at the rate of more than one a day.

It is something to be proud of, the businessman believes. Modern war was like an iceberg: for every visible aspect there were hidden immensities of production, purchasing, allocation, transportation, research and development, finance, and training. Without these, modern war couldn't be fought. Without these, there would be no victory to savor, this day in August 1945.

Still, the critics had droned on—about dollar-a-year men, for instance. Men like himself, who hadn't wanted to put their postwar careers with their companies and their current incomes from their companies at risk. OK, they hadn't preferred government pay to corporate pay. They became, instead, temporary federal bureaucrats (for a pro forma sum, to make the lawyers happy). Sure, their firms had profited from the war, but so had factory workers and farmers. In a capitalist country, you let people make money during war or they don't produce.

And just who, anyway, were labor leaders or disgruntled New Dealers to call businessmen like him selfish? Hadn't unions used their economic muscle in the very tight labor markets spawned by the war to push their total membership to 15 million by 1945? Wasn't this almost twice the number of only five years before, and wasn't it over 20 percent of the total labor force? If that wasn't angling for advantage, what was?

And what about the Democrats? Roosevelt is gone now, dead of a cerebral hemorrhage in April. But his successor, Harry Truman, is a broker and opportunist like FDR. He will bend to liberal winds if they start blowing again in earnest, just as Roosevelt had. A dying Roosevelt issued his "Economic Bill of Rights" message to Congress in January 1944, just before picking Truman as his new vice president. None of what he said boded well for the future: the right to a "useful and remunerative job," the right to earn "enough for adequate food and clothing and recreation," the right for farmers to enjoy a "decent living," freedom from "unfair competition and domination by monopolies at home and abroad," "rights" to decent homes for families, adequate medical care and good health, a good education, and "protection from the economic fears of old age, sickness, accident, and unemployment." It looks as though there are going to be lots of very expensive reform proposals around in Washington after the cheering stops.

It is not, then, a simply cheerful time, this August 14, 1945. As a manager, the businessman is paid to think about the future, and the immediate future looks as intimidating as reassuring. Will a renewed depression, for instance, follow the war? He has worried about that question for months.

But it is too late for all that now, long hours after President Truman announced Japan's surrender at 7 p.m. It is too late to worry about postwar depression, renewed New Dealism, and other dangers. The issues will still be there in the morning.

It is a long, long way back to the simpler world of his youth, the America of Huckleberry Finn, of newly invented telephones, electric lights, and automobiles; a nation in which Rudyard Kipling's poetry, Peter Ilich Tchaikovsky's music, and the Ferris wheel at the circus were all fresh and exciting and new. America has grown, it is a world power. Its economy is far more diverse, powerful, and vulnerable than it has ever been. The federal government is no longer just somebody you know by their first name selling you stamps at a post office. And the far-off Washington of yesterday has become a direct, immediate, and compelling fact of national life. Strikes and unions are no longer things you read about happening in faraway Colorado coalfields. Socialism and communism, words barely known in the United States in 1885, are now global forces. Much had been transformed in only sixty years; much more will be. That much, at least, is clear.

It will all begin, the businessman understands, with peace. Then reconversion can truly begin. But reconversion to what? It has been sixteen years since anything has been normal. What, now, was "normal" in America? That, as the celebrations continue on the evening streets in New York, remains the question—and the challenging reality.

1
DEFINING POSTWAR NORMALCY:
THE FIGHT OVER LABOR LAW

America in 1945 was an array of unresolved controversies about authority, status, and power. For sixteen years, the boundaries between the public and private sectors had been in flux; now, tens of millions simply wanted normalcy. Few of the most engaged political actors, however, agreed what normalcy now was, or should be. The nature and extent of union power, the nature and extent of the federal role in economic affairs, and the nature and extent of the U.S. role in stabilizing the postwar world all caused immediate and furious debate.

Unions challenged businessmen most powerfully: prearmistice labor struggles had produced a new industrial order, in which almost 70 percent of U.S. manufacturing workers were union members. Union leaders, however, still worried. They feared for the future more than the present. They were concerned about problems internal to organized labor and problems external to it. Internally, the decade-long civil war between the AFL and the CIO persisted, muted only by wartime union-raiding bans. AFL leaders, for instance, thundered at the NLRB for supposedly favoring CIO over AFL affiliates.

As leaders squabbled, the composition of the led shifted decisively: 17 million jobs had been created in America during the war, 15.5 million people had joined the armed forces, 20 percent of the population had changed jobs, and 11 percent of the population had migrated to cities to work in defense jobs. Blacks had abandoned the agrarian and poor South in droves and white southerners weren't far behind. Nontraditional workers flooded into factories: black manufacturing workers tripled in just three years, and 5 million women worked in war industries. Industrial unions thus became more heterogeneous than ever.

Meanwhile, external dangers remained, especially from reactionary big businessmen. Tom L. Girdler, president of Republic Steel, was nothing if not forthright: he was as horrified by wartime collective bargaining "as a physician is horrified when . . . a cancer has developed in the person of someone he loves." Strong unions were collectivist threats to capitalist innovation and vitality. Girdler's view was that of the mainstream of the

16,000-member National Association of Manufacturers (NAM) and the even-bigger United States Chamber of Commerce (USCC), the nation's two largest and most inclusive employers organizations. Received corporate wisdom had it that Washington's new taxing, spending, regulatory, social welfare, monetary, trade, antitrust, and labor policies were almost all bad. Moreover, budgets should be balanced annually, the domestic gold standard should be restored, and states' rights should take precedence over federal whenever reformers were powerful in Washington. Capitalism would provide jobs for everyone if left alone, government officials couldn't ameliorate economic problems, liberals were dupes who only encouraged creeping socialism, and only radicals fomented labor unrest. Competition, individualism, private property, and minimal government were the unchanging bases of economic justice. Such ironbound conservative credos threatened unions, among others, as fundamentally as ever.

Two new business groups, however, avoided the reactionary mind-set of the NAM and the USCC. These new organizations, the Business Council (BC) and the Committee for Economic Development (CED), opted for a truce with the new unions and the New Deal. They differed from their predecessors in matters of strategy and structure.

Structurally, the long-established NAM and USCC were general membership bodies, representing all industries and all sizes of firms. The BC and the CED were tiny and elite, overwhelmingly made up of big business CEOs (chief executive officers). They had between 60 and 200 active members. In other words, the NAM and the USCC represented everybody; the BC and the CED represented only presidents or board chairmen of the largest corporations. Strategically, the NAM and the USCC were "outside" pressure groups. They mounted grass roots protests and after 1934 focused their political attentions on Congress. The BC and the CED, on the other hand, were "inside" bodies, usually working with policymakers in the executive branch. The NAM and the USCC spoke in the idioms of conflict, the BC and the CED in those of cooperation. The BC, in fact, was *in* the federal government but not *of* it. Big business had created it as a symbiotic agency at the Commerce Department in 1933 at the request of New Deal leaders to maintain mutual advisory contacts as the NIRA, the Wagner Act, Social Security, and other important economic reforms were formulated, passed into law, and implemented.

The CED, for its part, was an offshoot of the BC that Commerce Department leaders helped interested businessmen midwife into being in late 1942 and early 1943. Unlike its parent BC, the CED was an independent organization with no formal affiliation with the government. Its informal relations with federal power barons, however, were extensive and improved its standing with more conservative groups like the NAM and the USCC. It couldn't be derided by corporate bitter-enders, as the BC often was, as a bunch of "tame millionaires" helping liberals do the New Deal's dirty work.

The CED also had different purposes than the BC. The BC was reactive, normally taking stands on domestic and international issues that presidents and their aides asked it to. The CED, in contrast, was proactive. Its main purpose was to create an agenda and organize a "positive business program" for postwar industrial development, economic growth, and social stability. It did this in cooperation with federal officials and, simultaneously, with the NAM, the USCC, and other capitalist organizations, many of whose members viewed the Democrats in Washington as the political Antichrist.

Despite such differences, the BC and the CED were two sides of the same coin. Membership overlap was substantial and far from accidental. Their policies were often made by the same men wearing different hats: corporate leaders who'd been around in Washington long enough to know that an expanded federal government wasn't going to disappear and that discreet symbiosis, accordingly, was a necessity. Such realism paid dividends. During World War II, BC and CED members provided most of the corporate representatives for the tripartite business-labor-public panels, which formulated and administered the crucial details of wartime economic mobilization policy. These panels mediated differences and, where voluntary mediation failed, often imposed binding arbitration judgments on contending parties. This left the rest of the government much freer to perform its traditional tasks and fight battles overseas.

A key arena for wartime mediation and arbitration was labor policy. And it was the CEOs of the largest and most technology-intensive corporations, not the far more conservative mainstream of the NAM and the USCC, who made wartime labor policy for business. NAM and USCC activists didn't like their exclusion from the inner councils of wartime labor policymaking one bit. The larger CEOs, castigated as "the country club set," had arrived early, when it counted the most. By the time the first NAM and USCC members were appointed in early 1944, they were, as one NAM official complained, "attempting to . . . lock a stable out of which the horses had already been stolen."

Such labor policy "theft" occurred because cooperative big businessmen faced facts, not theories. Tight wartime labor markets assured unions' power, so unions had to be persuaded not to hinder war production, increased profits, or victory. If workers and managers fought with strikes and lockouts, a Democratic administration might well punish big business far more than the unions, which were part of the New Deal electoral coalition. Large corporations had far too much to lose to risk union confrontations and wartime labor disorder. And the prewar status quo would not be enough: unions demanded new rewards in return for no-strike pledges and wage restraint during wartime. Policy was very often in the details. Union presidents understood that political truth as well as corporate presidents did.

A key policy detail agreed to by corporate, union, and public members on national war labor boards, therefore, concerned union security. Business was restrained from hiring millions of new workers and from using the customary threats and promises to keep those workers out of unions: war would not reinstate the open shop. Unions, meanwhile, couldn't strike to force labor-strapped firms to hire only members of their unions: closed shop conniving was also unacceptable. Both strikes and lockouts were banned "for the duration," and a "preferential union shop" compromise was worked out gradually over the fifteen months between January 1942 and March 1943. This compromise allowed employers to hire either union or nonunion workers at their discretion, but all workers who were hired at a unionized plant had to join that union as a condition of receiving permanent employment.

Such mutual accommodation wasn't easy. Evasion and straddle occurred over contentious details like employers' keeping on workers who quit a union after the union had negotiated a collective bargaining contract. Final terms, however, reflected wartime power balances. Managers couldn't play new workers off against old ones, or pit AFL unions against CIO unions, or bargain with only those workers who'd unionized before Pearl Harbor. Such policy agreements helped union numbers to almost double, to 20 percent of the labor force, in the four wartime years.

BC and CED members on war labor boards were not primarily concerned with the weakening of laissez-faire business creeds, but with their worldly interests. The Wagner Act had not only legalized unions, it had made workers, not management, responsible for deciding whether workers unionized or not. So BC and CED representatives declared an armed truce with unions for the duration, enrolled compromise-minded NAM and USCC leaders into their own ranks, and concentrated on benefiting from booming war economics. When peace broke out, however, emergency compromises soon decayed. Fear of a renewed depression was a root of the problem. Wartime cooperation had divided gains of affluence, but peace threatened renewed hard times and quarrels over apportioning scarcity.

Both union and corporate activists addressed postwar antidepression policies early. AFL and CIO leaders cooperated sufficiently to call for federal action to avert unemployment, curb inflation, and counteract cuts in take-home pay. Unions wanted a relaxation of the wage controls of wartime—but not a relaxation of wartime price controls, which primarily affected small business, agriculture, and service industries. Unions vainly demanded increases in the minimum wage, unemployment insurance benefits, and federal public works jobs. They also failed to get Congress to pass full-employment legislation, requiring Washington to be the employer of last resort in all future depressions. (The Employment Act that Congress did pass in 1946 was a hollow shell that committed nobody to anything, except the gathering of more national economic statistics.) These union demands were unpopular in all business circles, demands that embodied the Keynesian concept that government must maintain mass purchasing power and full employment when the private sector could not.

Activist businessmen, meanwhile, concentrated on the supply-investment aspect of economic growth, not the demand-consumption aspect. They wanted Washington to "unshackle business" to spur investment. They pressured for removing wartime price controls and maintaining wage controls. They lobbied for—and got—cuts in wartime corporate and excess-profits tax rates. They got an invisible but important tax change allowing them to write off losses from slack markets *or strikes* against their wartime excess profits.

Other postwar economic policy debates pleased the capitalists much less. They fumed at Truman economists' estimates that higher postwar wages were possible without higher prices because of higher productivity rates (lower unit costs) and higher production rates (economies of scale). Large capitalists opposed the CIO's income and wealth redistribution arguments as simplistic. High war profits and postwar profit maximization were necessary to finance the costly investments that underpinned economic growth. Businessmen strained credulity and misused statistics, just as unions did. And like unions they feared for the economic future.

As important, however, was what big business political activists did *not* do. They did *not* call for a return to the pre–New Deal past. The small business majority of the NAM and the USCC wanted to scrap statist "experiments," but their CED and BC counterparts kept on playing for power more than ideology. Such pragmatism had cause. Fifteen years of depression and war had obscured the boundaries between public and private, and business alone was not going to unmix them. CED and BC spokesmen, accordingly, talked about the "new role of government" in postwar America. To them the claim that all that was necessary for recovery was to "unshackle free enterprise" was irresponsible and businessmen who believed Washington's only role was as an umpire in a game where industry set the rules had "their heads in the sand." "The Federal Government," the CED added, "has a vital part to play in our capitalistic system." Washington must administer fiscal (taxing and spending), monetary, and other policies to help prevent both inflationary fevers and deflationary depressions.

Business and government were partners of necessity. Business should work to ensure that the compromises reached inconvenienced postwar capitalism the least. A mixed system in which corporations still made most major economic decisions and Washington was both umpire and economic guarantor was not socialism. Tax cuts, freer international trade, the expansion of unemployment insurance, short-term public works projects for the jobless, the promotion of small business through tax and other subsidies, and "realistic policies for dealing with monopolistic practices on the part of either business or labor" were all part of the new political image of the CED and the BC. U.S. capitalism was changing: corporate realists were replacing "yes, but," (or practical) politics for the "no" (or ideological) politics of previous years. They didn't seek to abolish New Deal fundamentals but sought, instead, to contain future federal expansion and to selectively roll back key wartime policies during the gradual reconversion to peace. Politically, matters were all in the details.

Such details, invisible to the 95 percent of companies employing fewer than 100 people, were worth literally billions of dollars to the firms the BC and the CED represented. By 1944, economists rich with federal experience had completed or gotten under way a dozen CED-sponsored "Transition from War to Peace" studies on subjects like the removal of wartime economic controls, manpower demobilization and reemployment, postwar international economic relations, and the sale of "government surplus" war goods and government-owned defense plants. The last item alone demonstrated just how profitable knowing the economic details was: $60 billion in surplus property plus war plant and equipment costing over $8 billion to build (and valued at twice that) was up for grabs. Washington had paid for one-third of all plants and equipment built in the United States during wartime; one-third of all war workers labored in these plants. Washington owned 10 percent of America's postwar industrial capacity, dominating major trades like aircraft, machine tools, synthetic rubber, shipbuilding, and nonferrous metals.

What the CED's economists understood, its big business members did too. One hundred and fifty large corporations and their subsidiaries had operated almost 80 percent of all government war plants and equipment (by dollar value); only 31 corporations operated more than 50 percent of these plants. The 100 largest companies ran three-quarters of all plants (by number). If Washington stayed in control of such massive capital assets after the war, the structure of American capitalism would be transformed. The TVA was peanuts in comparison. Washington could control high-technology manufacturing; if it sold its war plants to smaller firms, big corporations would be competitively disadvantaged. Similarly, if Washington dumped the massive amounts of surplus war property into private markets, prices would plummet and firms in industries like shipping and aviation would go bankrupt. Such postwar prospects were dismal to CED members. So they arrived early and proposed consistently about postwar reconversion in ways the smaller businessmen of the NAM and the USCC did not.

Such big business political action paid off. Two-thirds of the total value of all federal plant and equipment was eventually sold to only eighty-seven large firms. One company, US Steel, got 71 percent (by value) of all government-built integrated steel plants. High-technology synthetic rubber (polymers) facilities mostly went to the four largest rubber companies. Chemical plants were purchased by leading oil companies. Sale prices were minimal, often pennies on the dollar. Competitive bids from firms other than those that had run the plants in wartime were rarely allowed. Reconversion was therefore fine for big business—an almost unnoticed American version of Japan, Inc., that is, state-sponsored oligopoly.

While such lucrative private details were attended to, big business was active in other, far more public, ways, ones that highlighted cooperation between large firms and small. The CED worked with local and state affiliates of the NAM and the USCC and with many national trade associations to generate local community economic reconversion projects to plan for peacetime. Markets were appraised, investments budgeted, goods designed or redesigned, machinery retooled, and output projected. Businesses' interests in such uncustomary collective work was fundamental: if private companies failed to provide full-employment economic growth after largely risk-free war capitalism ended, social and political upheaval might revive the New Deal.

The postwar collective foresight orchestrated by the CED and others, then, was as necessary as it was ambitious, since it was very easy to be pessimistic about immediate peacetime prospects. Most Keynesian economists and liberals were pessimistic: they saw America as a "mature economy," which couldn't provide full employment without massive federal jobs and investment. Simple arithmetic fueled such concerns. The 12 million people in the military during the war had been a fifth of the total prewar labor force, 15 percent (or 8 million) of whom had been jobless in 1940. After Pearl Harbor, labor force participation swelled, creating a bigger labor force than ever before. Creating postwar affluence required an investment, output, employment, and income surge the like of which peacetime America hadn't seen since the 1920s.

The prospects for such a surge actually occurring were ambiguous, at best. Postwar economic challenges were so tremendous, in fact, that few big businesses wanted to add to them by trying to destroy powerful unions outright. Few if any CED or BC leaders liked unions, especially left-wing, CIO industrial unions. Big business tolerated big labor, just as it did big government; both were necessary evils. To contain them, however, big business needed a period of postwar political stability. They didn't get it. Powerful unions had other ideas.

Powerful corporations, accordingly, became more skilled in using federal power to restrain unions. As war ended, President Harry Truman's relations with CIO leaders rapidly deteriorated. In August 1945, CIO President Philip Murray stormed that Truman was "attempting to do the whole job of reconverting [the war economy to peace] without so much as asking [organized] labor to kiss his royal ass, so far as taking part is concerned. He [has] turned the whole job over to the industrialists."

Murray wasn't the only one capable of vivid expression. By September, Truman complained that, "like every 'new rich,' and person who comes into power suddenly, 'Labor' has gone off the beam." Greedy labor leaders were as bad as greedy industrialists.

Big labor unsettled the sixty-one-year-old president almost as much as big business or big government did. All had become central factors in American affairs long after Truman's birth in rural Missouri in 1884. For Truman, too, the United States in 1945 was far removed from the simpler world of Tom Sawyer and Huck Finn.

For the moment, however, the careful hypocrisies of power were preserved. Truman needed union votes, union money, and congressional support. So, despite his irritation about growing labor-management friction, Truman played the calm, paternal umpire. In November 1945, he created the National Labor-Management Conference of eighteen union and eighteen industry representatives to "settle wage questions and find alternatives to strikes." Here was traditional American minimalism. No federal delegation attended the meetings. Truman sought to midwife voluntary private compromises and to avoid spending his own public political capital.

Peacetime labor-management voluntarism hadn't worked for Truman's

Democratic presidential predecessors Woodrow Wilson and FDR, however, and it didn't work for Truman either. Union and management delegates agreed on nebulous generalities, which meant nothing, and disagreed about wage and union security specifics, which meant everything. The most important consequence of the Labor-Management Conference, in fact, didn't involve union leaders at all. USCC and NAM delegates met behind the scenes with BC representatives to hammer out proposals for labor law reform, which were supported by all corporate representatives at the aborted conference. Six of the BC representatives, significantly, were also CEOs from large firms prominent in the NAM, men whom the BC had recruited during wartime. Organized business clearly was seeking a united front to check postwar unions. None of this quiet corporate activity alerted unions. Truman's conference died stillborn; neither organized labor nor organized business could deliver constituencies for compromise. What remained was a likely gradual phasing out of wartime controls and an inevitable test of strength.

When the struggle came, it looked like the 1930s all over again. During the six months just after the war, more workers struck for lengthier periods than ever before (or since). For every workday lost to strikes in January 1945, 110 were lost in February 1946. Ten percent of all U.S. workers went on strike in 1946. Union leaders believed the best defense was a good offense, and assumed that without a successful offense, they'd be crushed between the hammer of dissatisfied union members and the anvil of reactionary business trying to undo everything unions had gained since 1935.

Organized business, too, thought that the best defense was a good offense, but they pitched their attacks differently. Despite the biggest strike wave the country has ever seen, employers did not attempt to operate their plants. They did not import strikebreakers, state troopers, tear gas, firearms, or the National Guard. They relied, instead, on economic pressure, lawsuits, public relations efforts, and (most of all) federal intervention. Business appealed to Caesar, not to Adam Smith. This difference later proved crucial.

Truman's presidency, meanwhile, decayed domestically. Massive strikes made for dreadful pocketbook politics. Policy vacillation didn't help—from war's end to March 1946, or seven months, the Truman administration changed its basic economic stabilization strategies three times. First it said wage increases should be allowed but price increases shouldn't be. Powerful unions used this as a blank check for strikes. Then it announced prices *could* be increased but only six months after wages increased. Employers remained distinctly unimpressed, and strikes only proliferated.

Contract negotiations between powerful corporations and large CIO unions subsequently broke down in the steel, petroleum, electrical manufacturing, and meat processing industries almost simultaneously. General Electric, General Motors, Westinghouse, US Steel, and Bethlehem Steel announced they would bear lengthy strikes rather than accept union demands—unless the Truman administration gutted the remains of fading wartime controls and allowed companies to raise their prices immediately after granting higher wages.

The country now faced a dismal prospect: strike-induced shortages of everything from automobiles to heating oil to hamburgers after four years of wartime rationing and scarcity. A quarter of the country's industrial economy would grind to a halt. Congress and the White House buckled. First, Truman temporarily prohibited oil refiners and meat packers from closing their doors and unions in these industries from striking, to buy him time to accomplish something more substantial. He failed. In the steel and auto industries, Truman enforced neither strict wages on unions nor strict prices on corporations. Congressional majorities opposed prohibiting strikes or reviving wartime controls. The White House dithered. Presidential economic advisers feared deflation one minute and inflation the next. Democrats exemplified national indecision on free markets and free collective bargaining versus continued wartime labor controls.

Truman paid an awful political price for this failure. By March 1946, remaining wartime wage and price controls were dead letters. Cost-push and demand-pull inflation boosted retail prices by 30 percent and wholesale prices by 50 percent over the next two years. More bitter strikes bloomed. By May 1946, a furious Truman threatened to draft railroad workers into the military to avert a nationwide rail shutdown.

Conservatives seized the political moment: 1946 was a congressional election year. By summer, Republicans were slashing at fractured Democrats with campaign slogans like *Had enough?* and *To err is Truman*. Voter majorities *had* had enough. The GOP ended up in control of both houses of Congress for the first time since 1930. Democratic losses were so great that one of every eight representatives and senators was a newly elected Republican.

When the new Republican congressional majority took power in January 1947, reining in unions was a priority. Unions had, by now, lost many political friends and the sympathy of the 80 percent of the work force not in unions. Union attacks on taxation and war property advantages that large corporations undeniably enjoyed were difficult for most citizens to understand; strikes that closed factories and enforced shortages on them were not. Most voters were innocent of economic theory. They personalized their economic fortunes and praised or blamed political leaders for them. In a strike- and inflation-filled year, this added up to severe political problems for Democrats, including those who survived the 1946 elections.

Truman's biblical homilies against the arrogant posturing of a handful of strike leaders like John L. Lewis of the United Mine Workers (UMW) hurt unions generally. Business was supposed to be selfish; organized labor was not. So when union spokesmen argued (honestly) that their members were relatively worse off than they had been during the high-rolling wartime years, millions of eyes glazed over: the eyes of returning combat veterans, for instance. Economic redistribution to veterans (e.g. via the GI Bill of Rights legislation) was very good bipartisan politics in the United States of 1945–46; economic redistribution to strikers who had rarely served in the military was not. An occasional active communist within the leadership of a minority of CIO unions only worsened matters, particularly as early cold war tensions gathered force.

The political climate, then, gave conservatives an opportunity. But how business politicians made use of this opportunity was crucial. Public opinion only wanted to "do something" about strikes; it did not select the precise legislative means to achieve that end. The formulation and passage of the Taft-Hartley Act demonstrated how corporate activists met these practical political challenges. Events unfolded as follows.

First, to accomplish anything, business had to transcend its laissez-faire slogans, since it did need Washington's help. It wanted the government to counteract the new legal and organizational powers of unions. It was not America's traditional "less government *in* business" but "more government *for* business."

The days of simply demanding the repeal of New Deal labor statutes were over. *Balance* became the slogan, and *revision* was the strategy. Instead of simply hollering "no," business had to say "yes, but." Just saying no to the Wagner Act was proven political suicide. You couldn't replace something with nothing. The votes for labor law repeal weren't sufficient to override the vetoes of Democratic presidents. In addition, the Supreme Court was now committed to enforcing collective bargaining laws. The fact of union rights, like federal might, was inescapable.

Politics, therefore, was compromise, not conquest. Because it was, virulently antiunion businessmen had to be removed from all labor policy leadership positions. All major national business organizations did just this: the BC and the CED had, unsurprisingly, muzzled the reactionaries in their ranks during the war. The USCC followed, after much internal bickering, by May 1946. After the Republican victory in the 1946 elections, the NAM did the same.

Once utter reactionaries were purged, practical politics began. Previously, corporate organizations normally agreed only on labor legislation they didn't want. Now they had to create workable compromises on what they did want. Aggressive unions, after all, threatened them all. A common (or common enough) agenda, once formulated, could then be presented to cooperative politicians. The CED had begun agenda building in 1943. During the Labor-Management Conference of 1945, the BC built bridges to the NAM and the USCC and expanded cooperation with smaller businesses. NAM-USCC cooperation was refined during the (mostly unsuccessful) 1946 labor law reform drives on Capitol Hill.

Efforts at corporate unity, however, couldn't be pushed too far. The big-business-only BC and CED and the panindustrial NAM and USCC, after all, represented very different business constituencies, with often very different opinions of unions. The more price competitive and smaller the firm, for instance, the less it liked unions. Larger, richer corporations, which had accommodated powerful unions, had to harmonize with smaller, poorer corporations, which had not. A wide, loose alliance allowed panindustrial cooperation; policy uniformity did not. So business interests combined agendas to create an amalgam of labor proposals, giving everybody but bitter-ender antiunionists something.

Business was also conveniently vague where necessary. A united front campaign to control unions did not foreclose future action by relatively accommodationist or relatively confrontational businesses. Marriage-of-convenience ethics ruled. Conservatives, sheer opportunists, and moderates all had to be satisfied enough with any final labor law package to support it.

Practically, this meant that what became the Taft-Hartley Act began as a something-for-everyone, Christmas tree bill in the more conservative and politically vulnerable Republican House. This same House (Hartley) bill was later pruned back significantly in the more moderate and politically protected GOP Senate, via the Senate (Taft) bill. This process of putting a conservative and a moderate bill together, to the overall advantage of the moderate bill, bought security for politicians. House Republicans put almost everything in their bill, knowing that parts of it were going to be thrown out later. Then they blamed the senators for being soft on essential conservative questions. Senate Republicans, meanwhile, traded off the least attractive elements of the House bill to gain the conservative Democratic votes they needed in both houses to override an inevitable Truman veto by the necessary two-thirds majorities. Bad cop (House), good cop (Senate) legislative choreography like this was as old as the Republic.

Achieving practical political results also required orchestrating external and internal political pressure on Republican and Democratic congressmen from voters back home, from state legislatures, and from official Washington. Orchestrating political pressure meant specialization. The CED and the BC were the corporate brains of Taft-Hartley; the NAM and the USCC were the brawn. Mass membership organizations like the latter had lots of clout on state and local levels and in the Republican House. Their local affiliates launched a nationwide propaganda campaign aimed at small businesses and those middle-class and other Americans without direct union experience or concerns. Both organizations targeted journalists outside of major cities.

Such opinion molding paid off. In 1946, twenty southern and western states passed restrictive labor legislation. Unions were put on the defensive. Rattled union leaders obligingly repeated the same mistake many a frightened businessman had made in the 1930s—they just said "no" to reform. They denied problems existed and thus handed the political initiative to their opponents. The NAM proved particularly adept at seizing opportunities to draft key sections of the hard-line Hartley bill in the House.

The elite CED and BC, meanwhile, worked the summits, not the foothills of politics. They had entree to the executive branch and the Senate leadership. They influenced the drafting of the soft-line Taft bill. They massaged opinion by influencing editors and reporters from major metropolitan newspapers and national radio networks, people who ignored free-enterprise boilerplate from the NAM and the USCC. These efforts only complemented the efforts of the USCC and the NAM, which—given a restive electorate, fractious Democrats, and nay-saying union leaders—was probably more important. The NAM and the USCC hit populist chords with the 95 percent of entrepreneurs employing fewer than 100 people in ways the elite groups could not. The combination of top-down and bottom-up corporate lobbying worked. Smaller business opened political holes through which big business ran, and vice versa. The NAM and the USCC emerged from almost fifteen years in the political wilderness once they moderated their reactionary stances and joined forces with the BC and the CED.

Unions, meanwhile, had many disadvantages. After congressional bargaining over a combined Taft-Hartley bill was over and the bill was resoundingly passed into law over a lackluster Truman veto, AFL and CIO leaders equated it with a "slave labor" statute. Rhetoric aside, Taft-Hartley did affect unions in powerful ways. While the Wagner Act prohibited employer practices, Taft-Hartley limited union practices. Taft-Hartley's limits were ones that Republicans, conservative Democrats, and middle-of-the-road Democrats had created. The most popular bipartisan elements of Taft-Hartley were actually parts of a bill passed earlier by a *Democratic*-majority Congress in mid-1946 (before being vetoed by Truman). These included

— creating the Federal Mediation Board to moderate disputes and decrease strikes
— giving presidents the right to limit unions' right to strike in peacetime by requiring sixty-day cooling-off periods, on national security grounds
— prohibiting jurisdictional strikes by the still-feuding AFL and CIO affiliates during the life of any union contract

These portions of the bill pleased the president, a vast majority of Congress, and business people of all stripes.

Business activists also overwhelmingly supported other segments of the final legislation, which caused more political division. These included

— denying federal collective bargaining protection to unions defined as communist dominated or communist led
— banning closed shop contracts
— banning unions of "managerial and supervisory" employees
— banning the preferential union shop in the antiunion South and West by allowing state right-to-work laws prohibiting the preferential union shop to take precedence over federal law allowing it, thus weakening union strike power and finances
— allowing employees to oust unions as well as select them by a majority vote
— strengthening employer rights to try to persuade workers that unions were not in their best interest
— restricting the NLRB through procedures that limited prounion administrators and complicated and lengthened appeals or litigation and that kept the NLRB from engaging in basic economic analysis or ensuring that unfairly fired workers were rehired

Taft-Hartley, however, did not always work exactly as business wanted. Its bans on secondary boycotts and on individual unions' contributions to federal political candidates proved legally ineffective. The NAM-inspired requirement that existing union shop contracts be reratified in special employee elections died stillborn after 94 percent of unionized workers affirmed they wanted unions. Further, the act did not include every item business hoped for. There were no bans on mass picketing, as the NAM and the USCC desired. Business attempts to cramp unions by excluding everything but wages and hours (e.g., working conditions) from union contracts failed. There was no prohibition on industrywide (instead of firm-by-firm or plant-by-plant) bargaining by powerful unions, as the BC wished. Nor did internal union finances and elections come under detailed regulation.

Plenty, however, remained—enough to contain industrial union power and to selectively roll it back over time. Weaker unions were smothered. Communist-led unions were suppressed. Organizing the unorganized became more difficult. These achievements satisfied BC and CED leaders. Neither made any effort—as the more opportunistic NAM and USCC conservatives soon did—to further weaken unions. Through Taft-Hartley, business politicians had used federal power to deny the initiative to AFL and (especially) CIO unions. This accomplished, large corporations generally operated within the status quo, in which powerful unions figured prominently. The BC was pleased with its work. Taft-Hartley was beneficial, it wrote to Truman privately in January 1949, because union membership had increased by 1,500,000 since 1946, wage rates had risen, strikes had decreased, and "union leadership has become more responsible."

When the BC submitted its report, Harry Truman had just won election on his own account against all the political prognosticators. His promise to repeal the Taft-Hartley "slave labor law" was a major reason for his victory in the low-turnout 1948 election. Before the election, Republicans had too often equated the antiradical AFL with the left-wing CIO; business organizations made the same cocksure mistake. Accordingly, AFL and CIO leaders stopped feuding long enough to work to elect Democrats; these union-mobilized votes regained the Democrats majorities in both houses of Congress.

However, neither these Democrats nor Truman gave business any hell on Taft-Hartley. Almost half of incumbent congressional Democrats had voted for Taft-Hartley in the first place. Repealing the act was risky; it could split the party wide open. Truman himself had long desired Taft-Hartley's bans on jurisdictional strikes, and he used the act's sixty-day cooling-off provision with zest. Simply revising Taft-Hartley instead of repealing it was also risky: labor issues and strikes had already cost Democrats plenty of votes. Cold war politics and their relation to the ongoing war within organized labor only further complicated matters politically.

At base, organized labor in the 1940s had the same problem that organized business had had in the 1930s—it wasn't very well organized. From

1930 to 1945, unions regularly used the split between businesses to their advantage, highlighting the violent actions and words of corporate primitives, while ignoring the deals they struck with corporate opportunists and moderates. Unions tarred all Depression-era businesses with a reactionary brush. During the cold war, however, the political advantage shifted; now business began to successfully brand unions as subversive. Corporations advertised the pro-Soviet stances of a small fraction of CIO union leaders, and ignored the nonradical mainstream of organized labor.

This guilt-by-association political technique often worked. The anticommunism and antiradicalism of postwar America produced the same lowest-common-denominator politics that the anti-business-as-usual anger of the 1930s did, especially among the millions of Americans who couldn't differentiate between a shop steward and a wine steward. By design, Taft-Hartley affected left-wing CIO industrial unions far more than right-wing AFL unions. The act's denial of federally protected collective bargaining rights to any union with officers who did not take anticommunist oaths was part of this design. CIO unions, already weakening relative to their old adversaries in the AFL, were further weakened. Several big CIO unions purged communists immediately after Taft-Hartley passed. By 1948, eleven other unions, with a fifth of the organization's total membership, were expelled from the CIO for being communist led. AFL raids on CIO unions intensified. CIO leaders were trapped: they were damned by Washington, organized business, the AFL, and portions of their own rank and file if they didn't purge radicals and savaged by AFL unions, business, and political conservatives if they did. They had a choice between looking either subversive or gullible.

It was not an enviable situation. What was branded as anti-Americanism in the house of Labor clearly weakened unions' ability to collect on political debts. Democrats whom labor had helped elect wanted to avoid being branded radical or their party being branded a class party, and they therefore made no strong effort to either repeal or revise Taft-Hartley. Truman-era Democrats became bastards, with a southern and western antiunion wing they wouldn't purge. But union leaders realized that Truman Democrats were *their* bastards, and that their own political position would weaken even further without them.

So no revision of Taft-Hartley ever occurred. By 1951, all hope of amending or killing the act was dead, even among union leaders. By then, most workers in mainstream unions no longer believed that Taft-Hartley meant slave labor anyway. Cold war political stasis had set in on the domestic front. A communist couldn't run for president of a union (because they might be elected), but a communist could still run for president of the United States (because there was no risk they'd win). Political stasis like this occurred because of cold war fears and also because fast-paced economic growth, not renewed depression, followed the war. A "mature economy" America was not. Events proved corporate optimists right and academic pessimists wrong.

The cheering and prolonged economic boom had many causes. Mammoth wartime investments generated income that ensured that postwar consumers anxious for normalcy didn't lack for means. Bank savings tripled in the four wartime years. CED-initiated postwar economic conversion planning helped businesses meet consumer demand for civilian goods, decreasing inflation. New mass-production techniques used during the war found ready peacetime applications. Contractors learned, for instance, to standardize buildings and erect them quickly and cheaply during the war. Postwar construction pioneers like William J. Levitt of Levittown did for suburban housing what Henry Ford did for automobiles, and what Levitt accomplished for residential construction, others accomplished for other basic industries.

Companies didn't just make old goods faster and cheaper. Large corporations had lots of war-created and federally financed high-technology products to develop postwar markets for. Aircraft (in particular, jets) were very visible examples. Other federally financed high-technology products included nuclear weapons, nuclear energy, and rocketry. The electronics industry found civilian uses for novel war devices like radar, computers, and improved television. Pharmaceutical, chemical, and food companies benefited from war products as varied as penicillin, synthetic quinine, sulfa drugs, synthetic rubber, plastics, insecticides like DDT, and frozen foods. Rivers of federal dollars buoyed up a technological revolution in the private sector. During World War II, Washington had supplanted universities and private foundations as the primary financier of basic scientific research (to create complex weapons like the atomic bomb). Washington subsequently subcontracted out more pure and applied military R&D (research and development) projects to growing numbers of academic and corporate laboratories and think tanks. By 1955, federal dollars paid for just over half of all R&D spending in America.

A largely military rationale also led Washington to underwrite postwar housing sales by guaranteeing the home mortgages of veterans and others. And in 1948, half of the 2 million college students were veterans whose education was paid for by the GI Bill. Postwar Military Keynesianism like this assisted economic recovery in ways academic pessimists had not expected. In 1946, for example, Washington spent $66 billion, two-thirds of it for the military. The low in postwar federal expenditure was in 1948, but the $35 billion spent that year was still 3.5 times the 1940 budget. In 1948 Washington spent $3.3 billion for veterans alone. This was one-third as much as prewar New Dealers ever spent a year for everybody. State and local government spending also doubled, from $10 billion a year during World War II to $21 billion a year by 1948, often to provide public services like schools, roads, sewers, and police to exploding suburbs.

A buoyed-up private sector, meanwhile, remained active on its own account. Not only did it have new products, it had many more places to sell them. America's postwar economic position was as fortunate internationally as it was at home. Exports tripled and then quadrupled over their prewar levels, while imports only doubled. Business—and the balance of payments—benefited because major foreign competitors lay in economic ruins. By 1945 America produced half the manufactured output of the planet.

Peacetime America, then, enjoyed unexpected, unparalleled, and reassuring affluence. That affluence and assurance combined with foreign fears and global military power to shift political energy and attention away from struggles over redistributing income, wealth, and power at home and toward the new frontiers of defending America and the world against the spread of communism abroad. Big business–government relations were affected profoundly by this change.

2

THE PATH TO THE MARSHALL PLAN

Elite politics and mass politics combined to achieve Taft-Hartley and what came afterward in America. Big business activists drew up a broad and inclusive labor law agenda, but small business lobbying and grass roots propaganda ensured that this agenda was largely achieved.

Propaganda proved particularly important in the Truman era because masses were easy to sway. Taft-Hartley politics illustrates the process. The majority wanted something done about strikes; the problem was how to gain popular and congressional support for specific restraints on unions. It was a means-ends situation common to all democracies: majorities specify nebulous ends; they do not select particular means to achieve those ends. The latter, politicians handled. The vaguer the popular understanding of laws and power relations, the easier to propagandize people and to lobby politicians to pass laws in elite interests. Elite power varies inversely with levels of popular interest, information, and concern.

In the case of Taft-Hartley, ignorance about labor relations policy was widespread. Thus, it was a prime propaganda issue. It was comparatively easy to equate strikes and other problems many people disliked with communists, whom most despised. A Gallup poll taken early in the Taft-Hartley struggle in January 1947, for example, showed that only 19 percent of the populace had a "generally correct" idea of the basics of the Wagner Act; 69 percent simply didn't know; another 12 percent gave utterly wrong answers. Since only one-fifth of the adults in the nation understood what the fundamentals of the Taft-Hartley fight in Congress were all about, 80 percent were fine subjects for anybody's propaganda, and corporations propagandized incessantly and successfully.

Taft-Hartley also illustrates a much wider truth. Public opinion on any economic issue could be swayed easily by elites because economics was unknown country to most Americans. If few understood the crucial details of domestic economic debates like Taft-Hartley, many fewer understood economic policy debates that transcended the nation's borders.

Educational scarcity was a major culprit. In 1940, the median level of schooling for all U.S. adults was only 8.6 years. Three-fourths hadn't completed high school; just one of every twenty-two Americans over age twenty-five had graduated from a four-year college or university. Educational standards were improving significantly for youth, but 1940s and 1950s America was not the relatively affluent educational society of today. In 1951, only 8 percent of adults correctly identified the meanings of the terms *monopoly, antitrust suit, Sherman Act,* and *interlocking directorates;* 46 percent identified none correctly. Half the electorate couldn't define any of the concepts used during the preceding fifty years in key policy debates between large corporations and the state. Few citizens understood basic public policies affecting business unless those policies immediately affected them.

Popular understanding was even more ambiguous about international economic policies. Factory workers knew about majority rule collective bargaining but not necessarily about international lending, foreign investment, world trade, exchange rates, or balance of payments. You could support your union because your boss was a bastard, but did you want an international monetary agency to protect you against volatile global currency swings? Popular ignorance of international economic issues was enhanced by basic geographical ignorance. *Where* international economic events were occurring was as puzzling as how or why or what was occurring. Two years after America's biggest global conflict ended, Gallup discovered that 72 percent of Americans could locate England on an outline map of Europe; 65 percent could place France; 53 percent Spain; 41 percent Poland; 33 percent Greece; 25 percent Czechoslovakia; and 18 percent Hungary. Terra incognita was vast.

Most corporate and government leaders involved in postwar international economic recovery issues, therefore, preferred very little popular involvement in the process. This was fine with the masses. Americans of the 1950s got energized about U.S. involvement in big foreign wars or about raising or lowering tariffs; everything else was left to a tiny elite of aristocratic, well-traveled, and much-schooled Americans: what we today term the *eastern establishment*. The creation and implementation of the Marshall Plan is an excellent example of such elite foreign policymaking. In international economic policy, a corporate and political inner circle cooperated to make America into the dominant economic, as well as military, policeman of the noncommunist world.

None of it was easy. Elites set agendas, but achieving them wasn't automatic. U.S. foreign policy traditions were ambiguous, oscillating between two poles. One pole was isolationist: although a strategically self-sufficient and historically neutral America was now a global economic power and a hemispheric political and military power, it should avoid entangling diplomatic or military alliances outside the Americas. When forced onto the world political stage, it should act as unilaterally, quickly, decisively, and temporarily as possible. Thus, government could remain minimal at home and abroad. This way, wily foreigners or wily Americans could not pervert the Republic. So said midwestern and western Republican conservatives and powerful segments of the Democratic party.

At the other pole were the internationalists who argued that hemispheric isolationism was passé. America was the biggest economic power on earth. In an era of modern technological war, the United States couldn't avoid multilateral global military and political responsibilities. Germany hadn't permitted America to be selectively neutral in World War I; the Axis hadn't in World War II. Military innovations like aircraft carriers and guided missiles were fast making America's geopolitical traditions obsolete. America needed international alliances to protect itself and avoid future wars.

To the internationalists, American traditions of economic unilateralism also needed changing. High tariffs, in particular, had to cease. Protectionism bred wars; free trade induced peace. A tariff-atomized international economy was an explosion waiting to happen. When goods couldn't freely cross borders, soldiers often did. A single dominant economic, political, and military power was necessary to nurture free trade and democratic politics in the world arena. Britain had performed this role from 1815 to 1914; now it was America's turn. To save Europe and the world from devolving into chaos again, the United States must create an American peace to reorder the world. So said eastern Republicans, low tariff Democrats, and many moderate and liberal New Dealers.

Unilateralist isolationists and multilateralist internationalists struggled constantly in elite policy circles after 1945. Outside Washington, the isolationists had the edge. America in the 1940s was a lot like Japan in the 1990s. Its people saw themselves as special and different. They didn't want any more trouble. They were on an economic roll and wanted to be left alone. "I can state in three sentences what the 'popular' attitude is toward foreign policy," a disgruntled Undersecretary of State Dean Acheson concluded in November 1945. "One, bring the boys home. Two, don't be a Santa Claus. Three, don't be pushed around."

Bipartisan congressional majorities reflected the popular unilateralist-isolationist habit of mind. In Eric Goldman's words: "Foreign policy was something you had, like measles, and got over with as quickly as possible." "It would be ironical," Republican Senate Majority Leader Robert Taft remarked early in 1947, "if this [newly elected conservative] Congress which really has its heart set on straightening out our domestic problems would end up being besieged by foreign problems." But irony it was. As Taft spoke, U.S. leaders were ferociously debating the necessity of American-led "collective security" and "containment" abroad. A nation that had fought a hot war to protect itself and its allies from fascist dictatorships moved on to fight a cold war to protect the world and itself from communist dictatorships.

The basic cold war military and political events are familiar. Less familiar is that the cold war had fundamental economic dimensions. Peace was not only proclaimed by America, it was underwritten and paid for by America. Four elements were central: foreign aid, foreign trade, development loans, and international monetary policy.

Of the four, foreign aid was easily the least popular. Foreign aid was U.S. grants to finance others' postwar economic recovery. It often appeared to be America-as-Santa-Claus, giving gifts to naughty overseas children. The United States had no tradition of foreign aid. U.S. government loans to Allied regimes in World War I became a widely unpopular form of de facto foreign subsidy when foreign nations failed to repay them. The first consciously designed foreign grant program in American history passed Congress only in March 1941. This Lend-Lease Act of wartime military gifts to other anti-Axis powers was rhetorically disguised as a loan, not a giveaway, to protect all who supported it.

After the war, foreign aid stayed unpopular. Three complementary banking and trade programs collectively known as the Bretton Woods system existed after 1944 to make global alms unnecessary. The first was the International Monetary Fund (IMF), a fledgling international central bank that restored a modified intergovernment gold standard to stabilize member nations' exchange rates. The IMF was designed to halt beggar-thy-neighbor currency devaluations. It formalized an American role as the primary guarantor of the stability of the value of money in the postwar capitalist world. The U.S. dollar became the most fixed and enduring unit of international financial account until 1971.

As the IMF stabilized currency values, the new World Bank made long-term loans to foreign governments. These loans were supposed to be relatively fast and relatively cheap. Governments with sound reconstruction projects, like the rebuilding of public sector transportation and communication networks destroyed by war, got capital to prime the pump for their postwar economic recovery. The third and final part of the Bretton Woods system was the General Agreement on Tariffs and Trade (GATT). The GATT, the first stage of an aborted International Trade Organization, gradually became the chief multinational forum to reduce trade restrictions and tariffs and to forward freer trade throughout the noncommunist world.

Subsidiary to the longer term reconstruction initiatives of the IMF, the World Bank, and the GATT were a series of ad hoc arrangements. These were grants to ameliorate starvation and other immediate postwar problems, largely undertaken by the United Nations Relief and Rehabilitation Agency (UNRRA). UNRRA's charities were temporary and short term. The concept fundamental to all immediate postwar economic assistance programs was that all major Western European industrial nations—particularly Britain, France, and Germany—would rely mainly on their own resources for their economic salvation. Bretton Woods was basically aimed at restoring trade and currency stability; the rest was up to the Europeans themselves. America's Santa Claus role was modest and reluctant. A $3.75 billion loan to Britain and a $1.2 billion loan and grant combination to France in 1946 helped both nations briefly approach prewar industrial production levels.

Recovery, however, miscarried. Between late 1946 and early 1947, all of Europe fell into deep recession. A basic problem was that European industry was not exporting enough to other nations to pay for the massive imports of raw materials and finished products that Europe needed for true economic recovery. The problem was especially acute in trade with America, because half of the earth's manufactured output was then made in the United States.

Buying U.S. goods, however, required U.S. dollars, and the availability of dollars very largely depended upon war-weakened Europeans' ability to sell goods to America. No-win irony abounded. Europe's ruined machinery couldn't be replaced by American machinery without American dollars to buy it with. Lacking such machinery, Europe couldn't strengthen its export position to earn dollars. Alternative ways of obtaining dollars were, likewise, difficult. U.S. corporations hesitated to build factories abroad until conditions stabilized. U.S. tourists rarely traveled in shattered and disorganized Europe. GIs were repatriated by the millions. American private loans to finance European purchases in America were the same credit card economics that had burned many large U.S. banks financially in the 1920s and 1930s: an interwar version of contemporary Third World debt. Public loans looked increasingly unlikely to be repaid.

All this left but one quick alternative: simply *give* Europe the capital required for its long-term economic recovery—a bigger jump start than the earlier loans to Britain and France, enough money to allow Western Europe to export enough to America to pay for the goods it imported from America. The logic of all this was not immediately obvious to most Americans. The idea that exports were always good and imports always bad was commonly held in a historically high-tariff and self-sufficient nation recently stressed by depression and war. The argument that U.S. taxpayers should finance the rebuilding of foreign competitors in key industries like steel—especially if the steel makers happened to be German—only one and two years after the end of a bloody war required finesse, gumption, and attention to economic fine points.

Enter big business, stage center. They were invited, they invited themselves, and many were working in Washington already. The names were legion. All had had either an acquaintance with federal power via previous membership in advisory groups like the CED and the BC, or service in economic mobilization agencies during the New Deal and the war, or repute and ability in the worlds of corporate law and investment banking. Often, the most successful business politicians had all three experiences.

W. Averell Harriman, for example, was a son of privilege who had also made a fortune of his own. He ran the giant Union Pacific Railroad his father had built. He was a driving entrepreneurial force behind Brown Brothers, Harriman investment bankers, a major American moneylender that financed foreign production and U.S. imports of many metals and foodstuffs. He was also a prominent BC member who had worked closely with the Roosevelt administration throughout the most bitterly divisive days of the New Deal. Harriman made it his business to know—and be known by—the powerful. He was involved in economic mobilization for war. He served as FDR's Lend-Lease administrator in wartime Europe. He was special envoy and ambassador to the Soviet Union from 1943 to 1945. He then served briefly as Truman's secretary of commerce, before becoming one of his close postwar foreign policy advisers.

Will Clayton's experience was similar. Clayton grew up poor and fast in the South, with a regional devotion to free trade as "the panacea for modern man." He built Anderson, Clayton and Company into the biggest cotton brokerage firm on earth in the 1920s. He joined the BC, broke with New Deal domestic reforms early and often, and was later brought back to Washington by mobilization and war. Clayton's conservative Democratic credentials and corporate connections were valuable in an era of war capitalism.

Clayton became the ever present economic man in official Washington: upper-echelon foreign and domestic lending administrator for the RFC, assistant secretary of commerce keeping strategic raw materials out of enemy hands after Pearl Harbor, briefly, the surplus war property administrator, postwar assistant secretary of state for economic affairs, chairman of the U.S. economic delegation to the Potsdam conference, Truman's invaluable liaison officer with powerful southern Democratic power barons in Congress, and advocate and architect of postwar emergency loans and grants to England. A courtly man who could persuade reluctant conservatives to get things done in international economic affairs, Clayton was someone even the young liberal economist John Kenneth Galbraith liked.

Will Clayton and Averell Harriman personified the business-government symbiosis during the war and the cold war. Manufacturers, merchants, lawyers, and financiers like them worked through the commanding heights of the big three cabinet departments of State, Treasury, and Defense. The roster of corporate lawyers and investment bankers in government included Secretary of State Dean Acheson (Covington and Burling), Secretary of Defense James Forrestal (Dillon, Reed), economic and military policy planner Paul Nitze (Dillon, Reed), Assistant Secretary of War for Air, then Undersecretary of State, then Deputy Secretary of Defense, and finally Secretary of Defense Robert A. Lovett (Brown Brothers) and Assistant Secretary of War John J. McCloy (a Wall Street lawyer). McCloy's responsibilities included overseeing the development of the atomic bomb. He later became American high commissioner to Germany and the first president of the World Bank.

Clayton, Harriman, Acheson, Forrestal, Nitze, Lovett, McCloy, and hundreds of others like them oversaw the details of America's rise to global power after 1945. They were essential to postwar policy and process. They knew the right conservative people inside and outside Washington. They were businessmen and couldn't be called wild-eyed or radical. They could mobilize the nation's corporate leadership to advocate uncustomary government programs like foreign aid.

Background was key. The investment bankers and corporate lawyers who so often designed and implemented American cold war economic policies were generalists. They did not make steel or automobiles. Their backgrounds were panindustrial, not industry-specific. They had advised many kinds of businesses on many issues and serviced many firms in many trades. Their range of acquaintance was wide. They had rich international experience. They waged America's economic war after Pearl Harbor. They were the closest thing the United States had to a landed aristocracy, and they knew how to bargain with corporate and political aristocrats from far less egalitarian lands. America's global reach was mostly economic before World War II. So big businessmen and their legal and financial consorts were the greatest pool of international expertise the nation possessed. They also possessed domestic advantages, building bridges between business and government, between widely varied industries, between export-oriented larger companies and import-fearful smaller ones, and between capitalists partial to freer trade and political and military leaders afraid a depressed Western Europe would breed bomb throwers and turn into a communist lake.

These internationalist businessmen also brokered bipartisan deals between risk-averse congressmen. Main Street America turned inward after 1945, just as after 1918. Wall Street did not. Republicans and Democrats anxious not to offend Main Street by backing postwar foreign aid could be persuaded to risk backing it by practical men of business and finance. If Truman intended to pay for an American peace, he needed conservative votes in Congress. To get them, Truman also needed men who spoke the idiom of hardheaded intelligent selfishness. Foreign aid, in short, had to "pay": Americans had to foresee clear returns on their money. Charity was a nonstarter—political support for it was insufficient to address the scope of postwar problems. Most Americans had had quite enough of global charity; now they wanted normalcy and (above all) peace. They had to be persuaded to pay for peace.

Paying for peace posed special ideological dilemmas for traditional, minimal government, American conservatives, whose standard minimalist theories did not explain cold war conditions. Now conservatives who wanted Washington to be less expansive, less interventionist, and less powerful at home had to ponder the necessity of Washington becoming much more expensive, more interventionist, and more powerful in order to wage an anticommunist crusade abroad. It took a lot of getting used to. Corporate activists in government nurtured this right-wing transition to a more global outlook.

The culminating stage of the process began early in 1947. Europe remained depressed. The Soviet Union threatened Turkey. Rebellion in Greece appeared to demonstrate a U.S.S.R.-orchestrated internal subversion. War-weakened Britain told Washington that it could no longer continue its police power role in the eastern Mediterranean and the Middle East. Truman stepped in with the Truman Doctrine in March 1947. "Primarily through economic and financial aid," he said, the United States should "support free peoples who are resisting attempted subjugation by armed minorities or outside pressures." America had become the economic, as well as the military, policeman of the world. Four hundred million dollars in emergency money went to Greece and Turkey, but only after Undersecretary of State Acheson scared hell out of Republican congressional leaders with the specter of communism triumphant if they refused.

Soon thereafter, Acheson, Clayton, and others at State went on to scare hell out of the Congress and the country alike to get much more money: money for Western Europe. In June, Secretary of State George Catlett Marshall gave a speech at Harvard in which he proposed a grand scheme of American-financed economic reconstruction for all of Europe. (Soviet pressure ensured that no nation they then dominated could receive this aid.)

In spite of the efforts of the corporate politicians, conservative congressional reaction to the Marshall Plan was distinctly cool. Congress was tired of foreign aid and wanted no more of it. It wanted Bretton-Woods-style loans, not U.S. grants, however euphemized, to accomplish postwar capitalist reconstruction. Taft Republicans feared liberal giveaway programs, global TVAs, and New Deal "socialism" for the world. Newly elected GOPers like young Richard Milhous Nixon parroted the old-time religion.

Truman administration leaders expected such a partisan ideological struggle. Marshall ordered his aides not to publicize his speech, and Truman did not initially endorse the plan. Private administration polls showed leading CEOs in anti-New-Deal industries such as steel and automobile manufacturing were not supporting Marshall's proposal. Oil industry executives were also reported to be skeptical. None of this boded well for bringing congressmen from both parties and powerful regional industrial interests on board for what Marshall forthrightly called a U.S. foreign aid program to revive "a working economy in the world so as to permit the emergence of political and social conditions in which free institutions can exist." It took nine months to persuade congressional conservatives that Marshall's foreign aid proposal wasn't wild-eyed political economics.

Without the corporate politicians, Truman's effort would have failed. Men like Clayton and Harriman arrayed foreign aid in procapitalist, anti-communist attire; they also formulated proposals, lobbied Congress to pass them, and administered the resulting programs. Forrestal, Acheson, Harriman, and fellow BC member and Secretary of the Treasury John W. Snyder, in fact, at Truman's request, began quietly recruiting big business support for a vastly enhanced U.S. grant program a week before the Truman Doctrine was officially announced in March 1947. Then, less than two weeks after Marshall's address at Harvard in June, Truman created a "bipartisan advisory council" to draw up a blueprint for America's foreign aid effort. *Bipartisan* definitely meant business-oriented. Moderate Republicans in Congress had told Truman that, without substantial corporate involvement in designing what was becoming known as the Marshall Plan, he could not obtain their support against obstructionist conservatives.

Truman acceded. He faced congressional deadlock otherwise. Harriman was promptly appointed to chair the President's Committee on Foreign Aid to draft proposals for Congress. Nine businessmen joined him on the committee. Five, like Harriman, were also BC members. Five of the nine also belonged to the CED, including CED Chairman Paul W. Hoffman, of Studebaker Motors. The remaining ten members included six college administrators (three of whom were members of CED's Research Advisory Board), two labor leaders (one from the AFL, one from the CIO), the president of the Brookings Institution, a Washington think tank, and an out-of-work midwestern liberal senator. Throughout, business members— particularly Harriman—set the agenda and the tone for the group's work.

After four months, the committee hammered out the practical details of the Marshall Plan. Congress was to vote $13–$17 billion in foreign aid for Western Europe over four years. The program, at Republican insistence, was to be administered by an independent agency headed by a safe and sound businessman, not by a pointy-headed liberal politician. This czar of foreign aid was also, however, to be as unconstrained by right-wing ideologues as by left-wing ones. Foreign aid, for instance, should not be used to bludgeon any Western European government (like the socialist one then in power in Britain) to adopt free enterprise on the U.S. model. Rotary Club oratory was irrelevant to the practical business of global economic reconstruction.

Anticommunist oratory, on the other hand, was very relevant. To convince or isolate Republican isolationists, foreign aid often became politics first and economics second. The Marshall Plan was not charity, the Harriman committee warned; it was a matter of self-interest and survival. If the United States failed to rebuild war-torn Western Europe, all of Europe, Scandinavia, North Africa, and the Middle East might devolve into chaos and fall under Soviet control. Even Britain might collapse. Such cataclysmic results would cause a "sweeping limitation of our economic and political life" and threaten "our very form of government itself." Communists menaced capitalism and democracy, and minimalist conservatives had to cease their opposition to bigger government and support foreign aid as a necessary antidote to Soviet imperialism. Clayton, Hoffman, and BC spokesmen repeatedly made "communist peril" arguments to Washington and corporate audiences in late 1947 and early 1948. These efforts succeeded as U.S.-Soviet relations worsened.

Smaller business forces of the NAM, however, fearful of imports and freer trade, helped keep the Marshall Plan bill Truman sent to Congress in December 1947 bottled up in Congress for four months. Billions of dollars in foreign aid grants, NAM fulminated, was creeping socialism, lousy economics, and a vain effort to interfere with "natural economic forces." The only real way to confront communism was to confront the U.S.S.R. militarily. Nuclear intimidation was preferable to more complicated economic "containment."

The CED, meanwhile, preferred an economic, as opposed to a nuclear, approach to national security and foreign affairs. It supported all the Harriman Committee recommendations it had helped create. The emergency foreign aid program should be *in* government but not *of* it. Business, not New Dealers, should run the program at all levels, in consultation with Congress. Admiring letters went out from corporate offices to massage the egos of conservative congressional power brokers. CEOs of large, technology-intensive, and export-oriented firms like General Electric testified before committees and lobbied legislators. In early 1948, the legislative logjam broke. A brutal Soviet coup in Czechoslovakia frightened fiercely anticommunist conservatives into backing an expensive economic containment strategy to avoid the more belligerent military responses vaguely advocated by the NAM. In April, Congress passed a bill creating the Marshall Plan by three to one. Truman and his corporate allies had won.

Had they ever. A week after Truman signed the Marshall Plan legislation, he appointed Paul Hoffman to be the czar of the new Economic Cooperation Administration (ECA) created to distribute U.S. aid money. Hoffman's job was mostly to keep Congress happy and annual appropriations flowing into the program during its four-year lifetime. Chief operating assistant to Hoffman was Harriman, who oversaw all detailed negotiations with foreign industries and governments. Hoffman and Harriman, in turn, recruited scores of BC and CED members to head specialized "industry divisions" within the ECA. These BC and CED activists then recruited thousands more industry experts from their own and other firms, often using the argument that only business expertise could keep foreign aid from devolving into political giveaways and waste. The prominent law firms and banks that had earlier sent the Nitzes, Forrestals, and Achesons to Washington also provided personnel for the ECA.

The days of minimal government in America were over, in fact, if not in theory. Big business, big government was the order of the day: the same corporate politicians who had mobilized the economy for war now mobilized America to fight the economic cold war. BC and CED leaders who had earlier allied with small business organizations and congressional conservatives to contain the spread of aggressive unions at home via Taft-Hartley now allied with the Truman administration to contain Soviet power and influence abroad by formulating and implementing the Marshall Plan—over conservative congressional and corporate opposition.

Big government with a big business accent definitely worked: $13.5 billion in economic grants went to Western Europe between 1948 and 1951; $22.75 billion in economic and military grants went abroad in the first seven years after World War II. In the same period, Bretton Woods agencies headed by corporate politicians like McCloy provided $8.5 billion in additional loans. Washington spent more annually in foreign aid to Europe during the Marshall Plan era than it had spent for everything in 1933. And it was big business in government doing the job.

Such symbiosis, however, remained a fact without any comfortable theory to explain it. The cold war, like the Depression and World War II, was a situation not considered in traditional American economic or political ideology. Many government and business leaders came to see the Marshall Plan as simple necessity, a down payment on the American Century. They created a de facto Keynesian pump-priming program, which paid for 25 percent of all Western European imports between 1947 and 1950. They reduced destabilizing dollar shortages in world trade. They helped begin the thirteen-fold increase between 1950 and 1990 in inflation-adjusted trade in global goods and services. They cut corners, raised alarms, and wrapped economics in rabid anticommunist politics to get congressional votes and to massage public opinion.

They sought to inaugurate, as McCloy put it at the time, a "Periclean Age" in which "a great nation with selfless ideals was led by great men with equally selfless motives." To accomplish this goal, many of America's nobility left their corporate estates to benefit their country, themselves, and capitalism, simultaneously.

3
OIL: COLD WAR SYMBIOSIS AT AN APEX

The cold war spurred the symbiosis between big business and government, just as the hot war had. Ad hoc accommodation was the norm. Corporate politicians moved to the right, domestically (to contain unions), and to the left, internationally (to contain communism). Central to both strategies was the permanent reality of federal power. Federal law checked and restrained the CIO at home. Abroad, government helped corporations fight the economic cold war. Washington mobilized its might to deny global strategic resources to its radical enemies, and oil was easily the most potent single factor in this global equation.

Truman and his successors were willing, if not always happy, to oblige strategic industries in ways that mixed federal power with private purposes. They couldn't do without big business. They might—indeed, often did—view large corporations as sinful, but they also respected the powers of the sinners. The specific terms for cooperation between big business and the state were often contentious; the overarching necessity of the symbiotic relation usually was not. Washington now helped guarantee economic health in America and underwrote political and economic health for the noncommunist world, but Washington couldn't do it by itself. Domestically the New Deal was a sequence of special deals, not a well-coordinated general deal. It certainly wasn't socialism. Democrats regulated capitalism; they did not replace it. And like Republicans, they cooperated with powerful business interests as a matter of sheer organizational, economic, and political necessity. They did it to do their jobs.

Globally, postwar oil policy made the same point. In 1947 and 1948, as Taft-Hartley, the Truman Doctrine, and the Marshall Plan became centerpieces of national policy, a key shift in America's energy circumstances occurred. A nation that had always exported more oil than it imported now began importing more than it exported. No longer was the United States a self-sufficient oil nation that could—as in World War II—supply all its own needs and part of Europe's as well. Foreign oil mattered: it was a primary component of national security in the petroleum age. Postwar international oil policy, Daniel Yergin wrote, "provided the point at which foreign policy, international economic considerations, national security, and corporate interests would all converge. The Middle East was the focus."

In the Middle East, oil-rich areas like Kuwait, Iran, and Saudi Arabia especially mattered. Britain had pioneered the oil era in the Middle East, and it had exercised prewar dominance in the region. Washington, which had never hesitated to support U.S. oil companies' exploration and development efforts in Latin America, shied away from backing American firms' penetration of Moslem lands east of Suez to avoid offending British imperial sensibilities.

In spite of Washington's deference, U.S. companies started prospecting in Saudi Arabia a decade before World War II began. Work went slowly because of the 1930s Depression and because Saudi Arabia was a poor and largely feudal land over three times as big as Texas. By 1939, however, two large U.S. firms felt optimistic enough about the future to purchase long-term monopoly rights ("concessions") to find, produce, and sell oil from an area in eastern Saudi Arabia as big as Texas and California combined.

The Saudi monarchy was chronically short of revenue and anxious to decrease British influence in the kingdom, so normal development equations ruled. In return for comparatively little, U.S. companies got comparatively much. The Sa'ud monarchy received small payments for granting the concessions, and its exchequer was kept afloat with regular loans from the companies, loans charged off against future royalties. Royalties—a percentage of the take levied only when oil was actually produced from a lease—were initially fixed at a dollar a ton of crude (unrefined) oil. The monarchy soon levied other taxes on oil production that approximately equaled the annual royalty payments, but Saudi Arabia held no ownership share whatsoever in the companies, nor did its royalty or tax payments initially relate to profits. Only in 1950 did the Saudis arrange a fifty-fifty profit split. Initially, such crucial facts were academic: early profits were minimal, due to the high development costs of drilling wells, building transport systems, and constructing refineries.

War, however, changed everything in the Middle East, as in America. Suddenly Saudi oil—present and potential—loomed large in national security calculations. These calculations were symbiotic from the start: before the war, U.S.-owned oil companies controlled half the world's then-known petroleum reserves. Washington did not want such control to decrease, since by World War II oil was clearly *the* strategic commodity. Without it, modern armies, navies, and air forces couldn't operate. After Pearl Harbor, the point was to ensure that threatening foreign powers (first fascist, later communist) did not gain more access to oil via external or internal pressures against weak oil states. Suddenly, American petroleum companies in the Middle East were primary players in both the hot war and the cold war. Equally suddenly, corporate and political leaders needed one another to safeguard global interests. War brought a formal and long-term integration of the petroleum industry into the inner circles of the government. Such symbiosis was a result of a long-standing ambivalence in U.S. politics: the federal government ought to *do* more but it ought not to accumulate more power in the process. It solved this paradox by sponsoring solutions created by the private sector.

During the war, the Petroleum Industry War Council (PIWC) was created. The PIWC was in the government but not of it. Petroleum industry executives streamed into Washington to man the eighty-three PIWC cooperating committees that created and implemented policies. In 1946, once the cold war replaced the hot war, the National Petroleum Council (NPC) was established, replacing the PIWC. It survived essentially unchanged for thirty years. The NPC was a BC for "tough hombre" oil executives alone. It set its own rules, elected its own members, picked its own chairmen, set its own agendas, and recommended the appointments of almost all the government bureaucrats it worked most closely with. Normally, no federal officials even attended NPC meetings, which were held every few months. Oil executives paid their own expenses, arrived at agreements by majority vote in committee, and provided an object lesson of the truth that information is, indeed, power. The NPC often provided the only expert analysis that Washington's military and economic planners depended upon to make energy policy during the quarter-century after the war.

In the Middle East, meanwhile, the instrument of cooperation, mutual aid, and a symbiotic political economy for world petroleum was ARAMCO, the Arabian-American Oil Company. ARAMCO evolved immediately after the war out of the desire of federal policymakers and corporate CEOs alike for secure long-term access to and control of the growing Saudi oil reserves. Saudi Arabia was turning into the mother lode of oil. Clayton, Forrestal, and Nitze (who handled international petroleum policymaking for Clayton), realizing that developing Arabian oil reserves would be expensive, strongly supported efforts by the two U.S. firms that had pioneered Saudi oil to bring in additional American partners with investment capital and established oil markets to develop the reserves quickly. Western Europe desperately needed low-priced energy for its economic recovery; the Saudi royal family desperately needed oil royalties to develop their country—and to help them survive politically; and Washington wanted political stability and economic growth in the Middle East. Above all, it wanted the Soviets kept out.

ARAMCO, a federally backed cartel of four of America's largest oil companies acting in concert to develop Saudi oil just as that bonanza began to be profitable, solved all these short-term political and economic problems. Saudi oil remained firmly under U.S. control via ARAMCO, which gained in return implicit U.S. government safeguards for their most important single foreign holding. ARAMCO was the linchpin of America Inc. in the postwar Middle East.

On March 12, 1947, Standard Oil of California, Texaco, Standard Oil of New Jersey (later Exxon), and Socony (later Mobil) finished lengthy legal and financial negotiations and signed agreements creating what became the largest oil combine in the world. By a fitting coincidence, the date was the same one on which President Truman enunciated the Truman Doctrine, highlighting America's role as the economic and political policeman of the noncommunist world, a belief that, only three months later, coalesced into the corporate-government campaign for the Marshall Plan. Thus the United States became the strategic economic defender of the Middle East (via ARAMCO) at precisely the moment it became the economic guarantor of Western Europe (via public money and private expertise). Multinational oil companies were now "essentially political as well as economic institutions."

Big oil, however, did not simply dictate policy in Washington: oil politics were as complicated as any other kind. ARAMCO was not the only oil game in town. The United States was then the only country in the world whose major oil firms simultaneously produced both domestically and overseas.

This unique characteristic of America's oil industry led to fundamental ambiguities in American oil diplomacy. Petroleum companies that were the most powerful abroad were often not the most powerful at home. The largest American oil companies were all multinationals by World War II: these big Five (Exxon, Mobil, Texaco, Standard of California, and Gulf) were major producers both domestically and overseas, but foreign oil (especially in developing, or Third World, nations) increasingly mattered more to them than domestic oil did.

In addition to these five multinationals were about twenty ambitious medium-sized companies and thousands of small companies. The twenty larger companies were powers in the domestic American oil market but did not (yet) have any significant Third World oil holdings—and they badly wanted them. The small oil companies owned oil reserves entirely or almost entirely in the United States. Although the Big Five controlled over half of Third World oil reserves by the early 1950s, they held only slightly over 20 percent of America's domestic reserves.

What all this entrepreneurial arithmetic meant was that what was best for large oil companies abroad was not necessarily best for smaller oil companies at home. Different firms' economic interests, in fact, could be entirely opposed. The Middle East was a mother lode: its oil was produced at exceedingly low cost. Forty-five gallons of Saudi crude cost far less than the steel barrels it was sometimes shipped in. U.S. oil, by contrast, was expensive to produce. This meant that imported oil could undersell U.S. oil if it could be imported into America freely. The Big Five had significant domestic oil holdings, too, so it behooved them to limit their imports to protect the value of their domestic oil. In the short term, then, small companies might not get hurt badly. In the long term, however, nothing was guaranteed. It was an optimistic oilman indeed who trusted big oil not to drive small oil producers out of business should it ever suit them to do so.

Over the next decade, accordingly, two protective strategies became central: small firms sought to exclude low-cost Middle East oil from America's domestic markets and medium-sized firms sought to improve their competitive positions by getting Washington's help in obtaining oil concessions in the Third World. These strategies succeeded more often than not. Reasons varied, but they often related to American politics, particularly congressional politics:

—There were lots more small oil people than there were big (or big and medium) oil people. They packed more wallop in voting booths. Any oil state politician who offended small oil too badly risked electoral defeat.

—All oilmen had money, the mother's milk of politics, and few were shy about using it. However, the money *and votes* of small and medium oil often counted for more than the mere money of big oil.

—Big oil was in a careful alliance with Saudi kings and others, whose votes didn't count in U.S. elections and whose money, if illegally contributed, was a political albatross—given U.S. support for Israel.

—Elected politicians often tried to avoid difficult oil policy questions (and votes-money trade-offs). They buried such disagreements in oil-industry-dominated agencies like the NPC as long and thoroughly as they could. Big firms, thereby, might control small firms *for* the politicians. When they no longer could, the pols had no easy choice but to do the small companies' bidding.

—Big oil paid taxes and royalties to foreign regimes, while small and medium-sized oil firms paid taxes and royalties to U.S. state and federal governments. Big oil, in addition, got a 100 percent write-off against its federal corporate income taxes for all royalty and income taxes paid to foreign countries. This meant that the federal treasury, and smaller oil's taxes, subsidized big oil.

—Workers employed in domestic oil, from production to retailing, vastly outnumbered U.S. workers producing, refining, and transporting foreign oil. These people voted. Plus, if they lost their jobs, it was clearly an economic and political problem for the United States. Furthermore, a jobless worker in Saudi Arabia could blame a Saudi monarch or a U.S. oil company. A jobless worker in the United States would more likely blame Congress, particularly if the widely reported reason was low-cost foreign imports.

Overall, then, the big-oil-first policy that military and diplomatic leaders deemed necessary to national security was politically risky to oil state senators and representatives, especially oil state senators and representatives running Congress at the time. From such disjunctions of interest grew debates about whether foreign and domestic oil policies should be related. Big, medium, and small oil thus pulled federal policy in different directions, even, as we shall see, regarding ARAMCO's dominant role in the oil-rich Middle East.

Initially, these debates were relatively even tempered and low profile. As long as low-cost imported oil was only a small threat to small producers, elected politicians could dodge policymaking and allow ARAMCO and the NPC to make oil policy. But once the bonanza days of Middle East oil production really began by the mid-1950s, matters changed. Politicians were called upon to help resolve intraindustry disagreements. Political and corporate leaders arrived at short-term accommodations, which were unworkable in the longer term. They closed more of the burgeoning U.S. market to low-cost foreign oil and opened up oil development abroad to more U.S. firms, which eventually eroded ARAMCO's bargaining power in Saudi Arabia. As is often true in political economy, however, short-term appearances were deceptive. The U.S. oil market grew so fast that allowing Saudi oil a smaller percentage of it still meant that total absolute amounts of Saudi oil imported into America rose steadily. At the same time, American power abroad seemed to be growing so fast that U.S. leaders thought they could protect almost all American corporate interests almost everywhere with relative ease.

Humane statistics illustrate the point. The United States became a net oil importer in 1947–48, just as ARAMCO was formed and the Middle East began to be a U.S.-dominated oil lake. But more than imports were going up: American oil consumption rocketed into the stratosphere, along with the economy as a whole. After a brief postwar dip, economic growth rode into the American Century on technological innovations, a sea of unspent savings, and another sea of low-cost petroleum energy. Oil, the least abstract of all these elements, changed the nation in the most obvious way.

The number of cars almost doubled (to 40 million) between 1945 and 1950, doubling and redoubling in the forty years thereafter. Huge tract suburbs like Levittown signaled the dawn of the auto age: one in every eight American families "went suburban" in the first postwar decade alone. There were eight shopping centers and a handful of supermarkets in America in 1946; forty years later there were 30,000 shopping centers, as many major supermarkets, and 45,000 convenience stores. Motor hotels (such as the Holiday Inn chain, begun in 1952), the 126,000 fast-food restaurants (such as the McDonald's hamburger chain, established by 1954), the over 100,000 miles of interstate superhighways (90 percent built and maintained by federal dollars and federal gasoline taxes), and even the 40 percent of marriage proposals that were made in automobiles all signified the postwar cheap energy era. In the first eighty years of the oil age (to 1950), American oil consumption rose to 5.8 million barrels per day. In the next twenty-five years, consumption tripled.

Domestic production surged to keep up with such explosive demand, but demand grew so fast that imports became progressively more important. As they did, feuds between small oil and big oil intensified. NPC-brokered compromises based on the principle that low-cost foreign oil would only augment domestic production, rather than replace it, frayed, then fell apart. By the mid-1950s small oil was in open revolt against the national oil policy made by the petroleum industry and called upon Washington to redress small oil for the favors it had done big oil.

Washington reluctantly obliged. Congress and the executive branch alike could no longer evade policy issues by calls for consensus and self-regulation. A Congress dominated by representatives from oil states supported small oil: a mandatory oil import quota program lasting from 1959 to 1973 froze foreign oil imports at about 12 percent of domestic production. Domestic U.S. crude oil prices stayed about 30 percent higher than they would have been without this exclusion. The big oil versus small oil controversy over Middle East oil was a repeat performance of the business debate over the Marshall Plan. Multinational firms unafraid of import competition were lined up against small domestic firms very much afraid of it—only this time, the multinationals lost more than they won.

As big oil lost policy ground relative to small oil at home, it was losing ground to medium oil abroad. The political agenda of medium oil involved pressuring Washington to ease its path to global oil concessions, à la ARAMCO—and they were succeeding. Some went multinational with a vengeance in the 1950s and 1960s in order to find and develop low-cost foreign oil before big oil could. Developing nations needing oil revenues to buy their way out of poverty possessed common interests with hard-charging medium oil. The more oil companies there were bidding for concessions, the higher the charges the host countries could levy, and the more likely oil would be discovered, pumped, and taxed. There were many hungry host countries, and they understood basic competitive arithmetic. Medium oil, meanwhile, did its capitalist arithmetic too. In global petroleum, reserves were (and are) the name of the game. Any medium-sized company that wanted to end up big had to develop lucrative oil fields before the competition. Grow or die was its competitive principle, and medium oil was willing to pay high prices to obtain foreign reserves.

Once medium oil had stakes in the Middle East, however, U.S. foreign oil policy became ambiguous regarding big oil and ARAMCO. American oil primacy had been achieved by big oil; it was now easy to argue that it didn't really matter how many American oil firms had Middle East concessions, so long as they were American. U.S. global economic and military power was at its apex in the two decades immediately after 1945; American power could surely protect all multinational oil, large, small, and in-between.

This was a false vision, even a self-defeating one, but it spoke to host country and oil industry aspirations, and it paid political dividends back home. Washington need not back only one international oil cartel—it could help lots of companies in expanding world oil regions. Thus free-market ideology could be forwarded. The more firms producing foreign oil, the more competitive oil prices would likely be, the less the United States would spend for oil imports, and the more its balance of payments would benefit. Federal favors started with big oil of necessity; they were expanded to medium oil as a matter of convenience.

The policy process at work here illustrates that America's corporate-government symbiosis is not the usual Western European, Japanese, or developing nation kind. It is different, often very different, even when postwar symbiosis was at its apex in petrodiplomacy. Oil, bluntly, is overtly statist almost everywhere else and only indirectly statist in America. Abroad, oil reserves are owned or controlled by central governments; only England and its former settlement colonies are partial or complete exceptions to this rule. In the United States, due to oddities in old English legal traditions and American federalism, oil is owned by individuals (via total subsurface mineral rights) or states (via offshore mineral rights that the federal courts awarded them in the 1950s). Only oil on federally owned lands are specifically federal, and even that oil is never produced, refined, or sold by the government. Instead, private companies purchase federal rights and pump the oil themselves.

In the rest of the world, affairs are quite different. Central governments often own all subsurface mineral rights everywhere in their home territories. A Saudi businessman can no more privately dig for or produce oil than he can open a saloon. France, Italy, and England have major or majority holdings in national oil companies producing oil around the world. Oil, a linchpin of national security, is also a linchpin of national power; it is a public utility, necessary to modern survival, and the private sector is not allowed access to any extent without very thorough regulation. Abroad, oil is often a state monopoly. Globally, it is often a thoroughly symbiotic cartel, which suits almost all foreign governments—and almost all foreign political traditions—quite well.

America's statism, however, is different. Although oil is a de facto public utility and necessary to survival, America's federalist and minimalist ideology is so strong that government regulation of oil is ad hoc, veiled, oblique, tacit, and ambiguous. At times it is schizophrenic. Big oil companies like those in ARAMCO, for instance, were regularly pressured to cooperate with international cartels abroad to help ensure continued Western control of Middle East oil resources (e.g., during the Iranian Revolution of 1951–53) at the very time that these same companies were being charged with hundreds of antitrust violations in their domestic operations. In 1952, antitrust officials even briefly attempted to prosecute companies for being in global oil cartels that the president had approved of. Frustrated free enterprisers could never quite decide whether cartels were the norm in particularly important natural resource industries like oil or whether they weren't. They were the norm, of course—as the rise of the Organization of Petroleum Exporting Countries (OPEC) and the steady erosion of foreign oil companies' ownership and production power in the Middle East in the 1970s and 1980s later amply demonstrated.

Still, U.S. leaders were constrained by marketplace mind-sets, and few ran the risk of overtly recognizing or acting upon the fact that oil and laissez-faire did not mix. Ideologically speaking, it did not do to challenge the myth of free enterprise, and almost nobody did. Instead, for twenty years after World War II, leaders of both parties repeatedly opted for industry self-regulation, voluntary solutions to oil import issues, and baf-flegab regarding government-enforced price fixing and market allocation. Corporate and political leaders opted for de facto government-industry symbiosis, which would give something to everybody without corporate divisiveness or political risk. Energy affluence allowed such obfuscation.

The policy mélange included oil depletion allowances (for everybody from 1911 to 1975 and only for small oil after that); domestic production quotas to boost prices for domestic producers (administered and enforced by the states, with full federal backing, from 1935 to the oil drought of 1973); foreign oil import quotas from 1959 to 1973 to protect small oil from big oil; genial acceptance of even more genial oil industry estimates that the postwar United States was not reaching the end of expanding domestic oil reserves—when it, in fact, was; help for every oil company that wanted to go after an oil concession in the Middle East. The underlying beliefs were that hard choices didn't have to be faced yet, that nonmarket controls would be exercised by somebody else (like states), that federal favoritism could be given through regulations (like depletion allowances) buried deep in the federal tax code, and that the United States would always be able to set most of the rules of the global oil trade in both corporate and government dimensions.

It didn't work out that way. It couldn't. A relatively decentralized and ad hoc government and a relatively private, contentious, and competitive oil industry gradually began losing ground to nations whose relations among oil, national power, and security were overtly state centered and often overtly monopolistic. Saudi Arabia, for instance, bought a 25 percent ownership share in ARAMCO in 1973, raised its share to 60 percent a year later, acquired full ownership in 1980, and obtained full managerial control of the world's largest oil company in 1989. By 1989, only fourteen of the top fifty oil companies (state owned and private) in the world were American.

Most American leaders, however, were obsessed with the military intricacies of the cold war in the 1950s and the 1960s, not with the intricacies of commerce. The key details of how American corporations controlled Middle East oil (whether through one huge ARAMCO or through numbers of self-defeatingly competitive medium-sized and large oil companies, all bidding against each other for exploration and production rights) was not of primary concern. In 1945, before ARAMCO was formed, Secretary of the Navy James Forrestal had said that he did not "care which American company or companies developed the Arabian reserves" so long as they *were* American. What mattered most was the Soviet army, not the Saudis or the Libyans or the Kuwaitis—or Saddam Hussein of Iraq. A reckoning would take place, of course. When it did in the oil-scarce 1970s and 1980s, government-industry symbiosis fell apart. Only the Gulf War of 1990–91 reversed the trend.

Such events were not even imaginable in the immediate postwar era, however. And as American business leaders in 1950 looked to matters foreign and domestic, a very different set of challenges loomed. Korea, communism, and the corruption of Democratic presidential leadership in both foreign war and domestic economic mobilization set the stage for renewed Republican and business ascendancy under Eisenhower.

4

KOREA, COMMUNISM, AND CORRUPTION: THE PATH TO EISENHOWER

Korea began it all. A limited war on the Asian mainland went awry, becoming America's first "Vietnam." The United States entered a war to contain Korean communist aggression, scored quick victories, went on to increase the stakes to roll back aggression and conquer the aggressor, and found itself pushed into a containment strategy in a grinding war of attrition with China, the most populous communist power on the planet. All this occurred within the space of only five months, from June to November 1950. The failure of this anticommunist liberation strategy in Asia soon poisoned America's domestic politics, produced civil war within Truman's Democratic administration and within the majority Democratic Congress, and led to a conservative resurgence in the nation's affairs.

Relations between big business and government mirrored these trends. Korea initially surprised almost everyone. It seemed the wrong war against the wrong enemy in the wrong place at the wrong time—a minor Asian variant of the major anticommunist theme in Europe and a diversionary probe in a wider Soviet world offensive. As such, the "police action" in Korea did not require total economic mobilization for war, as Truman insisted with wide bipartisan support. Partial, or creeping, mobilization was enough to allow the United States to fight a small war in Asia now and, possibly, a much bigger war against the U.S.S.R. elsewhere, later.

The gray area of partial economic mobilization for limited war in Korea, however, ran into immediate trouble among those small business people who thought in ideological black and white. NAM and USCC leaders opposed controls on industry or higher taxes on business or wealthy Americans and called for a purely voluntary approach to mobilizing business. The BC and the CED, however, understood the comparative corporate advantages of "positive guidance." "Policymakers, whatever their political bias or faith," as a CED and BC eminence serving as Truman's chairman of the Federal Reserve Board put it, "are sick and tired of [laissez-faire] counsel that begins 'we oppose' and 'we are against' and 'we object.' "

Thomas McCabe of Scott Paper Company and the Federal Reserve Board was exactly right—so right that big business moderates from the BC and the CED like McCabe, not NAM and USCC ideologues, dominated the emergency economic mobilization agencies created by Truman as Korea escalated. So wide was the dominion of BC members that all the top "government" officials who met with NAM and USCC spokesmen immediately after war began to institute cooperative relations were BC members: Treasury Secretary Charles Sawyer, Averell Harriman, and General George C. Marshall (recently retired as secretary of state and soon to become secretary of defense).

Much as limited war once again made public and private sector distinctions largely academic, limited economic mobilizations often proved unpleasant exercises for big businessmen in government. Korea first destroyed Truman's political stature, then his ability to lead, and finally his presidency. Congress openly rebelled. Republican right-wingers unseated many liberal Democrats in the 1950 midterm elections. Policies unraveled as stalemate followed the massive Chinese invasion into Korea in November 1950. Senator Hubert H. Humphrey of Minnesota remembered the period as one of virulence and "systemic distress." "Letters from constituents," Humphrey recalled, "reflected the craze. Do something about housing, do something about education, do something about [un]employment, but cut taxes, slash expenditures, cut the budgets, they said in obvious contradiction. Get out of Korea, but whip the Communist Enemy. There was little logic in the air." The national mood during Harry Truman's last three years in office, like Jimmy Carter's a quarter of a century later, was a howl of self-pity and frustration.

Logic was scarce, but politics wasn't. Military defeats toppled the remnants of New Dealism in Washington. Reactionaries demanded militant anticommunism, vastly increased arms spending, no deficits, and no new taxes, partly as a way to starve to death New Deal social welfare programs. The NAM had a hit list of social programs a mile long. It orated that the pinko Truman should avoid all wartime controls (except on unions), put a retail sales tax on everything, and fight a rigidly free-enterprise war. The USCC also opposed wartime controls, taxing, and spending bills, unless the controls hindered unions, the taxation was regressive, and the spending was for the military.

Given such views, it was easy to appear moderate. So the CED's and the BC's "yes, but" accommodations ensured that they, not conservative corporate ideologues, would run wartime mobilization. Both organizations were cautious: they supported controls as long as the government also dispensed economic incentives for wartime capital investments, kept unions from growing as fast as they had in World War II, and was moderate about taxing corporations. Both backed a relatively mild "rigid economy" in nondefense spending and balanced budgets. They wanted the middle class, not the corporations or the wealthy, to pay for the war. They did not advocate abolishing social programs.

Corporate politicians strove to control a semimobilization for a semiwar that became steadily more politically and economically expensive following Chinese victories in northern Korea. Corporate liberals recruited from the BC headed almost all the top economic stabilization boards created just after the Korean War began—and all the successor agencies reorganized and centralized after China entered the war. The Defense Production Act passed by Congress in September 1950 only increased big business's advantages. Accelerated depreciation, loan guarantees, and government-built plants were tendered to war industries as in World War II. Antitrust laws were again retired for the duration. To reassure business further, no civilian production was banned. Guns *and* butter became the limited war principle.

Advisory committees to recruit private industrial expertise also inevitably proliferated. By the end of 1950, there were 68 such symbiotic committees. By 1952, there were 554. To further entice business, union representatives were excluded from these committees. Although USCC and NAM spokesmen protested the controls, apparently seeing them as big business setting rules for small business à la World War II, BC and CED leaders stayed in Washington to ensure that the controls stayed unobtrusive compared with World War II controls. Truman's White House cooperated in this corporate effort. As Bert Cochran has written, Truman, like Jimmy Carter twenty-five years later, "initiated controls with the dedication of a man who starts looking for a job . . . hoping he will not find one."

Organized labor, however, was not nearly as accommodating. It didn't share Truman's small town economic assumptions. The roaring wartime economic boom was leaving many unions power poor, with union membership not rising significantly, as it had in World War II. Inflation fears were rife. Union leaders simply weren't winning on the crucial details of mobilization policy. Their discontentment soon translated into strong pushes for compensatory higher wages throughout industry. By 1952, the number of U.S. workers out on strike totaled 3.5 million, the most since ill-omened 1946.

As union leaders and members mounted picket lines, politics turned surly. In December 1950, Truman called together a triumvirate of BC and CED leaders: Charles E. Wilson of General Electric, Eric L. Johnston (also formerly president of the USCC), and Cyrus Ching of US Rubber to reorganize war controls. These three men called for a strict wage-price freeze as of January 26, 1951. Angry union leaders thereupon promptly withdrew from emergency wage stabilization boards, the only ones upon which they had any real representation. Most were enticed back for a pro forma year, before they walked out again, permanently.

There was reason for union leaders' anger. Truman's limited wartime controls usually let business control its own prices and to restrain wages as well. The problem for the unions was that price cheating is usually much easier to accomplish than wage cheating, particularly when business applies wage standards and makes the judgment calls (i.e., about fringe benefits). As wage limitations bit deeper, union leaders demanded Truman put himself on the line and give business hell on *their* behalf.

Truman tried not to oblige—until, that is, a national strike loomed in steel, a key war industry he could not ignore. Starting late in 1951, the steelworkers union issued repeated demands that he support a significant wage increase, to be paid for largely out of company profits.

While Truman had a wage stabilization board on which union leaders still (barely) served "study" the matter, big business leaders in government played some hardball of their own. Chaos in Congress had worsened, and the limited war in Korea had killed Truman politically, so corporate politicians by the hundreds beat a path to the Republicans. In December 1951, the CED withdrew its support for Truman's economic controls; in March 1952, the BC followed suit. Simultaneously, the wage stabilization board advocated a 12 percent hike in workers' pay without any compensatory increase in steel prices. The hard-pressed president accepted the wage board's recommendations, and steel producers were furious. BC member Charles E. Wilson of GE, director of defense mobilization, was also furious. On March 25, Wilson told Truman that if he did not reverse himself, Wilson would resign. Wilson went. Four days later, Truman's popularity within a by-now seriously splintered Democratic party was so low that he withdrew as a candidate for reelection (just as Lyndon Johnson would do after the Tet offensive twenty-six years later). The furious steelworkers union, meanwhile, struck.

Truman was also furious: about conservatives feasting on him in Congress, about big business in revolt against controls, about unions shredding him for conduct unbecoming a Democrat. Truman had become a lame duck president with nothing left to lose. He slashed back, especially at steel producers, who berated him for not controlling unions sufficiently on their behalf. Over the opposition of his own attorney general (who quickly resigned), Truman tried to temporarily and partially "seize" (nationalize) the nation's steel mills. The fox was in the political henhouse now. "Give 'em hell" Harry was going out with a bang. Truman sought to repeat FDR's dramatic World War II seizures of the coal and railroad industries and to pay off long outstanding debts to union leaders at one and the same time. In Truman's view, he'd been stabbed in the back by business when he was at his weakest politically, fighting communists abroad and Congress at home.

Corporate politicians' views, of course, differed. Seizure—however temporary and partial—made capitalism conditional upon good behavior as determined by presidents on national security grounds in an unprecedented state of constant crisis called the cold war. Business leaders pondered such notions like men ordered to play tag with sharks.

Relations got downright bloodthirsty after that. Lawyers contended in courtrooms and newspaper editors on editorial pages. Truman's squelching of a national rail strike in 1946 over union opposition had been statesmanlike, but his telling steel corporations that a union was going to get wage increases without their raising steel prices was dictatorship. Balderdash, replied Truman, the steel companies were unpatriotic war profiteers. Both sides verbally slugged it out. On April 9, 1952, eighty-five steel companies were told to expect seizure. Wage hikes were inevitable if Truman succeeded. Congress, meanwhile, was in an uproar; impeachment bills were introduced. And 95 percent of the nation's newspaper owners condemned Truman editorially.

Lawyers got even busier when, on April 29, a federal appeals court judge ruled Truman's temporary nationalization illegal, and constitutional gridlock threatened. The Supreme Court immediately heard arguments in the case and announced its decision on June 2, as the steelworkers' union vowed more strikes if the Court's ruling in a case known as *Youngstown Sheet and Tube versus Sawyer* went against it. The Court didn't blink. Its all-Democrat-appointed justices turned Truman and the union down cold in a six to three vote. For the first time since the beginning of World War II, an extension of presidential emergency powers was voided. Cold war was not (legally, anyway) yet hot war.

Conservatives were delighted. So were many in Congress, for it was Congress's legislative power that the Court majority said Truman had unconstitutionally usurped. Truman, added the Court, should have used the Taft-Hartley Act's sixty-day cooling-off period, powers Congress had already given him, before attempting seizure of private property.

Truman surrendered but delayed six weeks to avoid bludgeoning a livid (and still striking) steelworkers' union to the bargaining table via Taft-

Hartley. On July 23 he arranged labor-management talks at the White House. The very next day, Truman announced a settlement that gave the union its wage increase, but only at the price of giving the companies all the compensatory price increases they demanded. Truman's final effort to uphold unraveling wartime controls had signally failed: one of the biggest corporate-government confrontations in modern U.S. history ended in total defeat for the lame-duck president and the left wing of his party.

Inflation—given the demise of Truman's disheveled limited controls and the ire of frustrated unions—might now have become public enemy number one in corporate circles. But it did not. War was an engine of both cost-push and demand-pull inflation, but the business politicians of the CED and the BC no longer depended on weak Democratic presidents or ineffective Democratic Congresses for protection from such difficulties. Just before the Court scuttled Truman's steel seizure, a more independent Federal Reserve Board began to serve as a bastion of the business approach to utilizing federal power in cold war America. With increases in Federal Reserve power starting in 1951 and continuing under Eisenhower, two decades of Democratic efforts to control inflation via varied wage and price controls ended. For another two decades, inflation control moved toward far more traditional symbiotic techniques: central bank monetary policy.

Inflation had been an enduring corporate concern for a decade: first war, then skyrocketing prices after the armistice, then a brief period of relative price stability, then Korea loosing inflationary genies once again. Three-fourths of the wholesale price inflation in the twenty-five years following World War II occurred in the five years between 1946 and 1951. Business, particularly capital-intensive big business, liked none of it. Inflation eroded the value of income, assets, and wealth; made long-term investments riskier; increased corporate and individual progressive income tax rates; penalized savers and creditors; and reduced or undid profits. An obvious way to stamp out inflation was unemployment: decrease price pressures by decreasing the money supply, crunching credit, increasing interest rates, and lowering investment, output, income, and employment.

Decreased employment, however, also meant lots of discontented voters without jobs. Liberal Democrats to whom powerful unions were allied, therefore, preferred the longer term economic risks of inflation to the shorter term political risks of unemployment. Conservatives, meanwhile, preferred higher unemployment over higher inflation on the basis of very different calculations favoring more affluent voters.

Big business leaders also preferred unemployment to inflation once fears of a renewed depression ended by 1948. They were not elected by masses of citizens. Unemployment was something corporate managers very rarely mandated for themselves, as opposed to those they employed. Corporate managers had far more to fear, in institutional terms, from inflation than from unemployment. Profits and savings erosion, higher tax rates, and riskier investments could all hurt firms—and careers. Inflation also psychologically threatened employers more than unemployment did. They could easily control employment within their individual firms, but their individual powers to affect inflation via pricing were comparatively costly, dubious, or inconvenient to admit. Business leaders, finally, were far more likely than other groups to be both college educated and trained in economics; they knew there was an inflation-unemployment trade-off. They believed most nonbusiness people were economic illiterates or bunglers.

To minimize bungling, members of the BC and the CED also believed that managing the money supply was the easiest, least interventionist, and best single way to perk up or cool off a normal economy. Interest rates were the key: the lower they were, the more money bankers would loan and the faster the economy and employment would grow; the higher interest rates were, the less money bankers would loan, and the slower the economy and employment would grow. Controlling credit availability, then, was a fine way to control inflation. As banking and finance went, so went the economy; and as the money supply went, so went probable levels of inflation and unemployment.

All this, in turn, meant that business people, unlike most other political Americans, understood the supreme practical importance of Federal Reserve System policies. The Fed is America's central bank, its "banker's bank." As the Fed goes on interest rates, so goes banking generally. And as banking goes, so goes the rest of the economy. The problem was, in the view of big business, that the Fed's interest rate policy had made it an "engine of inflation." The Truman administration, like the Roosevelt administration before it, was committed to full employment, full employment was dependent upon high economic growth fueled by low interest rates ("easy money"), and easy money meant inflation. Worse, it used federal deficits to underwrite (possibly inflationary) economic growth.

This deficit financing system worked as a result of a long-standing gentleman's agreement between the Fed, a semiindependent central bank with both public and private financial characteristics, and the Treasury Department, the executive branch's chief bill payer and revenue raiser. The treasury, to service the vast federal debt created by deficit spending during the Depression, Korea, and (especially) World War II, wanted the interest rates it paid on money borrowed from banks and individuals kept low. This was made far easier when the Fed agreed to "monetize the debt." Translated from economese into English, the Fed supported (pegged) the market in treasury certificates of federal indebtedness (U.S. Treasury bonds) so that their prices remained high and the interest rates on fixed-return securities remained low. To do this it printed money and bought treasury bonds with it. Because treasury bonds were the least risky securities around, their low interest rates helped lower interest rates on all other types of debt. However, the Fed's antiinflationary hands were tied: it wrote checks to buy bonds, thus making easy money, low interest rates, economic growth, and low unemployment possible, but it couldn't tighten credit by reducing the money supply. Federal monetary policy was flexible in only one direction.

The White House, via the treasury, dominated the Fed, which many of the nation's leading bankers and businessmen regularly advised. The CED, the BC, and Fed Chairman and BC member Thomas B. McCabe backed a more powerful and independent Fed, after depression fears had subsided in early 1948. The Fed should crunch the economy as well as spur it. It should no longer be bound by the experiences of the Depression and World War II. Congress was also concerned about the Fed as an inflationary engine. Tight monetary policy looked increasingly necessary as a brake on the fiscal (taxing-spending) policy of the Korean War era. Congress, often oblivious to economic theory, regularly willed the end (federal spending) without willing the means (federal taxes). This meant that, lacking economic growth miracles, federal budgets and federal deficits were usually much higher than many preferred. If, therefore, the New Deal welfare state was not going to disappear (and it wasn't) and if Congress was going to continue passing new spending bills more often than new taxing bills (and it was), a more powerful nonelected Federal Reserve Board was necessary to choke off deficit-fueled inflationary pressure by the most traditional, least interventionist, and most politically protected means available—central bank monetary policy.

In March 1951, three years of CED-orchestrated effort succeeded. In a move understood by few, an important treasury–Federal Reserve accord was signed. Under its terms, the nation's business-oriented central bank freed itself of a decade-long treasury ascendancy. Relatively interventionist federal taxing, spending, and wage-price control policies were replaced by less statist and less interventionist monetary controls applied by a semiindependent regulatory agency manned by business leaders. Just as the Supreme Court had protected big business's pricing and ownership powers in the steel seizure case, the central bank now protected business from inflation. Government in America had undergone an organizational revolution during twenty years of Democratic crisis management. Corporate leaders again demonstrated that they, too, knew how to manage elite conflicts.

The politics of central banking, like that of foreign aid, showed how corporate power was often inversely proportional to an issue's visibility. Where policy was complicated and technical and, thus, involved relatively few members of the public or business, big business views often counted most. There was, however, another side to this coin, for where policy was clear, more immediate, more compelling, and energized large numbers of people and firms, big business's desires often counted for little. An instance of the latter political dynamic was the McCarthyite red scare of the early 1950s. Cold war routinized emergency in America; it made crisis perpetual. Traditionalist, minimal-government conservatives feared the condition, but they feared communism more. It was only a matter of time before this conservative dilemma boiled over into frustrated ideological wrath. Their idyllic Jeffersonian America was caught between the devil of big government and the deep blue sea of communism. Plainly, forces of statist subversion and conspiracy were at work.

Small business traditionalists in the NAM and the USCC launched an antisubversive offensive in the business community: as early as 1946, the well-financed Free Enterprise Campaign was under way in America, led by both organizations. Anticommunism was incessant in grass roots propaganda. "The Reds," a USCC leader fulminated privately in March 1946, "have a lot to do with our current, very serious labor situation." Strike waves, in fact, were bolshevism run rampant. "We will have to send some firing squads in[to] every good-sized city and town in the country," he continued, "and . . . liquidate the Reds and the Pink Benedict Arnolds." Publicly, the USCC issued a less bloodthirsty pamphlet, "Communist Infiltration in the United States," one month before the 1946 congressional elections. Unions and liberal Democrats were prominent radical suspects. Government regulation became, in this and other NAM and USCC publications, "inefficient, un-American, dangerous to national morals and the basic liberties enshrined in the Constitution."

National small business organizations weren't the only commie hunters. The AFL red baited the CIO; the FBI and the American Legion smeared the Democrats; the Catholic church used red baiting to accelerate a postwar religious revival; steel, auto, chemical, and electrical firms facing long and costly CIO strikes secretly contributed to extreme conservative pressure groups. Truman administration policymakers, meanwhile, used red menace arguments that were "clearer than the truth" to sell military and economic alliances like NATO and the Marshall Plan to Congress and to an American public they often considered ignorant, gullible, and unsophisticated. Ambitious Republican politicos like Richard Nixon of California ranted privately to GOP foreign policy eminence John Foster Dulles in 1948 that "under the New Deal communist affiliation was probably the best recommendation possible for a person who wanted to get ahead in government."

Initially, each segment of this anticommunist multitude had different political agendas. Rancor and bitterness was widespread, but it was often too diffuse and partisan to get very far. Efforts were fragmented, such as small business's efforts to undo labor unions and New Deal labor laws. Truman's second term, however, changed everything. First Truman was elected against the odds. That was bad enough. Then the GOP lost control of both houses of Congress after only two years. That was disastrous. The Republicans badly needed an energizing political issue.

Global circumstances soon provided the issue. The Soviets exploded their first nuclear weapon late in 1949. Fears of atomic spies became endemic. Two months later, China became the second communist super-power on the planet. Congressman Nixon, with the quiet cooperation of the USCC's chief red hunter, was in the midst of an ultimately successful prosecution of Alger Hiss, a former high State Department official, for perjury and past communist associations.

Republican elder statesman and Senator Robert A. Taft then brought the red scare into the mainstream of American elite politics. A beleaguered Truman and his aides, Taft argued, were too reluctantly antired. Events were showing they simply weren't tough enough. Democrats were "dominated by a policy of appeasing the Russians abroad and of fostering communism at home." Liberals were naive dupes who created subversion. Only hard-eyed conservatives could save the Republic. War in Korea, begun in early 1950, turned such partisan rancor into rebellion. The country, mired in the frustrations of cold war and containment, went berserk.

The best known and least scrupulous leader of the four-year political purge that followed was Republican Senator Joseph R. McCarthy of Wisconsin. McCarthy, unlike Nixon or Taft, ignored facts, legal or otherwise. McCarthy was a showman. He did not legislate, as Taft did, or prosecute, as Nixon did; he simply attacked. If one conspiracy smear didn't work, he found another. McCarthy understood how to demand that people participate in a logical fallacy known as proving a negative: *prove that you are not now and never have been or never have consorted with or assisted communists, knowingly or unknowingly: prove that you are not a dupe or subversive; prove you've stopped betraying your country*. Now, after twenty years of waiting, reactionary, small-government conservatives in America finally had their hour.

Big business politicians in the BC and the CED, meanwhile, sat out the great red scare. A handful of present and former CED and BC members publicly supported McCarthy; another handful publicly opposed him. The vast majority kept their mouths shut and their heads down. McCarthy had his uses, after all. His bad means might lead to good ends; Democratic liberals, for instance, went down to political defeat or lapsed into cautious silence, and voters deserting Truman might vote Republican, presidentially and congressionally. McCarthy's sledgehammer smashed two decades of Democratic dominance in Washington to bits. Finally, McCarthy wasn't yet doing anything to inconvenience businessmen: their anticommunist credentials were impeccable, and there were far more inviting targets around.

As long as the Truman administration stayed in office and the war dragged on in Korea, the logic of opportunism ruled in corporate America, as elsewhere. But then two things happened to change the political dynamic. First, weakened Democrats lost both the presidential and congressional elections of 1952 to the Republicans. For the first time since 1930, a GOP president *and* a GOP-majority House and Senate coexisted in Washington. Second, the new Republican regime negotiated an armistice that ended the Korean War by July 1953. McCarthy then outlived his usefulness: further unearthing of subversion only reflected badly on Republicans. McCarthy, however, would not stop his attacks, and moderate Republicans now became responsible for proving that they were not soft on communism. Conservative traditionalists were frustrated by Ike's unwillingness to destroy international communism by declaring war on it.

These reactionary loose cannons were also firing, finally, in the direction of big business. McCarthy, anxious to run all Truman era "appeasers" out of policy posts in Washington, attacked the corporate lawyers, financiers, and industrialists brought into government to create such bipartisan cold war fundamentals as the Marshall Plan. McCarthy pilloried Dean Acheson, Paul Nitze, John J. McCloy, and scores of others as "Wall Street operators" and communist sympathizers. By March 1953, McCarthy was attacking Averell Harriman (whom Truman had unsuccessfully supported for the Democratic presidential nomination in 1952) as a subversive "whose admiration for everything Russian is unrivalled outside of the confines of the Communist Party." Had matters stopped there, they would have been bad enough. But they soon got worse. McCarthy wanted not only to get rid of Democratic appointees, he wanted to select their replacements within the

Republican leadership by intimidating the non-McCarthyite conservatives around the new president. In late 1953 and early 1954, the increasingly frustrated McCarthy attacked "subversion" in the army officer corps. The message to career army General Eisenhower was obvious.

McCarthy's new intimidation campaign, however, misfired badly. To pillory the army, and to intimidate Ike, McCarthy and his congressional allies began by smearing a close Eisenhower military associate (and former BC member), General George C. Marshall of the Marshall Plan. McCarthy then attacked Army Secretary Robert Stevens, a former chairman of the BC. Stevens was attacked for not immediately discharging an army dentist from the service on McCarthy's demand after the dentist took the Fifth Amendment regarding past Communist party membership. Stevens counterattacked but then capitulated after being baited before McCarthy's Senate committee in February 1954. Stevens, McCarthy graciously concluded, was an "awful dupe."

Then another BC member, Ralph Flanders, a Vermont industrialist, Republican senator from that state since 1946, and cofounder of the CED, got involved in the fray. In March 1954, Flanders, capitalizing on the reduced political tensions after the armistice in Korea, strongly attacked McCarthy. Flanders' effort was the only one made in the Senate after 1951, when fellow CED founder William Benton, then a Democratic senator from Connecticut, frontally assaulted McCarthy. (He was subsequently unseated in a smear-ridden campaign in the 1952 elections.) By spring of 1954, Flanders was calling loudly for McCarthy's censure by the Senate. Benton and fellow-CED founder Paul Hoffman, meanwhile, provided extensive financial assistance to a lobbying group created to help Flanders topple McCarthy. Some of the nation's most prominent corporate politicians were out after McCarthy's scalp.

Eisenhower himself continued to evade confronting McCarthy. But the fact that Republicans were now openly attacking one of their own gave courage to previously cautious media corporations and the army itself. CBS television news, headed by a man who soon became a BC member, televised a documentary attack on McCarthy by reporter Edward R. Murrow, as Flanders launched his first attacks on Capitol Hill. The military quickly joined in. By April, thirty-six days of live televised Army-McCarthy hearings badly damaged McCarthy, especially after he defended the unethical actions of his possibly homosexual aides, Roy Cohn and G. David Schine.

Army Secretary Stevens's previous public crucifixion at McCarthy's hands, meanwhile, did not set well with the BC. As the Army-McCarthy hearings ended in May, Stevens attended a BC meeting at a resort near

Washington. He was met at the airport by a special delegation of corporate peers, escorted to the meeting, and given a conquering hero's welcome. Eisenhower administration officials at the meeting, meanwhile, were cold-shouldered for not putting McCarthy on a leash and keeping him there. Given that two of Eisenhower's top three cabinet officers were BC members (recruited for Ike by a longtime military associate, General Lucius D. Clay, also a BC member), it is unlikely that the lack of welcome by the assembled CEOs was lost on the administration. These two, Secretary of the Treasury George M. Humphrey (a Cleveland steel magnate) and Secretary of Defense Charles Erwin Wilson (of General Motors) could not ignore the fact that they too were now grist for McCarthy's mill—given that their BC peer and open shop advocate Bob Stevens was about as Marxist as apple pie.

Once corporate opposition to McCarthy grew in Congress, in the cabinet, and in important big business government advisory groups, McCarthy's days were numbered. Big business opposition alone did not undermine McCarthy or end the four-year red scare, but it legitimized dissent and made opposing America's chief communist hunter less risky.

McCarthy had many enemies, but most had stayed safe, obscure, and quiet, including rising young politicians Richard Nixon, John Kennedy, and Lyndon Johnson. Not until big business opposition grew did moderate Republican leaders do something about McCarthy and end the spasm of reaction that small business forces in the NAM and the USCC had helped unleash. Altruism was rarely involved. Big business internationalists had helped design and implement the bipartisan cold war policies McCarthy termed treasonous. They fought, finally, not to protect others but to protect themselves and the moderate, internationalist wing of the GOP, of which almost all were a part. In December 1954, McCarthy was censured by the Senate. His days as a reactionary anticommunist superstar were over.

A decade of reassuring political and economic security for American big business followed the brief McCarthyite spasm. *Security* in the 1930s had meant economic protection from the ravages of depression. In the 1940s, *security* came to mean military protection during global war, both hot and cold. America in 1936 and 1946 possessed relatively little of either sort of security. The 1950s, however, were in many respects a realization of American corporate dreams deferred for decades of crisis. *Security* was both military and economic, and there was more of it around than ever before.

Politics also looked secure. Postwar liberalism, after Truman's failed second term and the McCarthy era, no longer threatened to expand federal power. Such statist expansions as occurred were cautious and thoroughly rationalized in conservative terms.

Unradical America, however, was a mixed system. Although the New Deal was largely contained, the era of minimal government was no more. In the era symbolized by the cautious Dwight David Eisenhower, military-industrial and other symbiotic relations between business and the state grew.

5

EISENHOWER AND THE
AMERICAN CORPORATE DREAM

The same cold war tensions that conservatives used to weaken the left also, ironically, undermined the ideological foundations of the right. After two decades of depression, war, and anticommunist crusade, realists no longer debated whether the central government should be large; they debated why it should be large. Washington was now "a necessary agent for good in a hostile world."

Progressive conservatives accepted this cold war irony. Big government was hell, but the alternative was worse. The more conservative only grimaced: they were on the horns of a howling ideological dilemma—they wanted to kill lots of communists without big organizations or big money. The Republican right reluctantly supported cold war globalist military and economic policies "that had the domestic effects they most feared," but they believed that domestic conspiracies (not depression or war) had destroyed the America of William McKinley, Herbert Hoover, and Daniel Boone. Moderate Eisenhower Republicans yearned less for bygone minimalist days and accepted the necessity of American global military and economic action, but they sought to avoid a too big government by trying to do the job cheaply.

Alas, policing the world was not cheap. In an era of increasingly high-tech weapons systems, it became increasingly expensive. The point was made repeatedly to a reluctant Eisenhower. Ike intimate Arthur Larson detailed one such illumination, circa 1954–55:

> One day in the middle of the winter I was sitting with Eisenhower in his office when Secretary of Defense Charles Wilson came in to talk about his budget. The conversation soon turned into a one-way harangue by Eisenhower, whose sole theme was that Wilson had to stay within his budget at all costs. "Not one penny over, do you understand? Not under any circumstances!" "Yes sir," was about all Wilson could manage, looking almost like a school-boy getting a scolding. The session ended with the most solemn, sacred, immutable promise by Wilson that, whatever it took, the line would be held and the budget not exceeded.
>
> A couple of months later I happened to be with Eisenhower when Wilson

again appeared. To an incredulous Eisenhower, Wilson managed to blurt out his confession: he was already two billion dollars over his budget. I shall never forget the protracted moment of blank silence that followed, while the two men stared speechless at each other, as if in the presence of some gigantic, unknowable, uncontrollable force of nature.

The "force of nature" called *cold war* became an economic fixture after Korea. Eisenhower and Wilson sat flabbergasted as one year's military spending sailed over its budget by almost two-thirds of total federal spending of only twenty years before. A Republican general who had termed Truman's Korean War military expenditures "disastrous" and who had winced as federal budgets, military appropriations, and deficits doubled and more than doubled from mid-1950 to mid-1951, had eight years of military budgets averaging $44 billion annually. America's pre-Korea arms spending levels tripled, as an era of permanent high-technology mobilization began.

It was frustrating. An "intolerable burden," Secretary of the Treasury George Humphrey called it. But burden it remained: nuclear and other arms races stayed expensive. Congressional Democrats, meanwhile, pushed for increases in Republican defense spending in every year of Eisenhower's two terms except 1957. Ike, Senator John F. Kennedy often charged, mistakenly placed "fiscal security ahead of national security." The cold war should (and later would) be fought more vigorously on many more technological and geographic fronts.

Still Eisenhower conservatives persevered. Technological imperatives, however, were against them: rocketry, jet aircraft, long-distance bombers, spy satellites—the whole postwar aerospace revolution; computers in their prolific weapons systems applications; nuclear-powered submarines to deliver thermonuclear weapons with greater accuracy, stealth, and surprise; infrared night scopes for rifles; improved radar and sonar detection devices; helicopters innumerable. Wave after wave of innovations made generations of existing weapons obsolete. U.S. military spending, the conservative *Economist* magazine later estimated, increased by a factor of thirty in constant (1990) dollars in the sixty years from 1930 to 1990. High technology, America's way of war, drove this transformation. Military spending totaled about 70 percent of the budget in Eisenhower's era. When the costs of all past wars were removed, cold war defense still composed over half the budget.

By the end of Ike's presidency, only twenty companies received over half of the total dollar value of all prime military contracts, and only a hundred firms accounted for 75 percent of the total, up from 63 percent in 1953.

This military-industrial symbiosis is illustrated by the aerospace industry. Before World War II it barely existed. Airplane manufacturers employed fewer workers than candy and confectionary firms, and three-quarters of all their production went for export. Pearl Harbor changed all that. FDR called for and got 50,000 planes a year by 1942, seventeen times prewar levels. Without massive government financing, none of this could have happened. So it remained after the war. Air power and national security became synonymous. By the end of the 1950s, about 80 percent of the aircraft and aerospace industry's business was done with Washington.

Airplanes weren't all Washington wanted. Rockets stopped being science fiction and became hard military fact in World War II. The 1950s saw the start of the space age, particularly after the Soviets orbited *Sputnik I*, earth's first artificial satellite, in October 1957. *Sputnik* thoroughly upset the "delicate balance of terror" of the nuclear age in America, just as earlier Soviet advances in thermonuclear technology had done. The powerful Soviet intercontinental missiles powering the Soviet space program also ended the geographic isolation that was the historic basis of America's minimal government ideology. Missiles, moreover, could not be built by private investment and enterprise alone, since there were no profitable private markets for them. Washington had to underwrite them.

Research and development funding is illustrative of the way the government's role has grown. Until World War II, universities and private foundations financed most scientific and engineering research without immediate marketplace potential. Pure science was what academics did. Business financed applied science in industries like pharmaceuticals and telecommunications. World War II, however, shifted the financing of increasingly expensive R&D out of the private sector and into the public sector. The development of the atomic bomb vividly illustrated the phenomenon: pure science had awesome applications. In aerospace, electronics, nuclear weapons, nuclear energy, and other high-tech industries, Washington became the biggest source of science R&D money around. By 1955, it provided 53 percent of the $6.2 billion of total R&D spending; in 1961, it provided 65 percent of $14.3 billion. And by the late 1950s, 85 percent of federal R&D spending was for the military. Private industry did up to three-quarters of the work, and large universities and semiprivate research labs did most of the remainder.

Creating cold war weaponry mixed public and private in other ways. New federally funded research and development centers were created to organize the "perpetual technological revolution." These semipublic military R&D think tanks, today numbering just under forty, began with the Rand Institute in 1946, established to chart high-tech directions for the air force. Symbiosis here was thorough. Think tanks like Rand were in the government but not of it, formulating policy on contract.

Think tanks (which by 1990 received $6 billion in annual contracts, or about 10 percent of Washington's total R&D budget) were soon joined by another type of symbiotic agency, also oriented toward cold war science. Starting with the University of California at Berkeley's Los Alamos National Laboratory, which managed the Manhattan Project, universities and corporations built and operated ten major, federally funded, basic research facilities, half of them heavily oriented toward the military. DuPont Corporation, for example, built the Oak Ridge National Laboratory, which helped Los Alamos develop nuclear weapons. Today, the facility is run by Martin Marietta, a major Pentagon contractor. The Brookhaven, Argonne, and Lawrence Livermore national laboratories are all research institutions run by universities like Berkeley and the University of Chicago. The Jet Propulsion Labs in Pasadena, California, part of California Institute of Technology, manage all of NASA's unmanned deep-space exploration missions.

Federal R&D, weapons spending, think tanks, national laboratories, and other initiatives eroded the traditional boundaries between the federal government, industry, and academe. They were the components of the mixed system, which led Eisenhower to conclude his presidency in January 1961 by warning of the threats of a growing "military-industrial complex."

But in spite of his lame-duck swan songs, Eisenhower and other cold war leaders were faced with practical military-industrial conditions, not traditional theories, while in office and in power. The alternative to state-supported R&D in such strategic areas as rocketry, computers, and nuclear weaponry usually appeared to be Armageddon. So symbiosis it was. State-assisted development of new products, new technologies, and new industries—plus the deliberate use of scientific and technological R&D as a mechanism for corporate growth and national security alike—became characteristic of American government and American capitalism in the 1950s—so much so that the approach was intensively copied in Europe and Japan during the twenty years thereafter.

The Defense Advanced Research Projects Agency (DARPA) illustrates how cold war state dynamics regularly helped create new industries from scratch. DARPA, born after *Sputnik,* subsidized the development of *very* risky technologies with *very* high-potential military payoffs. For instance, $1 billion of DARPA money over twenty-five years went to what became segments of the modern computer industry, including fast microprocessor chips and ways to transmit data via telephone. DARPA encouraged researchers to establish firms in California's Silicon Valley to produce strategic hardware and software. In 1992 these companies employed 12,000 workers and had combined sales of $2.5 billion a year. DARPA's support for America's "defense technology base" finessed the normal boundaries between public and private, civilian and military. It confined its support to indirect financing (via R&D awards) rather than direct ownership (via purchasing stock in the companies). Thus, the public versus private proprieties were (barely) maintained.

Despite the fact that DARPA, the postwar Atomic Energy Commission (AEC) and other such symbiotic agencies strained political and economic tradition, they worked. Federal purchasing (mostly of a cost-plus-a-fixed-fee sort common to previous wars), government R&D, and quasi-public research and technology policy planning agencies all helped achieve unprecedented nationwide economic affluence. Washington didn't create boom times by itself, but it did encourage 1950s growth industries like aerospace, computers, and electronics through federal financing. For International Business Machines (IBM) in the 1950s, the federal government was the best single customer. The modern computer had originated out of federal R&D projects to improve artillery targeting of enemy aircraft during World War II.

Few political or economic leaders, however, agonized much about such symbiotic matters. High-tech arms races had to be run. Technology, many conservatives hoped, could even solve the problem of big government that war technologies had created. More bang for the buck, as Eisenhower advisers called it, would turn more arms spending into less. Wonder weapons would overawe the communists, the cold war would be won, and too much government wouldn't complicate American life permanently. Meanwhile, more should be spent on technology now, as a down payment on better cold war tomorrows.

Alas for rosy conservative hopes, cold war competition universalized during the 1950s. Not only was it waged everywhere, it began to be waged about everything. Education, economic growth, space exploration, and other matters became as vital as missiles, computers, and nuclear weapons. All symbolized victory or defeat in a total struggle between competing social systems. In such an atmosphere of universal conflict, new federal spending programs were often rationalized in terms of victory in this expanded cold war competition. In 1956 Ike supported the defense-oriented Interstate Highway Act, which eventually produced over 200,000 miles of main roads tying America together. In 1958, Ike signed the National Defense Education Act, a program that sent millions of students off to college via federally subsidized loans and grants.

By 1952, the ironies of cold war conservatism were evident in corporate inner circles. BC members, like all business people, regularly lauded economy in government, and they hoped, as Ike did, that eventually air power and nuclear weapons would accomplish this. Emigré rocket expert Wernher Von Braun understood this logic and how to appeal to it. When Von Braun addressed the BC in 1952 in a speech, "Space Superiority as a Means of Achieving World Peace," he added heavenly missiles and orbiting space stations to the *more bang for the buck* equation—so successfully that his arguments were reprinted for all BC CEOs in a special illustrated pamphlet. Again, via federally funded high technology, more became less.

The conservative masses of America also avoided agonizing about how state-subsidized high technology and national strength were related. The lives of the multitudes, meanwhile, benefited from the symbiotic relations between business and the state as immediately as many a military contractor's.

The homes millions lived in made the point. By the 1950s, residential housing construction was a "quasi-public activity" and "an important pillar of America's underwritten economy." The United States was literally built into a nation of homeowners with substantial assistance from federal financial regulations, subsidies, and guarantees. How all this came about is a story of federal regulations underwriting the banking system; political incentives to financial institutions to loan money on easier terms for home building; and federal programs insuring millions of home mortgages.

Federal guarantees for banking began during the Depression. The RFC and an expanded, more powerful Federal Reserve system became multibillion-dollar lenders of last resort to many failing banks. More important in the longer term, the New Deal guaranteed bank deposits via new Washington agencies, including the Federal Deposit Insurance Corporation (FDIC) and the Federal Savings and Loan Insurance Corporation (FSLIC). National insurance of bank deposits stopped panic withdrawals and facilitated lending, especially multiyear mortgage lending. Banks paid fees for FDIC protection to help maintain bailout funds for failed banks. These were government-brokered subsidies from stronger banks to weaker ones, undertaken for the greater good of the financial system as a whole.

Washington did more than stabilize banks by insuring their deposits. It also insured growing numbers of bank mortgages, especially after 1945. First via the Federal Housing Administration (FHA) and later via the Veterans Administration (VA), Washington promised to pay off mortgage loans if private borrowers failed to repay their debts.

In addition to insuring bank deposits and residential mortgages, the federal government also created a banker's bank, fully equivalent to the Fed, to loan money to those banks like savings and loans (S&Ls) specializing in mortgage lending. S&Ls used their mortgage assets as collateral during cash-short periods. The resulting Federal Home Loan Bank Board (as it was called until 1988), like the Federal Reserve System, required all member institutions using its credit facilities to accept regulations affecting the maximum interest rates they charged on loans, the amount of price competition from other banks for deposits, the types of housing loans they had to make in exchange for favorable income tax treatment relative to commercial banks, and the minimum amounts of cash they had to keep in their vaults to cover financial emergencies. Most housing lenders, like most commercial lenders before them, hastened to join the new federal system.

Washington also helped create financial institutions to get around state banking laws that prohibited interstate banking. It created national mortgage markets to spread economic risk. Banks in "mortgage rich" states batched together their loans and sold them to "mortgage poor" banks in other states. Washington also set up quasi-government organizations like the Federal National Mortgage Association (Fannie Mae) and the Federal Home Loan Mortgage Corporation (Freddie Mac), which today guarantee almost $2 trillion in de facto government-backed securities to develop national markets for federally guaranteed home mortgages. Lending institutions batch mortgages and sell them to Fannie Mae and Freddie Mac; they, in turn, package them into securities and sell them to investors everywhere.

Meanwhile, temporary emergency agencies underwrote housing markets in yet another way. During the depths of the Depression, nearly one-quarter of all home mortgages were in default. The Home Owners Loan Corporation (HOLC) dealt with the crisis; it bought up about one-tenth of residential nonfarm mortgage debt, bad loans that bankers were happy to get rid of. In return, the HOLC gave banks federally guaranteed bonds they were happy to hold. Millions of families thus avoided homelessness because of yet another symbiotic federal agency few knew about and fewer understood.

Washington did more. It financed construction of large-scale "defense housing" near war plants and military bases after Pearl Harbor. Via the FHA, it subsidized sixty-year mortgages to local governments building municipally owned housing for people too poor to pay for private housing. By 1970, about 2 percent of all city dwellers lived in about 1 million such housing units; by 1990, total public housing units increased to 1.4 million.

With the exception of this wartime housing construction and FHA-subsidized public housing programs, however, federal programs affecting the housing market, from the Depression to the advent of Eisenhower, were relatively nonstatist. In other countries, governments normally built and owned housing. In America, the preferred route was indirect government tax and credit incentives, financial guarantees, and subsidies to induce the private sector to lower mortgage interest rates, lower down payments on mortgages, and lengthen mortgage repayment periods. Such state enticements benefited banks, contractors, millions of middle-class home buyers, and the economy generally.

To see the difference that federal subsidies made, we need to know that the modern, quasi-public housing construction industry that federal policies made possible was and is one of the most important sectors of the economy. By the 1950s, residential housing construction was between 20 percent and 25 percent of total private investment. In peak building years, it wasn't unusual for total dollars spent for home building to equal or exceed the total spent on new plant and equipment in all manufacturing. Housing construction became a crucial economic variable, because home purchases became the largest single investment most Americans made in their lives. Additionally, home building employed millions of people, directly and indirectly: it had huge multiplier effects on other industries, such as furniture, appliances, and electric utilities. Its importance to economic growth is hard to overestimate.

Before state financial guarantees and incentives began during and after the Depression, however, the housing market was very different. Mortgages were much harder to get, and far fewer American families owned homes. In the 1930s, only about 45 percent of U.S. families owned their homes, a percentage almost unchanged since the 1890s. The rest rented, lived with parents, or just coped. About half of the owners owned their homes outright; the rest (one-fifth of all families) had mortgages. Not until the late 1940s did over half of all American families become home owners. By 1960, the number had risen to 60 percent; and from 1970 to 1993, to about two-thirds. In the space of a single postwar generation, one in five households achieved the single most valuable attribute of middle-class status in America.

This middle-class housing revolution was made possible largely by an even quieter revolution in mortgage financing. Before FHA and VA federally guaranteed mortgages and other government incentives to housing finance, purchase, and ownership came along between 1935 and 1950, down payments on mortgages averaged 40 percent of loans. Repayment periods were ten to twelve years at most. No sane banker then lent money at fixed interest rates for twenty, thirty, or forty years, nor did bankers loan to those who could put up only minimal amounts of the purchase price in advance. Home ownership, particularly new homes, was a comparative luxury. In the depressed 1930s, nobody got no-down-payment housing loans. But by 1953, 11 percent of homebuyers did; and only two years later, 48 percent. In the 1930s, no American families buying homes did so via thirty-year mortgages. By 1953, 5 percent did; and by 1955, 44 percent did.

In 1955, S&Ls (which by then made the majority of home loans) insured 44 percent of their mortgages through the VA or the FHA. By 1970, half of all single-family private homes sold carried mortgages guaranteed by either the VA or the FHA. In the 1980s, about one-third of single-family homes enjoyed federally guaranteed mortgage status. Federal guarantees and quasi-public strategies like these spurred housing business growth. The FHA and the VA were to housing what R&D funding and cost-plus contracts were to aerospace or the GI Bill and the National Defense Education Act were to college and university enrollments. In the 1950s, home ownership increased dramatically and the construction industry boomed. By 1960 there were 57 million family housing units, 25 percent of them built in the 1950s. The rate of 1950s home building was more than twice that of the 1930s and 1940s combined.

If all this wasn't symbiosis, nothing was. New financial environments were created in which a whole new spectrum of the population—loosely termed lower middle class—could afford homes and buy their way into an increasingly suburban American Dream. If any reader doubts that government has been thoroughly and permanently involved as guarantor of last resort in both housing and financial markets, the current $500 billion bailout of the nation's mortgage lending institutions—following simple-minded deregulation during the Reagan era—should make the truth of symbiosis starkly clear. Federal money without federal control has a downside.

Old-style free enterprise became passé in housing as in aerospace by the 1950s. But no entrepreneurial revolt ensued. Small NAM and USCC home builders, it seemed, liked the VA, the FHA, the FDIC and the FSLIC as enthusiastically as they disliked unions, agricultural price supports, and other examples of government "interference" and "inefficiency." Nor did the Eisenhower administration seek to abolish the mixed system, in which public money underwrote private housing financing and construction firms. The American formula was public guarantee or subsidy, private profit and control. Few conservatives, in business or without, quarreled with that kind of success.

America's underwritten capitalism was successful. State-assisted ascent to affluence in housing and high technology, however, was not the only distinguishing characteristic of the 1950s. Prosperity fueled a welfare capitalist revival, a renewed effort by major corporations to become focal points for social action.

Business had good credentials for the task. When the modern economic transformation of America began in the half-century following 1870, large corporations and state governments began formulating solutions to human problems in an industrializing society. Corporate and state efforts were minority phenomena usually restricted to prosperous states and prosperous firms operating in oligopolistic markets. Until the Depression, minimalist and revenue-poor Washington innovated little. "Laboratories of reform," such as the state of Wisconsin and innovative corporations like General Electric and Eastman Kodak, were where American leaders looked for social welfare solutions.

By the 1920s, as a result, hundreds of large companies had created a host of job-centered private welfare systems. What central governments pioneered elsewhere in the world, corporations often pioneered in the United States. Firms like GE and Kodak, for instance, built subsidized workers' housing, sold company stock to employees at below-market rates, and established bonus and profit-sharing programs. They instituted retirement pensions for longtime workers. They initiated medical and rehabilitation programs for employees with work-related illnesses or injuries. They created safety programs, recreation programs, and "company unions" to improve relations between management and labor.

All this and more GE, Kodak, and other firms did; and all of their actions mixed ideals and self-interest. Stock sharing, bonus systems, and retirement pensions not only boosted employees' compensation but aimed to increase their satisfaction and loyalty and thereby decrease labor turnover. Company unions gave workers a voice in grievance procedures, but they also discouraged independent craft unionization and strikes.

Until the Depression, welfare capitalism, together with spotty state-centered programs, was America's social welfare tradition. Only when local initiative and even a national employment-based corporate welfare system had no answers for millions without jobs did Washington abandon 150 years of minimalism and begin providing social welfare systems permanently and directly to America's civilian population.

Once affluence revived after fifteen years of economic and military emergency, however, welfare capitalism did too, and in more widespread ways than ever before. Fifties industrialists, wrote historian Eric Goldman, tried to "outbid the welfare state by welfare capitalism." Unions, too, were key elements in corporate social equations. If big business expanded employee welfare, big labor might lose its appeal. So powerful was the renewed welfare capitalist impulse that business analyst John Brooks argued in 1965 that "the biggest corporations have gone a long way toward converting themselves to welfare states." Pensions, medical programs, health and life insurance plans, chaplains, paid vacations, country clubs, and psychological counsellors were all part of the phenomenon. None of it came cheap. By 1959, the USCC estimated that welfare capitalist fringe benefits accounted for 21.5 percent of the total annual payroll costs of U.S. manufacturing.

The rebirth of fringe benefits began during World War II and Korea. Wages were controlled during and immediately after both conflicts, but nonwage benefits, or fringes, were not. Powerful unions, accordingly, sought to make up in fringes like paid vacations, health insurance, and pension plans what they could not obtain in pay envelopes. Fringes, however, cost employers a lot, so employers, particularly smaller ones, often fought them ferociously. Bigger companies like General Motors and US Steel initially did so too.

Between the passage of the Taft-Hartley Act of 1947 and the advent of Eisenhower, however, large corporations' attitudes toward fringe benefits began to change. In 1948, for instance, GM initially worried its BC peers by incorporating an escalator clause into a contract with the United Automobile Workers Union (UAW). The escalator tied wage increases to a new cost of living index calculated by federal economists. GM built expected worker productivity increases into its escalator contract as well. Workers thus got protection from inflation eroding their pay and promises of future wage hikes, in return for building cars at lower cost. GM, having defeated a long national UAW strike in 1946, now sought to avoid more by exchanging employer flexibility for employee efficiency.

Actions like GM's, soon copied by Ford and other large unionized corporations, adapted the welfare capitalist tradition to a changed industrial environment, in which big government and big unions now figured prominently. Welfare capitalism, 1950s style, was no longer unilateral. Managers did not simply award things to workers; they had to bargain about programs with unions representing their workers. Corporate welfare programs (e.g., retirement pensions) also now complemented government welfare programs like Social Security pensions. Welfare capitalism provided for the better organized and skilled segments of the labor force what were in most other advanced industrial nations almost wholly state-financed and state-run social programs.

The federal judiciary assisted this welfare capitalist revival. In 1949 the

Supreme Court ruled that fringe benefits like retirement pension and health insurance programs were proper subjects for collective bargaining. Skeptical or reluctant firms had now to provide more such services to bid against forceful unions. GM and many other large corporations, for example, quickly perceived the usefulness of providing workers' retirement pensions.

GM's pension plan became a postwar model for big business. When GM began company pensions in 1950, 2,000 American firms were providing them. By the end of 1950, 6,000 *new* plans were created, all along GM's lines. A special BC committee spread the word that a "national welfare state" along postwar Western European lines would corrupt America, while corporate-based welfare systems would not. Peter Drucker estimated that by 1976 "50,000 or so" private pension plans were in existence in the United States, including municipal plans created on the GM model. Pension funds "of the 1,000 or so largest companies had about $115 billion in assets, industry-wide or union-managed funds had about $35 billion, and [state and local government] . . . pension funds . . . about $50 billion." Total pension fund assets in America doubled every five years between 1950 and 1975. By 1990, their total assets of $2.6 trillion composed the largest single pool of capital in the world, covered 55 million workers, and owned more than half the stock of America's largest companies.

Federal policy further elaborated welfare capitalism. Tax exemption benefits now totaling $58 billion annually encouraged companies to provide health benefits for their employees. Health, like retirement protection, proliferated in the 1950s. By 1990 employers paid for 85 percent of the policies of the 173 million Americans covered by private health insurance. Pensions and health benefits became the twin cornerstones of the renewed welfare capitalism.

Conservatives approved such symbiotic arrangements between welfare capitalism and the welfare state. Immediately after World War II, thrifty Congresses let Social Security benefits lag far behind increases in the cost of living. Meager public benefits made private benefits like pensions more important. The defeat of pro forma Democratic national health insurance proposals in 1948 also made employer-provided health programs more attractive.

Public pensions were so low and so restricted that it wasn't until 1950 that Social Security became of primary significance to most elderly and retired citizens. Until that year, "welfare" doles far exceeded "earned right" social insurance pensions. In Ed Berkowitz's words, "Twice as many people received welfare as received social insurance. . . . The nation spent three times as much on welfare as on social insurance. . . . Nationwide, about one out of four people over age 65 received welfare." The average monthly federal-state welfare payment was $42 in 1949, compared to the average monthly Social Security retirement check of $25. Veterans benefits, meanwhile, "embraced about one-third of the total population" just after World War II. Until the mid-1950s, they also provided more money to needy citizens than Social Security did. It behooved workers—in unions or not—to welcome new employer-provided pensions and insurance, since the alternative could be small government pensions or old age on the dole.

As unions and management recreated welfare capitalism, Washington was not utterly inactive, but its activity often complemented the welfare capitalist view of the world. In 1950, for example, Congress very substantially modified and enlarged the Social Security old age retirement program because of widespread concern over swelling rolls of the elderly on state welfare, half of whose financing came, by law, from Washington. This seemingly liberal action had a basically conservative rationale. Postwar state governments, facing discontented elderly people, who very often voted, were doing what Washington would not do and new corporate programs could not do. They were increasing welfare benefits to keep needy retired voters happy. Since half of the funding for state-determined welfare benefits came from the general revenues of the federal government, what a BC report of December 1949 called the "fiscal integrity of the entire Social Security system" was about to be undermined by dole programs that state politicians were using to their own political advantage.

Corporate CEOs went on to specify what they meant, and what federal bureaucrats administering the Social Security system understood as well: no consensus existed regarding who the needy were. Louisiana, a political barony of the Huey Long dynasty, was "distributing old age assistance [welfare] to 82% of aged persons 65 years or over. This compared with 4.8% in the District of Columbia, 6% in Delaware, and 23% in the entire nation." No effective check on welfare programs or welfare spending existed.

What to do? Here, the businessmen of the BC and the bureaucrats of the Social Security Administration found common ground. Both wanted to decrease welfare payments and to replace welfare (whose eligibility rules and benefit levels Washington couldn't control) with social insurance (where Washington set benefit levels and eligibility rules). They would do this by greatly expanding the coverage of the federally run old age retirement program beyond the 60 percent of the employed it then covered. They would bring 8 million new workers, including the self-employed, into Social Security for the first time, raise the Social Security tax rate (half of which was paid by employers), and raise the total amount of wages liable to Social Security taxation (the Federal Insurance Contribution Act, or FICA deduction taken from paychecks). This extension of Social Security coverage boosted average retirement pension benefits by 80 percent. Shortly after the new federal law went into effect in 1950, the number of pension beneficiaries exceeded the number receiving state-supplied welfare—for the first time since Social Security began fifteen years earlier.

Thus, the conservative big businessmen of the BC and the CED supported the 1950 Social Security amendments, the most significant broadening of federal welfare responsibility since the passage of the Social Security Act in 1935. The BC, in fact, had supported the idea as early as 1941, partly to protect big firms from competition by small companies not then required to provide Social Security pensions for their employees. Big business support for expanding Social Security, however, nevertheless angered small entrepreneurs, not least the self-employed.

Marion B. Folsom of Eastman Kodak, who chaired the BC's Social Security Committee from 1935 to the early years of the Eisenhower administration, however, understood that a federally run program of social insurance that recipients had to help pay for was a closer approximation to private insurance than state-based welfare systems, in which recipients got something for nothing and where costs were far less controllable. Social insurance had private sector analogues; welfare did not. Welfare was a dole; a Social Security retirement pension was an earned right. Social Security bureaucrats understood the logic of private sector analogies for public sector programs, too. They, in fact, regularly dressed up Social Security in so much private sector clothing that the average American still assumes it is merely a private insurance annuity program being (badly) run for them by the federal government.

These Americans are wrong, of course. Social Security is not private insurance under another name. Social Security is a universal coverage system that cannot select its risks. No private insurance company ever operates that way. Social Security is yet another example of big business-government symbiosis. It is a public program often rationalized and understood in private terms. It is a system that businessmen like Folsom, bureaucrats, congresspeople, and presidents have tried to keep as businesslike as possible, in order that public funds will not be overprovided and in order that administrative decisions within the system can be kept nonpolitical. In 1950, America expanded Social Security to try and get rid of welfare. The idea that national governments should simply pay people in need out of general revenues on the basis of their right to live and without their contributing mightily to their own salvation was about as American as child molestation. America, recent "monster state" oratory aside, remains exceptional. The country today, in Sanford Jacoby's succinct words,

> spends a smaller proportion of its GNP on social security than any other advanced industrial nation except Japan. The structure of its social welfare programs also marks the United States off from other countries. Over 23% of total social welfare spending in the U.S. comes from the private sector in the form of employer-provided "fringe" benefits; in France and Sweden, the corresponding figure is about 5%. Much of the remaining 77% . . . by government is not composed of universal entitlements, as in Europe, but is linked to labor force participation and apportioned according to an individual's wage and employment history.

America remains so exceptional because private and public welfare programs have been designed and implemented to complement each other. Social Security and welfare capitalism never excluded one another. That's why most big businesses support Social Security. In 1984, at the peak of the Reagan Revolution, 70 percent of large firms stated they would remain in the Social Security system as it is even if they had the opportunity to get out.

The fact that Social Security is symbiotic, however, does not make it universally popular among business people. As we've seen, in 1950 small businesses did not want to be included in Social Security (even after the smallest got a lower tax rate). Social Security taxes, after all, added significantly to small business costs and competitive pressures.

Business organizations representing small businesses, therefore, counterattacked on the Social Security front almost as soon as a Republican president (Eisenhower) entered office in January 1953. The strategy favored by the NAM was to turn Social Security into a voluntary system. This approach, favored by Republican candidate Barry F. Goldwater in 1964 and by President Ronald Reagan in 1980 before his education in the finer symbiotic points, inspired no significant support in big business circles. A voluntary social insurance program is simply a dole, because wealthier and healthier Americans who can get better deals from private insurance will, and public programs will be left with only the poorest and weakest citizens—those least able to contribute to their own retirement costs. Social Security, therefore, will be left with all the minuses, without being able to redistribute pension income from pluses to minuses. For example, better risk individuals who are single might die one day after they retire, thus leaving money in the account to pay for lousy risk individuals who were, say, too ill to earn much money during their working lives and who, therefore, require a subsidy to receive the minimum retirement benefit.

Traditionalist laissez-faire forces, therefore, got nowhere politically in the 1950s or afterward, because they ignored symbiotic corporate-government realities and equated public programs with private programs. Other small business efforts, however, had greater chances of success. In 1953, USCC leaders began the most ambitious and considered counterattack yet made on Social Security and its big business and bureaucratic supporters.

After the 1950 reforms, Social Security participation grew so fast that Social Security taxes from 1950 to 1955 doubled the money in Social Security coffers. Social Security payouts in those years increased by 500 percent. A program that had involved $767 million in its cheap early start-up period in 1937 grew to over $21.6 billion by 1955. Still, because the U.S. economy was growing so fast in the 1950s, total payrolls (and taxes levied on those payrolls) rose so much that $8 billion more in surplus (unspent) money was in the Social Security retirement trust fund in 1955 than was in it in 1950.

The USCC had not liked Social Security to begin with, only reluctantly accepting it when the Depression era alternative looked infinitely worse: permanent and large universal doles for every elderly American. In 1953, USCC leaders took another shot at Social Security, since Ike and a newly elected Republican-majority Congress were in power. Its plan had three goals. First, to abolish all publicly funded "welfare" entirely; second, to extend Social Security coverage to all elderly Americans, whether they had ever worked or not; and third, to decrease the surpluses then accumulating in the Social Security trust fund by decreasing Social Security taxes.

These three goals aimed at three results. First, abolishing welfare entirely would stop state or federal officials from courting poor elderly voters by increasing welfare benefits or loosening welfare eligibility requirements. Second, extending retirement pension rights to everybody, with or without work histories, would clarify that there were significant income redistribution elements in Social Security and that many individuals got far more back out than they had put in. Third, decreasing taxes and the Social Security trust fund would gradually shift more of the financial costs of the program from higher income to lower income Americans and also inhibit politicians from using Social Security surpluses either to pay for big rises in current benefits or as a financial excuse to establish new Social Security entitlement programs that might not initially cost much but that would cost plenty later on.

At first, the USCC drive gathered momentum. Thousands of local affiliates called for reforms. The USCC got three of its own people on a five-person Social Security reform policy panel advising Oveta Culp Hobby, Eisenhower's new head of a federal agency that soon became the new cabinet-level Department of Health, Education, and Welfare (HEW) (today the Department of Health and Human Services, or HHS). Texan Oveta Culp Hobby and HEW, in turn, rode herd (or tried to) on the Social Security Administration. For a moment, it looked as if the USCC effort to stop cost, coverage, and benefits expansion of Social Security was a done deal.

The moment, however, was brief. Hobby knew little about the social welfare programs she oversaw and left office after she attacked as "creeping socialism" the free inoculation of all U.S. children with the widely popular new Salk polio vaccine, developed mostly at federal expense. The USCC's smaller business members, meanwhile, got nervous. Few understood why chamber leaders had committed conservative heresy by supporting expanded coverage of any federal social welfare program for any reason. The aim of controlling cost expansion, preventing new programs, and other details eluded them.

The details of the USCC proposal, however, did not elude two other political players for long. The first was Arthur Altmeyer, an FDR appointee who headed the Social Security Administration from its beginnings in 1935 until Hobby replaced him. The second was Folsom of Eastman Kodak, who had headed the BC's Social Security Committee since 1935. In 1953, Folsom was also the new undersecretary of the treasury, one of the few social welfare policy experts in Ike's administration, and the man who would soon succeed Hobby as secretary of HEW. In April 1953, on his last day in office as Social Security administrator, Altmeyer paid a special visit to Folsom to ask him to keep the USCC's proposal from getting Eisenhower's political support.

Folsom agreed to try. He and Altmeyer had often worked together on Social Security advisory panels, on which Folsom had informally led business delegations selected largely from the BC. He and Altmeyer both opposed providing Social Security old age pensions to people who hadn't worked (or their survivors)—for to do so would undermine the earned-right element of social insurance, by which workers contributed to their later retirement security by paying taxes over the course of their working lives. (The higher your paycheck, the higher the tax you and your employer paid, the higher your Social Security account, and the higher your pension after retirement.) Folsom and Altmeyer were comfortable with such similarities between social insurance provided by the state and private insurance provided by welfare capitalist corporations like Folsom's Eastman Kodak.

They wanted pensions to reflect the 'market value of the pensioner whenever possible. Finally, Folsom wanted Eisenhower to avoid political bloodshed over a program big firms like his had learned to live with.

Folsom fulfilled his promises to Altmeyer. He was already Hobby's chief Social Security adviser and one of the five businessmen on the Social Security reform panel she had just appointed. Folsom enjoyed excellent congressional connections from twenty-five years in Washington. He used what Altmeyer later termed his "great influence" to enlarge the reform panel to dilute USCC influence, to ensure that the Eisenhower White House didn't back the chamber's proposal, and to restrain Social Security's critics in Congress from passing the chamber's reform plan into law.

When Social Security reform did come, in 1954, it was a compromise that corporate and political accommodationists all agreed upon. They were the 1950 Social Security amendment all over again: coverage was extended to an additional 10 million working Americans, as part of another effort to limit the importance of welfare. These changes occurred at the margins— no frontal assault occurred. The USCC efforts had been frustrated. Symbiosis to the Folsoms of corporate America meant complementarity. They saw publicly provided Social Security pensions as one leg of a three-legged stool of retirement protection for working Americans. Private welfare capitalist pension plans and personal savings were the other two legs of the individual-state-employer approach.

If this, too, wasn't symbiosis, nothing was. The USCC's 1953 effort failed for lack of support among large corporations, without whose backing success was impossible. Big business CEOs, in forums like the BC, heeded experts like Marion Folsom, who argued that the welfare state and welfare capitalism were complementary. Folsom underlined his symbiotic point by becoming HEW secretary in Eisenhower's cabinet and overseeing the Social Security program. Organizations like the BC and the CED made the point by doing nothing to support the USCC.

America's social welfare state, meanwhile, continued to expand. Disability insurance arrived in 1956, then came enhanced vocational rehabilitation, and then the first powerful legislative stirrings of what became national health insurance for the aged and the poor in 1966. All of these federal efforts and more were dressed up in as much private and states' rights clothing as necessary to achieve their passage into law. Doctors, hospitals, insurance companies, welfare capitalists, state legislators, and governors all had to be satisfied, or satisfied enough. Contemporary national health insurance debates tell the same story. Only when swelling medical and retirement costs due to an aging population and the medical technology breakthroughs of the 1970s and 1980s caused the financial interests of care providers to oppose those of care financers and corporations did the symbiotic politics of welfare capitalism begin to develop severe strains. These strains led many financially strapped large corporations to call upon Washington to help restrain pension and medical cost increases and to mandate minimum retirement and health benefits (in other words, welfare capitalism) on all U.S. or U.S.-based companies.

As time progressed, more symbiotic features characterized America's mixed welfare system. In 1974, Congress did for welfare capitalist retirement pensions what it had earlier done for banks and home owners. Washington began guaranteeing pension benefits to employees whose employers either went bankrupt or ended their pension programs. The Pension Benefits Guaranty Corporation, which insures corporate pension liabilities (estimated at $800 billion in 1991), is yet another example of the symbiotic accommodation between public and private power in America during the postwar decades. The Marion B. Folsoms of big business understood why, political mythologies to the contrary.

Folsom, like many leading CEOs of the 1950s, rose to power in a new American corporate order that significantly changed the way firms made internal decisions and the way they related to others, including organized labor and the state. This new corporate order was managerial capitalism. It continued a long transition from the reign of people to the reign of rules in American big business. The administrative structure of many large corporations was relatively traditional before managerial capitalism and was loosely based on the hierarchical model of the lower levels of the military: long, vertical chains of command. At the top of the hierarchy sat either men whose names were emblazoned on the firms they had founded or all-purpose entrepreneurs who had inherited control of the firms from the founders. These leaders often tried to command all stages of production and distribution. Below them dangled subexecutives who reported directly and often informally to each other and to the chief executive. Underneath these subexecutives were middle managers and foremen, the company leaders and platoon leaders of big business.

This relatively simple and centralized corporate control structure began to evolve almost as soon as the twentieth century began. Firms began providing more varied products and services for wider and wider markets and diversified into more and more new industries. First, railroads operating far-flung national transportation networks evolved complicated managerial structures, whose parts performed specialized functions in a relatively decentralized fashion. In the 1920s, a handful of innovative firms—notably DuPont, GM, Standard of New Jersey, and Sears—began reorganizing in similar decentralized and functionally specialized ways. Central staffs became more organized, more powerful, and more bureaucratic. They set accounting, financial, employment, and other rules for a growing number of separate manufacturing divisions, each of which operated largely independently. A chief of staff approach common to the highest levels of the military replaced the chain of command style common to lower levels of the military. Central staffs planned strategies; generalists in the manufacturing divisions devised tactics to achieve the plans.

Before the end of World War II, however, all this remained a minority phenomenon. Changes were ad hoc and partial. But the rise of unions in the 1930s and 1940s, the onset of big government, and explosions of high-technology innovation in industries like aerospace, chemicals, electrical manufacturing, computers, rubber, automobiles, petroleum, steel, copper, food processing, and agricultural implements during and after the war sped the displacement of the reign of people by the reign of rules and accelerated the arrival of managerial capitalism.

Corporate reorganizations came in waves, particularly as technologically advanced companies became progressively multiindustrial. International Harvester, Allied Chemical, GE, Ford, and Chrysler, for instance, all changed to decentralized management between 1945 and 1950. Other companies swiftly followed. The fashion was for firms to undertake four or five major product lines, coordinated by as many as a dozen functional specialists in the head office of the corporation and responsible to the CEO. A signature of the managerial capitalist's new industrial state was investment plans reaching as much as four years into the future. In the late 1940s, only 20 percent of large U.S. corporations had such plans, but by the early 1960s, 90 percent did. Such dry administrative changes were important. They brought new corporate leaders to the forefront of both business and political life, men like Folsom.

Folsom and those he exemplified were staff men, not line men. Their expertise was in finance, marketing, or law. Staff managers worked in offices, not on shop floors. Staff managers organized, sold, counted, expedited, or organized things. Staff did not make things; many never had. They were strategists, not tacticians. They were functional specialists and planners, not line managers producing goods or providing customer services. Folsom, for example, was hired straight out of Harvard Business School at the age of twenty-one to create the Statistical Department at Kodak.

Staff managers were different from older, line production managers in other ways too. They not only did things differently, they often thought about things differently. They differed, as well, in class background. Staff managers of the 1950s (CEOs, almost-CEOs, or CEOs-to-be) were usually college or even graduate school educated. They had often started out in business wearing white collars and with BAs and MBAs after their names. They got things done by teamwork, by being flexible and smooth in negotiations. Such negotiations could be with central corporate staffs or with competing product divisions or with unions or with Washington.

Line managers of the 1950s, however, were quite different corporate animals. They did not manage parts of abstract systems; they solved concrete production problems. Normally, their education was a high school degree. They'd worn blue collars (or semiblue engineering collars) on shop floors before rising into upper managerial ranks. They were used to telling people far less schooled than they were to do things but not used to formulating proposals or trying to persuade people with as much or more schooling as they to consider things.

Line managers were like Henry Ford and his immediate successors frozen in amber. They did not respect unions, politicians, or bureaucrats much, including "bureaucrats" from the head offices of their own corporations. These latter were "bean counters" or "whiz kids," people with MBAs from Harvard, Stanford, or Wharton; people who didn't know one end of a machine from another; people who never did anything themselves but who increasingly limited the way "real" managers did things. Between the factory people and the systems managers, David Halberstam writes, "lay a chasm of class." The new breed of managerial capitalists had occupational experiences and world views that were increasingly different from those of the manufacturing men. Folsom, treasurer of Kodak, thought in terms of statistics, systems, and plans, including plans in which the federal government figured prominently. Shop-floor-oriented business people had a far more traditional view of corporate America, in which getting a job done through decisive, unfettered, hands-on entrepreneurial leadership was really what counted.

Corporate America was changing. Big business had long ceased being laissez-faire. The day of the managerial generalist was fading. Large diversified corporations were no longer conducted that way—thus the difference between the small businesses of the USCC and big businesses of the BC on Social Security in 1953; thus the phenomenon of symbiotic welfare capitalism in postwar America.

Welfare capitalism as it applied to labor relations during and after the

1950s demonstrated the ascendancy of managerial capitalist techniques. New doctrines of industrial psychology promoted faith in the essential harmony of employer-employee interests. Workers became variables to be measured, gauged, modified, understood, and incorporated into administrative equations. Corporate community and corporate citizenship became the trend. Large high-technology firms doing scientific R&D were pioneering in the application of social science R&D to corporate life.

The primary agent of this change, industrial psychology, had been around for decades. It was a child of Freud and Frederick Winslow Taylor and a uniquely American mixture of mental healing and scientific management, but its initial attractiveness in corporate circles was spotty. As late as 1946, only 30 percent of large companies had a professionally trained psychologist on their staff. To most businessmen, it was a blinding revelation that workers not only liked to be consulted but could be more productive when they were consulted.

World War II and its aftermath, however, was a watershed, after which "industrial social scientists finally came into their own." Only 30 percent of big firms may have had an industrial psychologist in 1946, but "over 50 percent thought it would be a good idea."

Change wasn't accidental. Big business's labor environment had altered decisively by the end of 1945. The reign of people was being succeeded by the reign of rules concerning workers, as well as everything else. Unions and federal agencies like the NLRB existed to regulate things; they expected businesses to formulate and abide by rules, too—rules about hiring, firing, placement, promotion, seniority, job classification, pay scales, work rules, and disciplinary and grievance procedures. The good old days of hire and fire at will were over. Henry Ford's benevolent feudalism was dead. Henry Ford II, who took over his grandfather's company in 1946, did not run it like a corporate barony. He spoke, instead, about "human relations" and "human engineering," through which staff (or managerial capitalist) power increased faster. What Ford was doing, many other large companies were doing too.

Ford and others bureaucratized labor relations for practicality as much as ideology. Government and union rules, for example, required corporations to maintain records for legal and contract negotiation purposes. People were recruited to manage the records. As centralized records were easier to use than decentralized records, employee data were organized within functionally specialized staff departments. These staff departments, in turn, systematized matters like corporate job classifications and wage rates, because ad hockery—workers doing what you told them to, or else—

was no longer feasible at the commanding heights of U.S. manufacturing industry. The existence of powerful unions, moreover, meant that unilateral force had to be replaced with multilateral negotiation and consent. Thus, it also became important for managers to know more about what employees were thinking and why they were thinking it.

In such efforts to know more, industrial psychology provided powerful tools and techniques. There were, for instance, attitude surveys to gauge relations between worker morale and shop floor productivity. Fifty prominent firms had used such attitude surveys by 1944; by 1947, another 200 had. Psychological testing, which the military had used widely during World War II, also boomed. In 1939, only 14 percent of companies surveyed used psychological testing as part of their employee hiring process. By 1947, 50 percent did; and by 1952, 75 percent. Modern motivational research was coming into its own, so much so that in 1953 *Business Week* trumpeted the entrepreneurial virtues of teamwork between management and workers. Knowing what workers thought and why they thought it paid dividends. It allowed management to identify and solve labor problems before unions or federal regulators did.

Psychology in American industry in the 1950s had widening applications. One was in the area of small group managerial dynamics. The "T-groups" (or sensitivity training sessions) of the 1960s and beyond, for example, evolved out of role playing and group decisionmaking training techniques pioneered in corporate America in the 1950s. Managerial capitalists heading large multiproduct, multiindustrial, corporations no longer just ordered things done: they bargained and they negotiated in groups, teams, and committees. In such a new and inevitably bureaucratic world, industrial psychology was but one part of a much wider structural process affecting all of American life.

Change had its humorous aspects. Industrial psychology approaches became so trendy by the 1950s that even the most hidebound traditionalists claimed to embrace them. As early as 1945, a rabidly antiunion former president of the NAM announced that industry was passing into a new era, "the age of industrial relations." The NAM, not to be outdone, changed the name of its antiunion journal, the *Open Shop Bulletin*, to the *Labor Relations Bulletin*. By 1949, a bombastic GE vice president named Lemuel Boulware, then instituting new corporate labor policies to weaken CIO unions, waxed eloquent about "selling" human relations. "You have got a product," Boulware orated to three men, including David Lilienthal, chairman of the thoroughly symbiotic Atomic Energy Commission (AEC). It's "just like selling flatirons," he claimed. "I was in charge of selling flatirons, and what did I do? I made my own product attractive. I advertised." Boulware went on at length about his prowess as a salesman. Then one of his listeners, a federal wartime labor arbitrator and corporate lawyer, said, "Mr. Boulware, I guess that I'm mixed up about your selling labor like . . . flatirons. I thought you were buying labor, not selling it."

For all of the pomposity and posturing, however, industrial psychology's techniques and tools helped spark a revolution, one in which the welfare capitalism of the Eisenhower era and beyond again served as an important counterweight to union power and federal regulation.

Big labor, meanwhile, had begun to fade. The 1950s, unlike the 1930s and 1940s, were years of stasis in union circles. Organized labor's weaknesses furthered big business's ascent to postwar power and influence. Labor's troubles were not just industrial psychologists taking attitude surveys or corporations instituting welfare programs that decreased union support for an expanded welfare state—plenty more challenged organized labor, both externally and internally.

External problems included affluence, automation, decentralized labor laws and standards, the gradual erosion of unions' core manufacturing power base, and a politically risk-averse Democratic party. Internally, unions contended with worker segmentation in a sprawling immigrant society, a growing preference for the status quo on the part of labor leadership, an inability to resolve internecine jurisdictional strikes, undemocratic union governance procedures; and occasional outright racketeering.

The external challenges hit unions hardest. War and postwar booms produced affluence enabling tens of millions of American workers to achieve middle-class status for themselves and their families. Average after-tax real wages for a production worker with a spouse and two children doubled between 1939 and 1958. Workers enjoying rising incomes and wealth had progressively less in common with unorganized and unskilled workers. High-tech workers labored at GE or IBM, bought houses, and hoped to send the kids to college one day, while their low-tech counterparts worked in laundries, rented apartments, and often lacked even savings accounts.

Automation also posed problems. The word entered America's vocabulary in the fifties. Labor was being supplanted by revolutionary self-regulating machines like the computerized devices that operated on electronic feedback principles. Such machines didn't require intensive tending by humans. Unskilled and semiskilled feeder, controller, handler, and operator jobs at the low end of the manufacturing spectrum, accordingly, began disappear. Barriers to occupational entry rose. A key issue—increasingly, *the* key issue—in collective bargaining became job security, rather than wages, hours, or working conditions. *Robots* was the most feared word in the industrial vocabulary. Science fiction come true eroded the work forces in manufacturing, mining, and transportation, where unions were strongest. Forty-six coal miners in 1963 produced what a hundred had in 1953; sixty railroad workers in 1963 handled as much traffic as a hundred in 1953; seventy-nine autoworkers in 1963 built the same number of cars as a hundred had in 1955; and on it went. Automation, additionally, limited the effectiveness of strikes in industries as varied as chemicals, petroleum refining, printing, telecommunications, warehousing, and longshoring. Computers and simple robots ran on despite picket lines. They were changing the world of work forever.

The computer electronics revolution of the fifties and beyond eroded union power not only in specific industries; it also eroded it generally. "At some point in the mid-1950s," economist Harold Vatter perceptively remarked at the time, "the number of persons engaged in goods-producing activities fell below 50 per cent of the civilian labor force." The service industry era had arrived in America. Total manufacturing workers in U.S. industry actually declined absolutely in the fifties, and by 1962, only 42 percent of American workers remained goods producers, compared with 58 percent in services. Numbers like these spelled trouble for unions, particularly because, in the fifties, three-fourths of all union members labored in manufacturing, mining, construction, and transportation. Unions also had geographical problems. Two of every three manufacturing workers were unionized, but over half of them lived in only four states: New York, Ohio, California, and Illinois. The proportions were skewed because many other states had laws hostile to unions. Taft-Hartley had made vast regions of the nation into an open shop mecca. Employers in labor-intensive industries like textiles headed south and west in droves in the fifties. As global competition intensified in other trades in the following decades, auto, steel, electrical manufacturing, and other firms followed—when they didn't go abroad in search of even lower cost workers.

The unions' chief political allies in Washington did little to counteract such systemic erosion of union power. Inaction was a matter of basic political arithmetic. Most union leaders were not radical and had no desire to alienate prounion Democrats by forming an independent labor party. This meant, given widespread Republican and conservative Democratic intransigence on the subject of organized labor, that unions in the fifties and beyond were like blacks after the 1960s—a captive of one political party, with nowhere else to go. Democrats didn't have to bid very high to keep unions on their side. So most didn't. They defended what was and risked little else. Important unions such as those in the construction trades, which had made many profitable industry-specific deals with Democrats over the years, liked this status quo just fine.

Chief among such union defenders of the status quo was George Meany, a plumbers union official who had risen through city, state, and national crafts union federation hierarchies for thirty years to become, in 1955, the first (and for the next twenty-five years, the only) president of the newly merged AFL-CIO.

AFL-CIO's 1955 merger sought to repair twenty years of rift between craft and industrial unions. Meany was a gut fighter and a thorough conservative. He was caste conscious but not class conscious. He believed that the central core of America's economy had already been unionized and that organizing the unorganized in new industries and regions was not a priority. Meany thought Democratic politicians were bastards but were at least *his* bastards. He liked to affect a bastardly demeanor himself by recalling that the only picket line he had ever walked was in protest of New Deal efforts to change legislation favoring construction unions building public works during and after the Depression. The New Dealers had wanted to lower wages to put more unemployed craftsmen to work. Meany had successfully demanded they pay union scale, even though many fewer union members got jobs as a result.

George Meany, as the story suggests, knew his union fundamentals but remained largely oblivious to the changing economic contexts in which unions operated. Despite this, he became Mr. Organized Labor in the 1950s, 1960s, and 1970s. His leadership nicely complemented the anti-reform and antiradical atmosphere of postwar America. Meany's critics within labor, like Walter Reuther, president of the UAW, complained that Meany would not even tithe every organized worker a dollar a year to spread industrial unionism to open shop states and unorganized service industries. But Reuther, in Meany's eyes, was a radical.

Meany's second year in office as the standpat president of the AFL-CIO proved, however, to be the peak of trade unionism in contemporary America. From 1956 onward, unionized workers as a percentage of the labor force dropped year after year, with only occasional interruptions. In 1956, 25.2 percent of U.S. workers were unionized; by the mid-1980s, the percentage had fallen to 20 percent; by 1991, to 17 percent. Absolute numbers were no more reassuring. Union workers peaked at 22 million in 1975 and declined thereafter, especially in the industrial core economy.

By the end of Ronald Reagan's presidency, only 19 million of 120 million working Americans belonged to unions, a lower proportion than in any developed Western nation except France. AFL-CIO membership was two-thirds of that total (12.3 million, only 80,000 more than in 1955). The AFL-CIO stagnated, despite an increase of over 50 million in U.S. workers over the same three decades. When George Bush assumed office, the AFL-CIO spoke for only 13 percent of those employed in private industry. Only in the local, state, and national government sectors (where unions enrolled 37 percent of workers) was the union record credible.

This fact, however, had nothing to do with Meany or the forces of complacency that he represented. Meany and union leaders like him not only resolutely ignored changing economic and technological conditions, they ignored changes in the composition of the work force as well. Women and minorities rarely influenced their views of who needed organizing. Females, supposedly, were working only temporarily until marriage and child bearing. Such stereotyping assumed a society that didn't exist any-more: 25 percent of the labor force was female in 1940; 45 percent of it was female fifty years later. Married women, only one-third of the total female labor force in 1940, became a majority of it by 1950, and from 1960 on, composed about 60 percent. Good-old-boyism and feminine nurturing traditions, however, led 75 percent of these women to hold female-only jobs in a variety of services. This sexual job segregation, despite the growing importance of services in the economy, caused many a union to blithely write off women and women's issues in the workplace. Such thickheadedness only further ensured that union ability to organize the often-female white-collar service workers would remain minimal. Whatever Meany thought about in the fifties, it wasn't equal pay or child care.

Instead, racketeering in unions—often ones unaffiliated with AFL-CIO—often focused labor leaders' concern. The 1950s were years of partic-ular despotism and violence in the independent International Brotherhood of Teamsters. The issue became front page news. *Labor* came to mean Teamsters. Teamster bossism and mob connections also accounted for the most important piece of labor legislation passed in America in the Eisen-hower era: the Landrum-Griffin Act of 1959.

The fight over Landrum-Griffin showed just how inept most unions had become in comparison with their corporate opposite numbers. The AFL-CIO made the same mistake it had with Taft-Hartley: its leaders enunciated no coherent position and often denied any political solution was required. Individual unions, meanwhile, lobbied for or against the bill independently, deluging Capitol Hill with labor lobbyists and offending many Democratic congressional leaders in the process.

Organized business, meanwhile, also repeated its Taft-Hartley performance. It formed an issue-specific umbrella coalition uniting big and small business organizations. It agreed on legislative basics enough to formulate basic policies for its far more organized and coherent lobbyists. Corporations complemented such inside efforts by paying for grass roots advertising and letter writing campaigns to put outside constituency pressures on congressmen. Inside and outside pressures alike focused on swing vote politicians, especially those from open shop southern and western states. While Meany dithered and the Teamsters Union stonewalled, Ike and a young congressional investigator named Robert F. Kennedy went on nationwide television to damn violence and intimidation in labor-management disputes and in internal union governance. "The best ally the management groups had," a contemporary analyst of Landrum-Griffin concluded, "was the AFL-CIO."

Nineteen-fifties labor legislation, accordingly, was far different from 1930s labor legislation. Landrum-Griffin didn't address the management side of labor-management relations at all. Instead, it strengthened federal regulation of internal union practices in ways Taft-Hartley had begun twelve years before. Again like Taft-Hartley, Landrum-Griffin was passed by a majority Democratic Congress against most labor leaders' wishes. Unions in America were becoming politically marginalized.

The internal weaknesses and external challenges facing organized labor were lost on most big businessmen, who simply put their old whine in new bottles. Many CEOs ignored reality as thoroughly as union leaders did, and their continued grumbling sometimes alienated even the defenders of corporate America in the Eisenhower administration.

Eisenhower arrived in office telling his close friend and BC member Lucius D. Clay that "frankly I do not consider either race relations or labor relations to be issues." Ike didn't want to do anything liberal *or* conservative. The status quo was good enough; efforts to roll back unions didn't make sense. In the first burst of Eisenhower Republican normalcy, however, the status quo wasn't good enough for full-blooded opportunists in the BC. BC's Labor Committee pontificated in May 1953 that administration of the Taft-Hartley Act had been "partial to labor," that preferential union shop contracts, which had become commonplace in U.S. industry during World War II, should be prohibited by law, that presidentially mandated Taft-Hartley cooling-off periods for strikes should be extended from sixty days to some vague much longer time limit, and that a secret vote of workers should be required before the government "allowed" a strike to take place.

Such old staples of corporate thinking didn't end there. Unions were monopolies and should be curbed by antitrust laws, according to a BC report in December 1958, as if Ike could bring back the open shop everywhere (or as if a New Deal Supreme Court majority would let him). And so it went. Even when Landrum-Griffin was passed, BC's Labor Committee would have preferred to have appended all sorts of pre–New Deal, pre–Wagner Act, wonderments to it that defied political logic—and that never did appear in the final bipartisan legislation. Business had legitimate complaints: featherbedding, for one, misuse of union pension funds, for another. But in labor policy, as nowhere else in the fifties, the private expressions of the BC and the public utterances of the NAM and the USCC often appeared interchangeable.

The bovine stubbornness evident in BC labor policy was largely self-administered solace. Big business was learning to live with big unions, but the living wasn't always easy. Realism was frustrating; and on important symbolic occasions such as the delivery of confidential reports to Ike's White House, old grudges sometimes replaced newer analysis. In the process, corporate rhetoric frustrated practical Republicans who were dealing with the reality of Democratic congressional power. On November 22, 1958, for example, Raymond Saulnier, chairman of Ike's Council of Economic Advisers, wrote to Frederick Mueller, secretary of commerce, regarding BC's requests for "clarifications" of the antitrust laws as they applied to unions. Ike's own attorney general had just sensibly announced that none were needed. "Why," Saulnier complained to Mueller, "is this recommendation made year after year by the BC?" Mueller replied that he certainly didn't know, but that he'd ask BC for written clarification of their own request. None apparently ever came.

It was just as well that the BC kept its mouth shut. Private mutterings about power-mad unions aside, the fifties were very good for corporate political sensibilities. A mixture of tired liberalism and Eisenhower's new Republicanism constrained most New Deal initiatives and limited the expansion of others like Social Security in ways amenable to welfare capitalism. Cold war anticommunism, meanwhile, legitimized peacetime symbiotic elaborations of high-tech war capitalism in strategic industries— America's peculiar version of Japan, Inc.

Corporate-government relations, however, were fluid. Though most BC members saw the difference between America's two political parties as "steadily narrowing" on the eve of the 1960 elections, the return of a Democratic president to Washington renewed uncertainties about what future the symbiosis between big business and the state would be. When answers to such questions came, they were hardly always to corporate politicians' liking.

6
CORPORATIONS ON THE NEW FRONTIER

John F. Kennedy didn't wish to alienate America's largest corporations when he became president in January 1961. He'd won a hair-thin victory. House Democrats *lost* twenty seats with him heading their ticket. Moderation, accordingly, was realism. Also, Kennedy's primary concerns were global, rarely domestic. His first Inaugural Address mentioned no domestic problems at all; instead he called upon a "new generation of Americans" to defend freedom abroad "in its hour of maximum danger."

Kennedy's global cold war assumptions and his desires for political accommodation with big business were understandable—he had no wish to repeat Truman's unhappy experience but wanted to lead as Eisenhower had, on America's "New Frontier" abroad. The New Deal was old news to Kennedy. He was only twenty-one years old when the domestic reform phase of FDR's presidency ended in 1938. For twenty-two of the next twenty-three years, until JFK's presidency began, American capitalism operated under conditions of war and cold war, and dynamic fusions of corporate and state power were normal. Private and public blended together in such economic sectors as transportation and communication; banking and securities markets; housing; agriculture; petroleum, natural gas, and nuclear energies; aerospace, computers, and other defense-related technologies; and higher education. Kennedy had no populist or progressive desires to humanize or abolish trusts, no socialist aspirations to replace capitalism with a more egalitarian system. Kennedy's was the liberalism of affluence and the politics of adjusting big business to big government, and vice versa.

In all this, Kennedy was a child of his times. He rose to political prominence during the 1950s, as business regained a central legitimizing role in America's economic affairs. Big business, as postwar liberal analysis had it, retained considerable dominion but could no longer abuse this authority, because big government and big labor now counterweighted unbridled corporate political power. Economically, meanwhile, big producers engendered big buyers to counteract them. Oligopoly manufacturers such as GE and Westinghouse were huge but so were the chain retail stores that sold their products like Sears Roebuck and Montgomery Ward. To liberal pluralists, Daniel Boone was dead. Organized groups competed now, not individuals. Old-fashioned leftists worried about giant businesses trampling popular liberties; practical liberals like Kennedy sought to manage the clashes between the economic Titans in the national interest.

All the Titans played essential roles in the liberal drama. Big government had saved capitalism from itself. Big labor (post-CIO purges) had saved workers from alien radicalism. Big business had mastered depression-free productivity, which served as what David Lilienthal called a bulwark "between freedom and the tidal wave of Communist militarism threatening the world with a new era of darkness." Lilienthal's words, written in 1953, were hardly unique. They echoed postwar views of other left-liberal New Dealers like Adolph Berle, Stuart Chase, John Kenneth Galbraith, and Carl Kaysen. All saw large corporations as essential to economic struggles against renewed depression and totalitarianism.

Moreover, prominent postwar liberals argued, obvious and growing differences existed between innovative big business and hidebound small business. Trendsetting managerial capitalists like those in the CED disagreed with liberalism only in degree, not in fundamentals. They knew laissez-faire was dead. They read urbane magazines like *Fortune, Business Week,* and the *Harvard Business Review.* They were responsible for the comparative conservative enlightenment of the Eisenhower administration, which had not tried to dismantle America's mixed system of public and private power. Small business and its organizations like the USCC and the NAM, in contrast, lived in the provinces. They supported Joe McCarthy and the reactionary wing of the GOP. They retained traditional entrepreneurial creeds, which were revivified Social Darwinism pining for a late nineteenth-century golden age.

To liberals like Kaysen, Lilienthal, and Berle, on the other hand, the direction of change in corporate America (industrial psychology, welfare capitalism, long-term and generally peaceful labor contracts) was the right direction. Capitalism was underwritten in important ways now and was depression free (though not recession free). "USA: The Permanent Revolution," *Fortune* magazine titled a special issue in 1951—the great transformation of American capitalism to be more democratic, more popular, and more affluent than ever before.

A majority of the populace agreed. Three of every four people polled in the 1950s in the most thorough survey of U.S. attitudes toward big business said the beneficial effects of large corporations far outweighed the detrimental effects; only one in ten said the opposite. *Big business* was not a scare word anymore. Fewer than 10 percent believed that big business had too much control over government; almost 20 percent were fearful of government subjugating business.

Affluence bred optimistic assumptions. America's mixed economy became an incredible growth machine in the fifties; almost nobody gainsaid that. For the twenty years following 1950, the economy expanded at a faster rate than at any time since the 1880s. Per capita output and income did likewise. Real weekly earnings for production workers leapt 70 percent between 1950 and 1970, and annual earnings (including times of layoffs) rose 41 percent. The average family's pretax income doubled between 1945 and 1973 (rising from $16,000 to $33,500 per year in 1987 dollars). Sixty percent of U.S. families were earning middle-class incomes, and 75 percent of union workers under the age of forty were living in suburbs by the mid-sixties. Half as many families were classified as poor, in income terms, at the end of the fifties (20 percent) as at the end of the thirties (40 percent).

Gross national product quadrupled between 1940 and 1955. Business profits soared compared to Depression or wartime levels. Although the war had helped big business more than small business, the fifties boom was good for nearly everybody. Eisenhower adapted wartime accelerated depreciation and other tax benefits for peacetime use by 1954. These supply-side incentives made corporate investments less risky and investment capital easier to raise within corporations, as opposed to stock or bond markets: by the end of the fifties, about three-fourths of corporate plant and equipment spending was generated internally, compared with less than 50 percent a decade before.

Investors, meanwhile, were optimistic: the boom times were here, and capital gains was the name of the game. People reluctant to pay more than seven times annual earnings for a share of common stock in a highly rated corporation in 1950 were eagerly paying eighteen times earnings ten years later. Government at all levels benefited from such economic expansion, just as the private sector did. The more investment, output, employment, and income swelled, the more tax revenues cascaded into federal, state, and local accounts, without unpopular income tax increases. By the mid-fifties the public sector was spending more money than total spending, public and private, in the depths of the Depression only twenty years earlier.

A "great divide in the history of humanity," contemporaries observed, was being crossed. The belief that poverty had become a "dated proposition" was widely shared. Relative skeptics like John Kenneth Galbraith only lamented the pockets of regional and racial poverty in an affluent society that need no longer allow misery to exist. An era of managerial, scientific, and technological innovations, corporate-labor and business-government accommodations, cheap energy and other natural resources, international economic expansion by U.S. firms, and economic stabilizers like cold war military spending and New Deal social insurance programs replaced the anxious years.

No successful politician could ignore affluence and optimism like this, and John F. Kennedy certainly did not. The bad old days were long gone. Pundits were aglow again with the promise of American life. Kennedy promised to get America moving even faster than a too-cautious Republican president had allowed. There were gaps aplenty between America's promise and its performance: missile gaps, space gaps, education gaps, economic growth gaps. Kennedy would harness national affluence and energy to close such gaps.

The first thing Kennedy required to achieve his goals was leadership in his own executive branch. He did as Eisenhower had done—he selected big businessmen and corporate lawyers to staff his cabinet in the big three departments of State, Defense, and Treasury. The similarities between Eisenhower's and Kennedy's cabinet recruitment processes are instructive. Ike delegated cabinet recruiting to two aides whose careers mixed public and private interests. One, Herbert Brownell, was a Wall Street lawyer and one of Ike's closest links to a key political ally, Thomas E. Dewey, the GOP's presidential candidate in 1944 and 1948. Brownell had managed both of Dewey's unsuccessful campaigns, had been Republican National Committee chairman in the 1940s, and was flush with business connections. The second member of Eisenhower's candidate selection team was even more networked into corporations than Brownell, and was much closer to Ike.

This man was General Lucius D. Clay of the U.S. Army, the Continental Can Company, and the BC. Clay and Ike first met when both were staff officers in the Philippines in the 1930s. Ike went on to become the wartime supreme commander of Allied Expeditionary Forces in Europe, mixing military and political supremacy in about equal proportions. His friend Clay, meanwhile, as procurement director for a wartime army totaling 8 million, had mixed military and industrial power.

After 1945, Eisenhower's and Clay's paths crossed again. Ike, with an assist from old Washington hand John J. McCloy, helped convince Truman to appoint Clay military governor of a defeated Germany in 1946. In 1949, Clay stepped down and McCloy replaced him. Clay retired from the army, but he didn't stay retired long. In 1950, he became chairman of the board of Continental Can and was immediately elected to the BC by CEOs who knew him well from the World War II mobilization effort. Within months, Clay was assisting fellow BC member Charles Wilson of GE to create other symbiotic mobilization agencies for Truman after China entered the Korean War. Clay's particular value was his long-standing influence with key southern Democratic leaders in the Senate.

Clay also played Republican politics. In April 1951, Eisenhower, then commander in chief of all U.S. military forces in Europe, secretly began running for the 1952 GOP presidential nomination. Clay, together with Dewey and Brownell, midwifed a "draft Ike" movement into being. Clay quietly recruited powerful southern Democrats to Ike's cause and stayed in Eisenhower's innermost circle throughout the nomination and election campaigns.

Once Ike triumphed, the president elect treated Clay as an alter ego regarding cabinet selections. Clay's corporate associations now became crucial. Unlike Brownell, Clay didn't want cabinet office himself; he would rather broker behind the scenes. He also ignored the Republican right and its small business allies in making his cabinet recommendations. Rather than right-wing politicians, Clay recruited big businessmen who had backed Ike against his Republican challenger, Senator Robert A. Taft, for the nomination and against patrician Democratic conservative Adlai Stevenson during the election.

Such corporate support paid off at an immediate postelection BC gathering at a Georgia resort. Clay, together with longtime BCer Sidney J. Weinberg of Goldman, Sachs, went political head-hunting in earnest. Eisenhower quickly ratified their choices. Charles Erwin Wilson of GM became secretary of defense, to manage the biggest bureaucracy in Washington. George M. Humphrey of the Hanna Company of Cleveland managed Ike's fiscal policies as secretary of the treasury. (The only non-BC member among the big three of Ike's cabinet was John Foster Dulles, a Wall Street lawyer ineligible for BC membership.)

The effects of these BC selections on Ike's administration were profound, as new BC cabinet officers recruited other BC members as their aides. Humphrey picked Marion Folsom to be his number-two man, until Folsom moved on to his own cabinet post at HEW. Wilson selected Robert Stevens and Robert Anderson as secretaries of the army and the navy, respectively. Only Wilson's air force secretary was not a BC member, although he had served on the boards of two long-time BC companies. And so it went. When Humphrey retired from treasury in 1957, BC's Robert Anderson (Dresser Industries) replaced him; when Wilson left defense in 1957, BC's Neil McElroy (Procter and Gamble) replaced him. John Foster Dulles at state, meanwhile, cared little about the economic elements of diplomacy, ensuring that the corporate appointees in Ike's cabinet had great influence in key policy arenas like the oil-rich Middle East.

When John Kennedy recruited the big three of his cabinet, the process and the results were very similar. Ike had picked many more political associates from business than Kennedy did during his briefer presidency, but JFK selected a larger proportion from large corporations (65 percent from Fortune 500 firms) than Ike did (56 percent). Eisenhower, on Clay's advice, got the CEO of America's largest auto company to ride herd on the sprawling Defense Department. Kennedy, on the advice of his broker, investment banker and Truman-era Secretary of Defense Robert J. Lovett, selected the CEO of America's second-biggest auto company, Robert S. McNamara of Ford, to run the Defense Department.

For the Treasury Department, Kennedy and Lovett chose C. Douglas Dillon, former board chairman of Dillon, Read, the same New York investment house that had earlier supplied James Forrestal, Paul Nitze, and others to Roosevelt's and Truman's administrations. Dillon's was an unusual appointment, to say the least. For the preceding eight years he had worked for Eisenhower, mostly at Nitze's old post as undersecretary of state for economic affairs. The reassurance to corporate America was obvious.

Finally, at the State Department, Lovett proposed Truman's Secretary of State Dean Acheson. Here Kennedy bridled. Acheson was too conservative. Lovett then asked JFK whether he would rather be his own secretary of state and appoint a good auxiliary to the post? Yes, Kennedy would. Former diplomat Dean Rusk's name surfaced. He had survived the McCarthy purges without being branded "soft," and he had deep bipartisan coloration. John Foster Dulles had supported him—in 1952, at the height of the red scare—for his current job heading the Rockefeller Foundation in New York. Lovett called Rusk an "ideal staff man." Kennedy, once again, took Lovett's advice.

Kennedy further reassured business regarding economic policy by appointing another Republican holdover, William McChesney Martin, as chairman of the Federal Reserve Board. Now taxing, spending, and monetary policy alike were all the primary responsibility of Eisenhower appointees. Martin, like Dillon, had come to Washington from the New York Stock Exchange to make the nation's central bank "independent of politics" by implementing the Department of Treasury–Federal Reserve accord of 1951.

In recruiting corporate lawyers and CEOs as Ike had, Kennedy played unsentimental politics. He had outmaneuvered congressional Democratic leaders to get nominated and had barely won the election; he needed political midwives like Lovett to vet major appointees and reassure seniority-rich southern Democratic power barons in Congress, exactly as Ike had needed Lucius Clay. Eisenhower used big business appointees to forward a moderate Republican–conservative Democratic coalition, which isolated conservative Republicans and liberal Democrats alike. Kennedy used big business appointees to try to buy himself sufficient conservative support to accomplish the same moderate and bipartisan result.

Kennedy, unlike Ike, stumbled almost as soon as he began. He delivered on his election promise to raise the minimum wage and to significantly increase workers covered by minimum wage legislation, but then he ran straight into the sand. The Bay of Pigs fiasco in April 1961 made him look inept only three months after his presidency began. In three more months, Kennedy had so alienated the BC that it ended its official symbiotic association with the executive branch. How the quarrel between the BC and Kennedy developed demonstrates both how much corporate and government leaders needed one another and how tense their associations could be.

The trouble began with a small businessman in Kennedy's cabinet, Secretary of Commerce Luther Hodges. Hodges, a textile mill manager from North Carolina who had later become the state's governor, distrusted large corporations. In particular, he distrusted the BC for its big-business-only membership, for having a "special channel to government thinking," and for being America's most elite club. Washington harbored many such symbiotic agencies, including the National Petroleum Council; the BC, however, was unusual in that it was a panindustrial body. The BC, besides, resided within Hodges' department. Hodges' determination to do something about BC's quasi-public role was strengthened because BC's current chairman, Ralph Cordiner of GE, was in severe antitrust trouble. Early in the 1960 presidential campaign, damning written evidence had surfaced about long-standing price-fixing practices among electrical manufacturers. These practices, aimed at driving smaller competitors out of business, included simultaneous identical bids and predatory, below-cost, pricing for expensive electrical generators sold to public and private utilities.

Cartels and oligopoly were nothing new, but getting caught dead to rights fixing prices was. Eisenhower, after viewing the evidence implicating over forty firms, grumbled that "the only thing those sons of bitches forgot . . . was: 'Don't take notes.' " Out of a mixture of fair play and expediency, Ike ordered antitrust prosecutions. Taking on GE, Westinghouse, and others during an election year would also inhibit restive Democrats on the Senate Antitrust Committee from branding Ike's vice president and would-be successor, Richard Nixon, as pro big business.

So, in an unusual move, Ike's Justice Department hammered offending corporations in ways almost never seen since the 1930s. Republican Attorney General William Rogers and his aide Robert Bicks attacked forty-seven companies. Normal antitrust niceties were not allowed. Federal antitrusters levied criminal charges, not the hitherto traditional civil complaints. Firms could not plead nolo contendere (a legal evasion allowing defendants to avoid pleading guilty to charges by promising never to do what they were charged with ever again and thus protecting themselves from future civil suits from angry customers). Ike's Justice Department wanted blood.

Blood it got. The third-largest U.S. electrical manufacturer (Allis Chalmers) soon confessed, and the case blew wide open. Pious statements to the media and to angry senators by the CEOs of the number-one and number-two companies (GE and Westinghouse) got nowhere politically. GE's hiring of Eisenhower's recently retired attorney general, Herbert Brownell, to "talk turkey" with his former associates at the Justice Department didn't work either. A week before the election, with political clocks ticking and fears of a Democratic presidential victory growing, nine companies and fourteen corporate officers caved in, pleading guilty to criminal antitrust charges—the first time such charges had held in U.S. history. Antitrust violations ceased being a gentleman's misdemeanor. In another legal first, a dozen second-tier corporate officials went to jail; 300 more got suspended sentences. Most companies eventually entered guilty pleas. Fines, by previous standards, were huge: $2 million, half of it levied against GE and Westinghouse alone. Two thousand civil suits were filed by utilities and state governments. The judge, in final sentencing hearings in February 1961, came down especially hard on GE, then the fourth-largest corporation in America. He characterized GE's CEO Ralph Cordiner as being an unindicted coconspirator against the free-enterprise system.

Commerce Secretary Hodges, watching all this unfold, decided he also wanted to teach Cordiner some lessons about capitalism. Hodges expected GE's board to fire Cordiner. When that board (60 percent of whom were also present or former BC members) did not, Hodges pressured Cordiner to resign as BC's chairman and in March replaced him with Roger Blough of US Steel. Cordiner was not amused, nor were many other BC CEOs for whom oligopoly pricing was a fact of life. Many Republican newspapers, however, were lambasting GE for "deceit, evasion, and double-dealing," so the event produced no howls of outrage.

What Hodges did next, however, did. Not content with removing the BC chair, Hodges attempted to alter the structure and operations of the BC itself by making four major changes: he wanted to have final approval on the acceptance of all members into the organization; he wanted to appoint twenty businessmen from small and medium-sized businesses to the hundred-member group; he wanted to control the agendas of BC meetings; and he wanted all BC gatherings addressed by government officials to be open to the press. Agendas, membership, media access: the list hardly seemed extreme, if you presumed—as Hodges did—that the BC was a government body.

It was not, and BC members did not presume that it was, either. They presumed that they were in the government but not of it. They presumed the BC had been a symbiotic advisory agency since 1933—one that selected its own members and officers, set its own agendas, and operated as confidentially as it wished. When Hodges lectured BC about capitalism and tried to control the BC politically, BC members lectured Hodges right back. Hodges snubbed them, and matters soon got subcortical. George Humphrey fumed that Hodges was naive and wrongheaded. Hodges countered that he would turn over all secret BC minutes to Justice Department antitrust officials for investigation if people like Humphrey didn't shut up.

By July, the BC had had enough. Council leaders paid a public visit to Kennedy. BC chairman Blough laid a memo on the surprised President's desk informing him that the BC was "disaffiliating" itself from the federal government and would operate as a "purely private" group in the future. "Gentlemen," sneered one of Hodges' assistants who was present, "you have just murdered yourselves."

Such rhetoric meant little, after the fact. The business of politics and the politics of business didn't suddenly cease because of the Luther Hodges—BC spat. Quite the opposite. Kennedy soon sandbagged his own commerce secretary, and BC stayed as quasi-public as ever. BC remained a recruitment center for corporate expertise, its meetings were still addressed by high-level administration officials without reporters present, and no antitrust probes were ever launched. The BC simply left its Commerce Department offices and moved to new accommodations down the street. Kennedy White House aides went on goodwill missions to corporate America; new economic liaison committees were created to replace the old ones; and by September 1961, Kennedy's right-hand man, McGeorge Bundy, told the BC that

the whole notion of drawing a line between anything as large and varied as the business community of the United States, and anything as complex and multifarious in its machinery as the Government of the United States is foolishness. You know that it's foolishness—we know that it's foolishness. . . . The questions which come up day in and day out between thousands of men

of affairs and hundreds of men in the various [government] departments simply do not yield to these easy slogans [probusiness, antibusiness]. You know
it and we know it. And it's a game we ought to stop. And it's a game which
I assure you this Administration will not play unless it's forced on us. It is
important that we give up the easy contests between the business interest
and the wicked Administration which have been part of our folklore before.

Just before Bundy spoke, a party for forty BC members was held at the
White House, during which Kennedy and his cabinet—including Hodges—socialized with corporate leaders and echoed Bundy's message of
pragmatic symbiosis and cooperation. Kennedy needed all the allies he
could get in September 1961. A summit meeting with Soviet Premier
Nikita Khrushchev in June had gone badly awry. By July, Kennedy and
Khrushchev were locked in a war scare over Berlin. On August 13, the
cold war turned frigid, as construction of the Berlin Wall began. Meanwhile,
anticommunist campaigns in Laos and Vietnam were becoming ever more
complicated. Kennedy had enough difficulties in foreign affairs without
facing whispering campaigns from corporate boardrooms at home. Not until
October, when Kennedy sent Defense Department officials to a BC meeting
to announce the official demise of his nonexistent nuclear missile gap with
the Soviets, did cold war tensions start to relax.

As cold war tensions relaxed, tensions between big business and government did too. Kennedy did nothing to save the tax reform legislation he
had introduced in 1961 from being shredded in Congress. Instead, he
backed tax cut legislation targeted on large capital-intensive corporations.
First came accelerated depreciation in July 1962. In October an investment
tax credit was passed. Business ended up with tax incentives on both
existing and future capital stock. The program was supply-side (investment,
not consumption, oriented) all the way, and through numerous incarnations,
reincarnations, and sweetenings until its eventual abolition in 1986, it
marked a "historic new [probusiness investment] commitment for the Democratic Party."* Only Democrats, Washington cynics said, could pass tax
cuts for business while gutting the tax hikes on upper-income individuals
that were originally supposed to finance them.

For all the Kennedy administration's devotion to sweetening corporate
taxes, however, no love feast between it and big business leaders ensued.
The same price-fixing problems that caused the Hodges-Cordiner-BC tiff
in 1961 soon resurfaced, this time in steel.

---

*In 1992, Democratic presidential candidate Bill Clinton strongly advocated restoring
the investment tax credit, one of his few clear preelection economic proposals.

By the time Kennedy arrived in office, the competitive model no longer described wide reaches of America's economy. Instead, Kennedy advisers had to deal with what Robert Averitt later called "center" versus "periphery" firms in a dual economy and what Galbraith christened the new industrial state.

Central to these ideas was the indisputable fact of oligopoly in key business sectors. There were several hundred high-tech price makers (oligopolies) surrounded by far more numerous price takers (traditionally competitive firms). This dualism helped clarify disjunction between traditional economic theory (which solved problems of power by denying they existed or by denying they could exist for long) and the fact of corporate bigness in the nation's affairs. For bigness there was. Throughout the 1950s, the United States was in the midst of the third of four great merger eras in its history. Like the 1890s, the 1920s, and the late 1970s and 1980s, the fifties were go-go years for takeovers and buyouts. Large managerial capitalist firms diversified across industry lines, often by purchasing smaller companies in other trades.

GM, for instance, expanded into diesel locomotives and refrigerators, and GM wasn't alone. In the eleven years between 1950 and 1961, the 500 largest industrial companies in America acquired 3,404 other U.S. firms, an average of 7 apiece; the top 200 absorbed 1,943 companies, an average of 10 apiece. Most mergers were of a large company and a medium-sized one. But mergers of two large firms weren't unusual: 14 percent of the 1,000 largest industrial firms disappeared by merger in the fifties, and 20 percent of them between 1950 and 1967 (1 percent of these firms went bankrupt).

Profits polarized as mergers accelerated. In fiscal year 1957–58, 572,936 corporations reported taxable incomes to the Internal Revenue Service. The largest 574 (the top .1 percent) received 53 percent of corporate net income. In 1958, a bureaucratic innovation within the Commerce Department signaled which way the corporate winds blew. The Small Business Administration was created to provide financial, procurement, and technical assistance to small companies in a big business economy. Now that small business was a special interest requiring special protection from government, bigness was inevitable to capitalism's future.

With growing bigness came oligopoly. The phenomenon wasn't universal, but it characterized most expanding postwar industries like chemicals, petroleum, rubber, primary metals, machinery, electrical manufacturing, automobiles, computers, and aerospace. By 1958, 55–80 percent of total sales were accounted for by the top four companies in these industries. Oligopoly replaced price competition with price "leadership." In this way, companies maintained their market shares and their rates of return on investment. In the mid-1950s, for example, the remaining Big Three U.S. automakers competed fiercely through style changes and advertising campaigns, but they priced their products like public utilities. None wanted bloody price wars or to destroy competitors in ways that risked antitrust investigations.

Similarly, steel companies controlled their market prices and market shares. They had achieved important efficiencies in mass production and mass distribution but were not quick to innovate, so compared to other high-technology industries, they lagged in overall economic performance. Steel remained, however, a powerfully symbolic industry. As such, it received far more political attention than most, particularly whenever nationwide union contracts were being negotiated. Harry Truman, as we've seen, had his very public struggles with steel in 1952. Eisenhower acted more subtly: he leaned on steel producers privately, pressuring them in 1956 and again in 1958 to make wage, price, and work rule concessions. In 1959, steel executives balked, and the steel strike that year became the only major industrial dispute of Ike's presidency. After 116 days, steel executives settled the way Eisenhower and Vice President Nixon wanted them to: they increased wages but didn't raise prices. They expected to recoup their fortunes after Nixon was elected president in 1960.

Nixon lost, however. Partisan steel executives were left with no political chips to cash in with Kennedy. Worse, a steel wage-price spiral began. After-tax profits as a percentage of shareholder's equity were down. American-made steel was being priced out of foreign markets, and at home it faced growing competition from substitute materials, including aluminum, paper, and plastics. Steel was in such undistinguished shape that, industrywide, it spent more money for memo paper than for alloys to make steel with. Something had to give. America's post–World War II seller's market was starting to come to an end.

The political problem remained that Kennedy owed steel nothing. Moreover, JFK's new administration soon proposed dealing with steel's wage-price spiral in a fashion that wouldn't allow the companies to cash in on their previous economic and political favors to Republicans. Kennedy's economic advisers, ironically, weren't that interested in steel: they simply saw steel's wage-price spiral as part of the wider problem of cost-push inflation. So they proposed a solution to steel's problems that might curb big business's and big labor's appetites by moderating inflationary price increases emanating from three important and heavily unionized industries: steel, autos, and construction.

The Kennedy inflation solution was known as wage-price guidelines. Via these guidelines, Democrats would do something they'd never done in peacetime—they would jawbone labor leaders into accepting lower wage increases before the steelworkers union and the companies bargained. Union wage increases would be tied to worker productivity increases as measured by government economists. Thus, unit labor costs wouldn't rise, companies wouldn't have to raise prices to maintain profits, and U.S.-made steel wouldn't price itself out of foreign or domestic markets. Important to the administration, inflation would begin to be addressed in a high-visibility industry. If union and management voluntarily moderated wage and price rises, economic life would be better for everybody.

Kennedy's assurances were all very well. But when it came to working out details, things got complicated. Early in 1962, US Steel and other large corporations sat down for industrywide bargaining with the steelworkers union. Kennedy's men got union leaders to accept a much lower wage increase than any they had accepted before, hitched it to projected productivity increases, and promised that steel corporations could pay the extra wages without increasing steel prices. On this basis, the union agreed to sign a new three-year national contract.

Then Kennedy's men visited industry representatives. Did they like what a Democratic administration had accomplished with organized labor? Yes, they did. Did steel accept the symbiotic principle upon which the deal with labor had been made? Well, it wasn't free enterprise. OK, but did steelmakers intend to raise their prices independent of the guidelines agreement Kennedy had just worked out? Silence. This evasion, alas, was taken as consent, as was the subsequent silence from individual CEOs when Kennedy officials queried them if they had any last-minute second thoughts. The steelworker's union, accordingly, signed new contracts with all the largest steel companies by April 7.

Then, on April 10, US Steel chairman Roger Blough dropped a bombshell—a memo to Kennedy announcing that his firm was raising prices on all its goods across the board, effective immediately. Within twenty-four hours almost all other major steel producers in the country fell into line. Kennedy seethed at this direct public challenge to his authority. His political credibility with enraged union leaders was also on the line. Blough and the other steel executives were logic chopping and cheating on the antiinflationary deals Kennedy had just worked out with the unions. "My father always told me," Kennedy commented to aides, "that steel men were sons of bitches, but I never realized till now how right he was." Blough had heard worse talk from Democrats, and from Democratic presidents.

But big steel soon rued the day it decided to recoup political debts owed by Republicans at Kennedy's political expense. The telegenic JFK used live television to address the country. Playing judge, he said that big steel had conspired against the traditional ideological rules of the capitalist game. (That Kennedy had ignored free markets with his guidelines was ignored.) As Kennedy demonstrated with dramatic flair, oligopoly in America was a normal way of life. "Simultaneous and identical actions of US Steel and other leading steel corporations" in raising prices after they had apparently agreed not to was "a wholly unjustifiable and irresponsible defiance of the national interest" and "showed utter contempt for the interests of 185 million Americans."

These were strong words and produced a storm of criticism from big business. Only a year after the first big criminal antitrust convictions in U.S. history, Kennedy was reminding the nation that the oligopolistic economy (which satisfied most Americans in practice) did not satisfy traditional capitalist ideology.

Blough, of course, understood that economic ideology and corporate reality were not related. That the pure competition beloved of American economists applied only very imperfectly to large high-technology corporations was no news to the CEOs of the big business BC, either: in 1952, the BC had issued a report called "Effective Competition" to counteract abstract and impractical academic doctrines. Central to the BC argument was that price competition per se was passé. What mattered was technological competition. Technical innovation and size of firm, the report said, advanced together. Technological progress was oligopoly's most important product: new and better products, not price, was the economic barometer that really counted. The logic could have come straight out of John Kenneth Galbraith's *American Capitalism*, published in the same year.

The BC's logic and Galbraith's logic diverged, however, in a crucial way. Galbraith, a JFK adviser, also argued that big business could no longer have it both ways: CEOs could not defend the necessities of bigness in business and then decry bigness in government or labor. It was illogical to advocate oligopoly one minute and wrap yourself in laissez-faire the next.

The sudden face-off between President Kennedy and Roger Blough only restated the problem Galbraith posed. Blough and other BC members argued that Kennedy was conducting class war and destroying business (i.e., investor) confidence and that the president had called all businessmen, not just steel executives, nasty names. Kennedy countered publicly that big steel and its allies were reasoning very selectively. They couldn't welcome federal intervention into union contracts to stabilize industry's cost structure and then argue that Washington should have no say at all in industry's pricing decisions. That was not the way the real world of antiinflationary politics worked. In only three days, it was all over. Kennedy cast himself as the savior of patriotism, free enterprise, and the national interest and said that big steel and Blough had flouted all three.

Simultaneously, Kennedy aides threatened the use of federal purchasing and regulatory muscle to penalize large steel companies that maintained their across-the-board price hikes. Similar threats applied to second-tier companies that later followed big steel. Within seventy-two hours after Blough left his memo on JFK's desk, three medium-sized firms—Inland, ARMCO, and Kaiser—decided not to raise their prices. US Steel and its allies promptly rescinded their increases. Big steel had been given a very visible black eye, and Kennedy appeared utterly victorious.

But appearances, as often in politics, were deceiving. Kennedy won the status contest, but he soon traded away most of the financial penalties he had assessed against errant steel men—and sweetened profits for corporations generally—to forward wider policy goals. It was a matter of cold political calculation—Kennedy might not like big businessmen but he still needed them. Kennedy's administration was organized around a promise to "get America moving again." This involved increasing economic growth. Without corporate cooperation, or at least toleration, the short-term expansion Kennedy sought might not happen.

If any were in doubt, a brief stock market crash made the point. Six weeks after the steel struggle ended, a speculative bubble burst. Investors lost more equity value in a single day than they had since Black Thursday in 1929. Panic induced the standard logical fallacies: politics had caused the Great Depression and Kennedy's meddling was causing another, post hoc, ergo propter hoc. Equally self-serving was the corporate view that capitalism was at once an unconquerable force of human nature and yet a fragile reed that could be broken by television politics that undermined business confidence.

However, depression frenzies soon subsided, stock markets reached new record highs within six months, and the Kennedy administration worked to avoid offending corporate giants any more than it already had. Kennedy had enough trouble directing the national mission abroad. By October, he and Nikita Khrushchev would be teetering on the very brink of war over Soviet nuclear missiles in Cuba. Anxious to reach economic accommodations at home, Kennedy detailed subordinates to reassure big business leaders of cooperation from the White House.

Tax cuts were a key item in Kennedy's political arsenal. To increase corporate investment levels, the investment tax credit and accelerated depreciation tax bills were signed into law within several months of the sharp drop in the stock market. Steel was exempted from none of these economic incentives. Price-fixing also became acceptable. A year to the day after the steel price hike of 1962, the Kennedy White House pointedly looked the other way when steel executives—now wiser in the ways of oligopoly—avoided price hikes on all their products at once and began, instead, gradual item-by-item increases that by April 1963 negated most of the rollbacks of a year before.

Even better was yet to come for big business. Again, it came via a tax cut. Kennedy and his successor, Lyndon Johnson, dressed up liberal demand-side Keynesian economics in conservative supply-side clothing and enrolled thousands of the nation's largest businessmen in a profitable symbiotic association with Democrats, who were planning to use general affluence to improve national economic prospects and their own political prospects.

To understand the Kennedy-Johnson tax cut of 1963–64, it is necessary to briefly discuss the economics of John Maynard Keynes. Keynesian economics arrived in America with the New Deal and allowed Democrats to comprehend what they were already doing. Pre-Keynesian economics saw the economy as a naturally self-regulating system, one in which severe and prolonged economic catastrophes were impossible. Free markets caught colds, even severe ones, but they did not get pneumonia, and they did not die.

Keynes viewed matters differently. The star performers in economic theory, before Keynes, were interest rates, wage rates, and money supply. All three variables were believed to change instantaneously enough to ensure that the economy naturally tended toward a normal state of full-employment economic growth. Thus free markets were automatically self-regulating systems and did not require active or continuing government involvement, except for modestly empowered central banks to stabilize currency values and to oversee bank operations. Keynes, however, argued that the instantaneous changes and natural self-regulations so beloved of his predecessors were balderdash. His star performers, economically speaking, were total investment, the multiplier effect, via which changes in investment or consumption spending translated into larger changes in income, and government taxing and spending policy. Keynes was no social-ist; he simply argued that public economic policy was a necessary counter-weight to private economic activity. State and market were not separate universes nodding to each other across the void but, instead, partners in creating and maintaining a stable and growing economy.

Government taxing and spending policies were central to the Keynesian vision. When the economy went bust because of insufficient private investment or consumption, Washington should spend more or tax less—or both. During booms, a reverse strategy ruled: tax rates should rise, and government spending should decrease. The private sector was still the crucial engine of economic growth, but the public sector was like the governor of that engine—it added or blew off economic steam to ensure that the mechanism wouldn't break down.

Before Keynes, American business was used to operating without thinking about federal taxing or spending policy. Washington taxed little and spent little more. Government's job was to stabilize the value of money and regulate trade to trade's advantage; otherwise government was dangerous or irrelevant. Of necessity and natural law, fundamental economic decisions were the private sector's supreme responsibility. Not so, however, after Keynes, or after the Depression, war, and cold war. Now economic destiny was shaped in Washington, too. Now Washington was as indispensable as it was unpalatable, and now corporate and government leaders shared power and responsibility in a symbiotic relation.

Adjusting to such changed realities wasn't easy: power shared was, as John Kenneth Galbraith remarked, power decreased. Throughout the 1940s and 1950s, big business struggled to accommodate the unavoidable fact that Washington would intervene more economically, via taxing and spending, than it ever had before.

A basic conceptual problem here concerned deficits. Conservatives, like everybody else, supported deficits in wartime to assure victory. In peacetime and cold war, however, conservatives equated deficits with sin. Deficits allowed Washington to spend more without immediately taxing more. It gave citizens illusions about free lunches. Government grew through IOUs, which taxpayers, especially wealthy and corporate taxpayers who paid higher tax rates, would have to pay interest charges on later. Feckless Democrats bought (or rented) votes with borrowed money and left it up to thrifty Republicans to pay the tab.

Liberals, on the other hand, viewed deficits as technical, not moral, questions. Deficits were economic management tools, not sins. There were good deficits and bad deficits. Good deficits increased economic growth and affluence; bad ones did not. Deficits were not evil in and of themselves; it depended upon what they accomplished. The public interest, not political payola, was involved, and conservatives were selfish in insisting otherwise.

So long as the deficit-as-economic-sin versus deficit-as-economic-tool scenario was played, economic debates had a basically political purpose.

They were arguments over minimal noninterventionist government versus large, interventionist government. Debates like this have a long and powerful history in the United States; by the early 1960s, however, big business began to realize that politically, as economically, the meaning of things like deficits usually resides in the details. A key detail about Keynesian deficits was this: there were different techniques to manage them, and these different techniques determined who gained economic prestige and political power. Imagine, for example, a period of economic sluggishness, a recession: investment and consumption down, unemployment up. In this situation, Keynesians believed that deficits were essential. How you created the deficit, however, was crucial.

One way to run a deficit was relatively statist and interventionist. Keep taxes constant and increase expenditures; target federal spending on economic sectors or occupational groups that needed help; pump out subsidies or construct public works. Conservatives opposed such "liberal Keynesian" subsidies unless they went to sectors (e.g., higher education, military aerospace, and housing) the conservatives favored. Jobs and income programs that more thoroughly substituted public for private economic power were almost always opposed.

Another approach to deficits, however, was much less state oriented and interventionist. Conservative Keynesian strategy kept responsibility for deficit-financed economic growth in the private sector. It did this by keeping spending constant and decreasing taxes (either for favored clienteles or across the board). Now Washington, instead of spending more money to do more things, performed only its existing duties; it did not need to increase in scope or scale—it simply left more money in private pockets via tax reduction. The private sector could then make use of this additional income to boost savings, investment, consumption, output, and growth.

Until Kennedy became president, neither liberal nor conservative versions of Keynesian countercyclical deficit financing won plaudits in large corporate circles. For years CED economists had advocated conservative, tax cut, Keynesianism (with the added desire to balance the budget over the course of the business cycle), but many CED members—and their BC counterparts—embraced Keynes gingerly, at best. As one result, no ambitious Keynesian policies of any sort were initiated during the Eisenhower era. Recessions, however, helped deny the Republicans control of Congress in 1954, cost them massive numbers of Senate and House seats in 1958, and helped lose them the presidential election of 1960 as well. By mid-1959, even minimalist conservative Herbert Hoover admitted to Eisenhower that "constant expansion of the economy" was essential to conservative political fortunes. Recessions slaughtered Republicans and undermined their ability to "flatten the curve" of government growth.

By 1960, therefore, many business leaders also began doing some equally pragmatic economic policy calculations. Democrats were not going away, nor were doctrines of more interventionist government. The thing to do, then, was not to "just say no" to taxes, spending, and deficits. Better to say "yes, but," so that when intervention occurred it did so in ways that expanded the frontiers of government's economic authority the least. Conservative, tax cut, Keynesianism was a possible way out of a political situation where Republicans were crucified by Democrats as do-nothing depression brokers every time the economy faltered.

Growing corporate economic pragmatism soon interfaced nicely with Kennedy's political pragmatism. Kennedy wanted faster economic growth, he was willing to use Keynesian techniques to accomplish it, and he was not wedded to liberal readings of Keynes. Indeed, quite the reverse. After his high-profile fight with steel and the stock market minipanic in early 1962, Kennedy wanted to buy better feelings on the domestic policy front. Tax cut Keynesianism was a major tool to accomplish this goal.

The process, as usual in American politics, occurred gradually. By June 1962, Kennedy was pushing hard for across-the-board cuts in individual and corporate income tax rates. Kennedy had not originally favored such tax cuts. His Keynesian tax cut proposals, however, were as political as they were economic. Cutting taxes for higher income individuals or groups was becoming good politics for presidents moving to the right in search of elite support.

Passing Kennedy's big income tax cut, however, still required careful choreography. Much as conservatives liked tax cuts, many also wanted spending decreases and no deficits at the same time. These right-wing traditionalists wanted what they'd always wanted: tax cuts as a way to inhibit government from doing anything they disliked. Then there were the frustrated liberal Keynesians like Galbraith. They didn't want tax cuts at all, but spending increases. Failing that, they wanted tax reforms that could pay for more generalized cuts. They wanted to end special tax deals like the oil depletion allowance to allow a better deal for the economy as a whole, while keeping federal spending up.

Kennedy, therefore, had to mollify right and left alike to position conservative Keynesianism as the golden mean of policy discourse. This is exactly what he did. Liberals were told that Congress wouldn't buy expenditure increase deficits in peacetime. So, tax cuts it had to be. Then promises of tax reforms baited the policy hook. Tax cuts, not tax reforms, however, remained Kennedy's actual priority and that of most congressional Democratic leaders as well. Reform could come "later." It was Kennedy's 1962 investment tax credit and accelerated depreciation tax cuts all over again.

Conservatives, meanwhile, got very different assurances, packaged to fit the occasion. Reactionaries got straight pre-1959 Herbert Hoover. Almost any tax cut was good; the bigger and closer to congressional election cycles, the better. Ritual promises were made that federal deficits would not increase, because of the growth explosion that tax cuts would set off. Kennedy was no radical; liberal New Deal dogmas were passé; no expensive new federal programs unrelated to defense were forthcoming. Federal mandates like minimum wages and civil rights there would be, but as Kennedy himself announced to a largely big business and union audience in May 1962, before the stock market fell, the "great national movements" that polarized workers and management in reform eras like the 1930s were "now rare" among the "general public." The "complexities of life today generate sophisticated technical questions which affect our economy and on which we ought to work in the closest concert." Kennedy wasn't going to demagogue anything. He wasn't going to orate any more about selfish businessmen defying the will of the people. Instead, a mandarinate of organized groups was going to sit down and make policy without the us-versus-them polarities of the past. Mass or class politics was going to be replaced by the politics of cooperating elites.

Most of this impressed corporate traditionalists favorably. They listened to the young president, they made their ritual complaints about deficits and runaway liberal spenders, and then they made sure economic assumptions and conservative dogmas didn't get in their way. Yes, tax cuts would be fine—across-the-board cuts for corporations, large and small; permanent cuts, not temporary ones.

Corporate moderates, meanwhile, got a more nuanced message. Kennedy was out to expand the economy not by spending more but by promoting growth in the private sector. No Democrat had done that for thirty years. The bad old days of unsettling structural changes in the economy like the Wagner Act, Social Security, and the TVA were over. Now, private power and public power would expand simultaneously. Democrats and business could stop quarreling about dividing the economic pie, because both would concentrate, instead, on how to steadily and quickly expand the size of the pie. Growth would replace redistribution under JFK, just as it had under Ike. Government had to grow bigger to wage anticommunist struggles abroad. At home, however, tax incentives would take precedence over tax increases or increases in public sector spending and investment. Keynes and capitalism weren't antithetical.

CED economists had been saying that for fifteen years. Now it was time for CED's and BC's CEOs to really listen to what their staffs were telling them. No, Kennedy was not going to decrease federal spending to avoid deficits. But deficits weren't going to end Western civilization, either. They were going to spur economic growth and increase public and private revenues. Deficits, Kennedy's chief economic advisers even allowed, were a " 'down-payment' on future [budget] surpluses." The deficit problem would be solved over the course of the business cycle—as the CED desired. Later.

Kennedy's salesmanship worked. The CED and the BC jumped onto what fast became a policy bandwagon. Tax cuts for wealthy individuals and business alone would be nicer, both organizations agreed, but Kennedy was a Democrat, after all, and so cuts for wider clienteles were an unfortunate political necessity. Restraint in future federal spending, likewise, was required. But increased deficits now were something big business could live with. By January 1963, the political foreplay was concluded. Kennedy men often arrayed Keynes in pre-Keynesian garb, using Reagan era supply-side rhetoric to sell Kennedy era demand-side economics.

Congress, however, was not to be rushed and spent a year finalizing tax cut legislation. Kennedy's advisers had promised something for everybody, and their promises conflicted. Simple tax cuts versus not-so-simple tax reform; more for everyone versus more for some at the expense of others; probably permanent cuts versus maybe temporary ones; deficits that would be paid later versus deficits that wouldn't—and didn't have to be; no more spending at all versus flattening the growth curve. Clarifying such policy tangles took time. But as Congress debated the economics of Herbert Hoover versus the economics of John Maynard Keynes, businessmen did not sit idly by. They had billions riding on the details of this tax bill, and they were not shy about making that fact known. With White House support, BC activists created an umbrella organization called the Business Committee for Tax Reduction (BCTR). It soon enrolled almost 3,000 corporate CEOs in a panindustrial coalition that lobbied Congress hard and long.

The BCTR proved especially useful in winning over Republican traditionalists and southern Democrats, who, for sometimes very different reasons, wanted to get Washington to do lots less of whatever it did by throttling spending and killing off programs. Liberal Democrats were already isolated. But for Kennedy's conservative tax cut Keynesianism to win, politicians anxious about uppity Negroes or wild-spending Democrats in Washington had to be won over as well. Kennedy men like Treasury Secretary Dillon cooperated by saying that severe recession and left-wing agitation would run rampant unless Kennedy's tax bill was passed. Reactionaries were the real radical dupes in government.

Once red baiting in reverse and Kennedy's assassination (in late 1963) isolated the most vehement right-wingers in Congress, it was all over but the shouting as far as conservative Keynesianism was concerned. The BCTR helped eviscerate the pro forma tax reform and tax increase elements of the Kennedy promise. Individual tax reductions were tilted toward the wealthy. Bipartisan opportunism ruled—the political economy of the least-common denominator.

In the process of creating the tax cut of 1963–64, Kennedy unleashed a conservative genie in American politics. Across-the-board tax cuts inevitably favor the affluent. A 10 percent income tax rate reduction means a lot more, in dollars, to a wealthy person paying $10,000 in taxes than to a poor person paying $500 in taxes or to the very poor not paying any income taxes. The wealthy, therefore, applauded Kennedy's individual and corporate income tax cuts, while the less affluent often didn't notice them at all. An affluent spin was put on Keynes, as understood in America—a spin that liberal spenders later profoundly regretted.

The tax-cutting drum was beaten repeatedly and successfully during the Carter, Reagan, and Bush presidencies. Encouraging the economy with tax cuts became, as Galbraith later remarked, "an uncontrollably popular measure with conservatives." Taxes could initially hardly be raised even to pay for the Vietnam War. Without big business support, belated and reluctant though it was, Lyndon Johnson would have found the chore impossible. As it was, he and his corporate allies barely got supposedly temporary war surcharges through a refractory Congress in June 1968, over two years after deficits and war-induced inflation had started ascending into the stratosphere. Not until 1969 was a liberal Keynesian tax bill rammed through Congress; it significantly increased the regular tax burden on corporations and higher income individuals and survived, with proliferating special interest tax loopholes, for eleven years.

America's Kennedy-brokered marriage of Hoover and Keynes, ironically, became a new variety of free-lunch economics. Reagan era supply-siders made this irony clear when they successfully revivified the Hooverlike aspects of the Kennedy tax cut message. It was the conservative old-time religion on taxes with a conservative Keynesian spin. Almost any tax cut was good, especially if it was for higher income individuals and businesses. Growth miracles would solve all deficit problems—later. When deficits did not magically disappear and the federal debt actually tripled during a decade of Republican presidencies, an even older old-time religion was revived. Tax cutters who had helped swell the size of the deficit and the debt in ways never before seen in peacetime now argued for more strenuous efforts to limit public spending. Kennedy was not Reagan, not by a long shot, but his decision to buy popularity in business circles in the wake of the steel price hike imbroglio via a conservative Keynesian tax cut nevertheless set the stage for the decades of economic conservatism that were to come.

7

THE TIME OF TROUBLES BEGINS:
FROM LYNDON JOHNSON TO GERALD FORD

There was no corporate triumph during Kennedy's brief presidency. Although business did well on taxes under JFK and LBJ, taxes were a special case: tax cuts increased economic growth, and economic growth had basic cold war dimensions during the sixties. The Soviet economy was growing fast. By 1961, Nikita Khrushchev regularly boasted that the U.S.S.R. would "bury" the United States economically by 1970. Both Kennedy and Johnson economists therefore regularly promoted their tax cuts as a way of keeping Soviet industry from overtaking American industry until 2010. Fears of a Soviet-led world economic order seem ridiculous now, but they were quite credible then. Liberals often acted conservative on taxes to stymie the reds.

Tax cuts, however, were not all of politics. Many other issues arrived in Washington in the 1960s to upset the status quo: civil rights, affirmative action, the environment, energy, consumer product safety, sexual equality, the energy crisis, stagflation, economic controls. Widespread political alienation and unrest following the failed war in Southeast Asia and the failed political sabotage and cover-up of Watergate shifted political power relations. Economic laws and global economic power balances stopped behaving the way big business assumed they always would. The decade from 1965 to 1975, for America's leaders—corporate and otherwise—was a time of troubles.

Some of the difficulties facing business leaders were organizational; others resulted from new social and economic policies the government was called upon to create. Structurally and conceptually, CEOs lagged behind circumstances—they reacted to events rather than led them. So even though business did well or was able to limit business taxes, elsewhere it lost more battles than it won. Big business knew how to play the politics of the 1940s and 1950s, but these were restricted, ad hoc, and informal. Its presence in Washington was limited and informal: few big firms had permanent full-time lobbyists. Far fewer had political affairs offices to plot corporate strategy in dynamic policy environments.

Numbers can only hint at the circumstances, but they provide a picture:

in 1961 only 130 firms had official Washington representatives, and only 50 of these had Washington addresses. Most of these lobbyists operated informally and without staff; their personal connections were what forwarded their company's interests, particularly regarding sales to the federal government. In 1970 only a handful of large corporations had political affairs divisions (80 percent of the largest 500 manufacturers had such divisions ten years later). Most big corporations' concern with federal political and administrative details in the 1960s and early 1970s was sporadic and episodic, compared with present practice.

What was true of individual companies was also true for corporate organizations. There were peak policy groups like the BC and the CED. There were panindustrial bodies like the USCC and the NAM. There were relatively well-organized trade associations, such as the American Petroleum Institute, staffing advisory agencies like the National Petroleum Council. There were ad hoc coalitions like those that lobbied for the Taft-Hartley Act, the Kennedy-Johnson tax cuts, and LBJ's war surcharge. And there were product divisions of large companies lobbying for or against specific legislation independent of one another without any corporate grand design. As the troubled 1960s and 1970s progressed, none of these organizational strategies worked well politically.

The BC exemplifies the problem. It was elite and well connected; it could have become a forum for developing potent corporate political strategies, but it rarely did. Power and influence it had. But the BC was more reactive than proactive, and it was often not well focused. For example, when BC representatives met with cabinet and White House officials in the era of Kennedy and Johnson, they didn't always arrive at compromise positions in advance. Discussions stayed informal unless specific BC reports were discussed. One CEO would prefer this issue or option, another would prefer that one. Organization was evident regarding unifying issues like lower taxes and unions, but that was rare. Strategy often wasn't plotted out in advance or revised in postmortems afterward. Agendas either sprawled or were focused by political managers, not corporate ones.

The BC's and the CED's lobbying was also informal and decentralized. Member corporations of both organizations lobbied individually, not as a group. The 1968 BC chairman told a fellow BC member who had been Truman's secretary of commerce that "one of the distinguishing features" of the BC was that "it does not speak for its members collectively; they speak for themselves individually." The CED was more public than the BC, but its modus operandi differed little. In 1962 it wouldn't even deliver its conservative Keynesian tax policy reports to Congress, when a sympathetic JFK asked it to, for fear of appearing too directly interested in legislation. Kennedy finally arranged the distribution himself, via congressional Democratic leaders. As Grant McConnell remarked at the time, "A multiplicity of intimate contacts with government is the essence of the process." Elite corporate organizations and business interests generally were "rarely united and . . . most often fragmented."

If elite bodies like the BC and the CED were many-headed beasts, the same was much more true of far larger general membership organizations like the USCC and the NAM. Lacking the access that BC's elite symbiotic status allowed, both often ducked major issues, like freer trade versus tariffs, which split their members. Their official legislative positions weren't amended in the give-and-take of political discourse but were based on their intransigent ideologies, in which unions and communists figured as their enemies. Their politics was mostly posturing. Senator Kennedy, for instance, who had cosponsored the Landrum-Griffin antiracketeering act of 1959, was no New Deal laborite. Kennedy's aide for labor-management issues later recalled that the NAM and the USCC staff he met with were "usually really scroungy bastards. . . . I guess they came in to us with a chip on their shoulder, and we reciprocated."

Because the BC and the CED were poorly organized and the NAM and the USCC were political fossils, business often fell back on trade associations to lobby specific issues collectively. This approach, however, was difficult when major new issues arose. Trade associations outside of a few industries like oil were "ill-funded, ill-staffed, ill-informed," and couldn't get well organized on short notice. Single-issue coalitions created on an ad hoc basis sometimes did better, and they worked especially well when ambitious politicians first helped midwife them into being. Big business performed best, in fact, not in doing things itself but in keeping others from doing things. It didn't usually put issues on agendas—it usually kept issues off agendas. Business's main political role was prophylactic.

It also strongly influenced new economic policies during the crucial implementation stages. Both Eisenhower and Kennedy, for instance, recruited business leaders in droves to set up various mini-Marshall-Plan economic aid programs for developing nations in the 1950s and 1960s, using the BC to select leading personnel. But directing and implementing policy, however important, was not the same as making new policy. Business—and big business—tended to respond to political initiatives, rather than generating them itself.

All this wasn't difficult as long as federal economic policy mostly involved cutting tax rates. But after Eisenhower and Kennedy departed the scene, conservative disaster came. Conservatives lost the 1964 election; then came the Great Society; then waves of new social regulations backed by, of all people, discontented elements of the upper middle class; and finally came economic controls instituted by a Republican president.

The 1964 election started it all with Senator Barry Goldwater of Arizona's presidential bid. Goldwater was an insurgent conservative, frontier populist, and small business traditionalist par excellence. His beloved West was a "colony" of mammoth eastern corporations and banks, which "bled the region of . . . natural resources, then abandoned us as soon as the riches ran out." The federal government stood in unholy alliance with the eastern financial and business establishment. As distant and uncaring moguls raped the West, a distant and uncaring Washington oppressed entrepreneurs by coddling unions at home and communists abroad. It refused to give up control over half the land area of the West to states and local business. To Goldwater, and to the millions of conservative Americans he spoke for, the times had got very badly out of joint. America's foreign and domestic policies had rarely been right, in fact, since the onset of big government and the cold war.

Establishment Republicans resembled liberal Democrats in Goldwater's populist vision. Democrats undermined America with no-win conflicts against communism and with rampant welfare statism; Republicans like Eisenhower and Dewey had spinelessly accommodated to big government, big business, and big labor. They had abandoned the small business and middle-class majority of Americans, who had made the country great. Mainstream conservative leaders had acquiesced in the already too big getting even bigger.

Corporate America was also spineless. It was off whoring after false gods and federal money. The big business establishment "centered in the boardrooms of virtually all major companies and businesses—banks, insurance firms, financial institutions, steel and auto companies, the works," wrote Goldwater, "called themselves Republicans but sought a GOP-run government not to lessen its intrusion in [citizens'] lives but to control more of how the federal establishment spent its funds." Big business was on the state payroll. It had been bribed to forget that big government was almost always the problem and that state, local, voluntary, or small business answers were almost always the solution. Social Security old age insurance and the Wagner Act (even as limited by Taft-Hartley), for example, must be undone. There was also "no substitute for victory" in the war against communism. The "containment" of reds abroad and New Dealers at home that corporate politicians like Marion Folsom, Lucius Clay, and others had accomplished after 1945 wasn't enough. The time had come to roll back creeping socialism everywhere before it destroyed America.

Goldwater's forthright challenge to the symbiosis between big business and the state was as old as Andrew Jackson and William Jennings Bryan. It was, and is, a faithful reflection of America's relative lack of a statist tradition and of the nation's historical experience of minimalist and decentralized government until the onset of the Depression.

Goldwater's broad-gauged attacks on bigness scared most big business leaders to death. They knew where Barry was coming from: they didn't like commies, liberals, or unions much either. But they also knew what minimalist conservative frontal assaults on America's mixed system of public and private power might cost them, politically and economically. Large corporate CEOs, accordingly, deserted to Democratic presidential candidate Lyndon Baines Johnson in droves. True, the now-retired price fixer Ralph Cordiner of GE was chief corporate fundraiser for Goldwater; the recently pilloried price fixers in steel also backed Barry; and a small handful of the nation's largest firms supported him. Most big business, however, raised money for LBJ. Scores of BC and CED notables headed the National Independent Committee for President Johnson and Senator Humphrey, which enrolled 3,000 CEOs. Many other firms contributed to LBJ privately.

Campaign cash reports demonstrate massive big business disaffection from Goldwater: in 1956, for example, BC CEOs had contributed $300,000 to Ike and $4,000 to Democrat Adlai Stevenson; in 1960, Nixon received $250,000, to JFK's $35,000; Goldwater, however, shifted the money equation away from the GOP for the first time in modern presidential history.* He received only $90,000 from BC CEOs, to LBJ's $140,000. The many unreported corporate contributions quite probably only worsened the campaign finance odds against Goldwater. Johnson intensified the corporate recruitment efforts he'd begun with BC delegations only twelve days after Kennedy's assassination in November 1963. As Election Day 1964 approached, Johnson addressed hundreds of businessmen a night at White House dinners. "In your heart, you know he's right," Goldwater partisans pleaded. "Yes, and in your head you know he's crazy," quipped LBJ's.

After the votes were counted, 1964 was a rout for the GOP on a par with 1932, 1936, and 1974. Goldwater won only 27 million of 70 million

*The Clinton-Gore Democratic presidential campaign of 1992 also apparently repeated this unusual achievement.

votes cast. Republicans lost thirty-seven House seats, a fifth of their strength. After the smoke cleared, a Democratic president was in the White House and the GOP was outnumbered just over two to one in both houses of Congress.

Lyndon Baines Johnson now had a golden political moment, and he seized it. LBJ, few realized, was "possibly the richest man ever to occupy the presidency" to date. He had achieved that wealth via federally awarded radio and TV station operating licenses within a symbiotic system that had existed in telecommunications since the 1920s. And Johnson was from Texas, then the major corporate center of the U.S. and world oil business, and he knew oilmen; he had raised money from them for many a Democratic candidate for decades. He recognized, as did the oilmen, their dependence upon the symbiotic system governing matters like foreign oil import quotas. Like other Texas power brokers, LBJ had protected oil's overall taxation, output control, price-fixing, and other regulatory advantages throughout twenty years of very successful political practice in Congress, a success that had made him majority leader of the Senate by 1955. Johnson, a regulated and license-protected radio and TV magnate, knew how to speak regulated and price-protected political language with not only oil but with construction firms bidding on federal projects; with real estate, housing, and S&L firms with stakes in federal mortgage financing policies; and with aerospace companies dependent upon military contracting.

Goldwater hated such influence peddling. His high-rolling western entrepreneurs weren't LBJ's variety. Goldwater got most of his money from smaller business people who wanted to return to the halcyon days of minimal government (that often hadn't existed, particularly in the publicly irrigated, owned, and underwritten western states). Johnson focused on big business (and segments of middling and small business) in the Midwest, West, and South. He reassured CEOs that he was no spoiled son of affluence and Harvard who had never met a payroll. He told them he was, in many respects, someone much like themselves: an entrepreneur, a doer, a maker of things. He knew the value of a dollar. He was a self-made man who had triumphed over adversity, a leader who understood big government and big business, a practical fellow you could do business with, who had his picture taken with you at the White House, and who made sure you received your autographed trophy shortly afterward.

LBJ's politics-as-business approach initially worked well. Big business not only supported his election, it supported him for almost three years afterward. There were no repeats of Kennedy's very public troubles with steel or the BC. Difficulties stayed private. And the BC was esteemed; a businessman who was the number-two man in LBJ's Commerce Department later recalled that Johnson equated business with the BC. He had to be reminded of the existence of the NAM, the USCC, and other national business organizations; for him they counted for much less, domestically or internationally, and they were, besides, Goldwater's base of support, not his.

Johnson consciously nurtured a big business–Democrat alliance: he passed Kennedy's tax cut with a rush, grandly assured business audiences that federal regulatory, taxing, and (especially) spending decisions would be to their liking, and labored hard to wean more corporate leaders— and corporate money—away from the Republican party. He seemed, for a time, to have succeeded. Harvard's Theodore J. Levitt hypothesized early in 1967 that "the Johnson treatment" was creating "what may turn out to be the most remarkable ideological transformation of the century," because America's leading businessmen had "finally and with unexpected suddenness actively embraced the idea of the interventionist state."

Big business–government cooperation was riding high. Yet, like the rest of America in 1967, it was also riding for a fall. Only a year after Levitt's laudatory article on the Johnson treatment appeared, Levitt published another, one with the grim title "Why Business Always Loses." What had happened? Vietnam. And domestic antiwar, racial, and regulatory unrest. Johnson's responses to such problems shifted corporate loyalties back toward Republican presidents from 1968 on.

Lyndon Johnson wanted to be a great and remembered president. He wanted more guns to fight communism abroad and more butter to erect a Great Society on New Deal foundations at home. He wanted to be another FDR, waging successful wars against domestic poverty and foreign enemies alike. The key to Johnson's hopes, like Kennedy's, was peacetime affluence and accelerated economic growth.

At first, all the economic, political, social, and military indicators seemed to go Johnson's way. The 1960s, after a slow start, saw growth that eclipsed even that of the 1950s. For five and a half straight years, the U.S. economy performed better than it ever had since 1929. Inflation-adjusted annual GNP growth rates more than doubled (to 5.3 percent) compared with those of the 1950s. No recessions like those that discomfited Ike occurred. There was another limited war in Asia to contend with, but it was limited precisely to avoid the domestic wartime economic controls and the bloody Chinese intervention that had harried Harry Truman during Korea. The economy after 1962 was on an escalator, improving the lot of all income groups. The rich got richer, and the middle class and many of the poor did, too. Now the gaps in America's affluent society that Galbraith had lamented in the 1950s could be closed.

Social welfare programs numbering 135, collectively called the Great Society, were LBJ's effort to close poverty gaps. The Great Society targeted problems that growth alone couldn't solve—because of educational incapacity, poor health, disability, or racial prejudice. While Keynesian tax cuts alleviated cyclical unemployment and economic growth lowered poverty rates, Great Society programs lowered both structural and technological unemployment and poverty rates via targeted social programs.

The Great Society came in many forms. The federal government, often acting with states and localities, did one of five things: (1) mandated and enforced minimum standards regulations, (2) provided income supports via social insurance programs or from general revenues, (3) provided remedial and rehabilitation services, (4) provided jobs and job training to particularly disadvantaged groups, (5) empowered the poor to engage in "maximum feasible participation" in locally based poverty programs aimed at improving their lives.

The Civil Rights Acts of 1964 and 1965 and the federal "poverty line" indicator created in 1964 to measure want, to determine eligibility, and to set benefits are examples of Great Society minimum standards initiatives. Medicare and Medicaid were primary income support programs. Medicare paid for health care for the elderly via the relatively popular means of "self-financing" social insurance. Medicaid did the same for the poor through the relatively unpopular technique of subsidies paid from general tax revenues. Office of Economic Opportunity (OEO) grants for needy college students and others were also examples of income support. Remedial and rehabilitation programs included Head Start (for preschoolers) and expanded support for vocational rehabilitation (for the disabled). Jobs and job training went to educationally disadvantaged people via the Job Corps. Empowerment initiatives included the federally funded Legal Assistance Program to aid poor appellants or defendants, and particularly the Community Action Program (or CAP). The CAP was contentious, loud, and occasionally fraudulent; and it so visibly threatened local politicians that federal support for community organizing became by far the least popular component of the Great Society.

Though locally oriented empowerment programs like the CAP were the most publicized, the most discordant, and shortest-lived type of Great Society programs, they were not, ironically, the ones that caused big business the most grief. They could be controlled or starved to death by denying them funds, and this control was exercised after conservatives' political fortunes began recovering from the Goldwater disaster of 1964. The protests, rioting, and assassinations of 1967 and 1968 and the failed Vietnam War split the Democrats wide open by 1968, putting another Republican president in office.

Congressional and executive branch conservatives, therefore, pared many Great Society programs after Lyndon Johnson's administration met its economic, political, and military Waterloo during the Tet offensive in Vietnam early in 1968. Federal money for community organizing went. All jobs and most job training programs went. Remedial and rehabilitation services were pared. Some large income support programs like the OEO died.

Most income support programs like Medicare and Medicaid, however, survived. All the new federal minimum standards programs did too. The basic corporate problem with income supports and minimum standards was that they couldn't be changed simply by denying them funds. They were entitlements. Laws, not annual congressional funding levels, had to be changed. Or the enforcement of laws had to be avoided. Liberal Democrats, however, retained enough control in both houses of Congress until 1981 to make conservative assaults on federal mandates and income supports unsuccessful. Income support laws like Medicare enjoyed the political cover provided by popular concepts of Social Security. The elderly thought they were only getting what they'd paid for.

Minimum standards laws, meanwhile, didn't even cost Washington much. Such regulations involved—as they always had—government forcing the compliance costs on others. The Civil Rights Acts were just like minimum wage laws—they set floors below which corporations couldn't operate. An even more important corporate difficulty with minimum standards laws was their sheer number and scope. They regulated business life in many uncustomary ways. The new federal minimum standards were of a panindustrial, not an industry-specific, type, which business had rarely seen since the passage of laws like the Wagner Act and the Social Security Act.

Another problem with the proliferating minimum standards laws was that they were supported by powerful groups of the upper middle class, whom CEOs had difficulty controlling politically. Unions had been corporate America's chief legislative opponents since the 1930s. Upper middle-class Americans of the 1960s and 1970s, however, had advantages over unions. They proved much harder to marginalize. The changed political environment that these people operated in was unfamiliar and confusing to corporate politicians. Organized business, then, not only failed to roll back minimum standards and income support laws in the 1960s and 1970s; it couldn't contain their expansion. The new social regulations were their real Waterloo.

Some background may be helpful. From 1938 to the early 1960s, corporate leaders had gradually accommodated to the changed realities of federal power. They had learned how to contain government expansion, sometimes in cooperation with smaller business, accepting large-scale federal economic responsibility only when Washington confined its role to providing economic incentives and financial guarantees to private firms to accomplish desired social purposes. America's corporate leaders rarely believed in unilateral government power. But they came to appreciate symbiotic public financing and underwriting of loan guarantees, military spending, research and development grants, tax incentives, subsidies, and national-security-related preferences for industries like oil, aerospace, and computers. In these arrangements, Washington was passive—it underwrote and subsidized, but it didn't control. Whenever politicians got too activist (as steel, for instance, thought Kennedy had when he briefly applied voluntary wage-price guidelines), CEOs bridled.

Between 1938 and the early 1960s, business had successfully contained government's unilateral use of its power. From the end of the domestic reform phase of the New Deal in 1938 until the passage of the Civil Rights Acts of 1964 and 1965, only one major new peacetime regulatory agency was created in Washington, the Federal Aviation Administration (FAA) in 1948, and even the FAA was established along the traditional industry-specific lines governing almost all federal regulatory activity in America.

This industry-specific tradition included industries like banking, telecommunications, and civil aviation, each of which possessed their own technical, structural, economic, and regulatory problems. Only rarely had Washington created a regulatory body (like the NLRB) to oversee all corporations in all industries. In 1964, however, regulatory norms again became panindustrial. That year, the Equal Employment Opportunity Commission (EEOC) was established to forward civil rights in the economic, as well as the political and social, realm.

The EEOC affected how *all* business hired and promoted people. It redefined management prerogatives the way unions, with federal muscle behind them, once had. Had EEOC been unique, it would have been bad enough, but the new social regulations that EEOC soon mandated regarding equal opportunity and, later, compensatory action were far from unique. Between 1964 and 1973, federal social minimum standards affecting all businesses were passed into law in other key areas, including consumer product safety, the environment, energy use, and workers' health and safety. New federal regulatory agencies like the Environmental Protection Agency (EPA) of 1970, the Occupational Safety and Health Administration (OSHA) of 1970, and the Consumer Product Safety Commission (CPSC) of 1972 were created to administer and enforce these panindustrial regulations.

Business failed to halt this new regulatory upsurge for many reasons. Its lobbying remained ad hoc, and the Goldwater candidacy had weakened congressional conservatism. The new federal minimum standards laws were a very cheap way to keep the reform momentum going as growth slowed after 1968 and taxpayers wrangled about paying for Great Society spending programs. Corporate profits between 1965 and 1969 were at their post-1945 peak, so corporate complaints about the economic costs to them of regulatory compliance could be ignored.

The 1965–75 decade, then, posed new regulatory challenges to American business. The new social demands regarding equality and quality of life originated not from industrial unions but from Americans with white-collar, professional, social status. Mimicking the early civil rights movement, environmental pioneers like Rachel Carson (*Silent Spring*, 1962), consumer product safety advocates like Ralph Nader (*Unsafe at Any Speed*, 1965), and women's rights spokespersons like Betty Friedan (*The Feminine Mystique*, 1963) called upon favored Americans like themselves to organize grass roots movements to change the world. Advocates like these focused the concerns of college graduates, a group whose numbers had tripled in the wake of a quiet higher education revolution begun by the GI Bill and *Sputnik*. They were publicists. They energized and empowered. They pioneered the use of television and computers for organizing, fund-raising, and lobbying. They invented modern mass political mailing techniques.

The middle-class reformers that Nader et al. spoke to and spoke for were more than innovative. They were also shielded from organizational pressures that business regularly applied to unions. Nader was a lawyer, Carson a biologist, Friedan a publicist. None was dependent on NLRB decisions or the fine print of the Wagner Act or Taft-Hartley. None worked in a factory, where they could be pink-slipped. Few cared about vested interests in existing jobs making existing goods in existing industrial environments. Middle-class professionals, unlike union leaders, rarely thought of themselves as having any special interests to protect. Instead, environmentalists, feminists, and others were part of a diverse public interest movement, which coalesced nationally just as political power centers and access points in official Washington started to proliferate. Panindustrial social reformism opened up, in short, just as American politics did.

Vietnam and its discontents fueled political reforms that changed structures and balances of power in Washington in important ways. In particular, they changed power balances in Congress and between Congress and the president. Imperial presidents had got the nation into trouble at home and abroad. Traditional congressional leaders, an elite based on seniority and deference, had allowed this to happen. Constitutional checks and balances hadn't worked as advertised. Reformers, therefore, changed the political rules. They altered key elements of the congressional power system via a series of legislative reform acts passed between 1970 and 1974.

They weakened the seniority system. They increased the number of committees and (especially) subcommittees. They decreased committee chairs' powers to bury legislative proposals or to punish refractory junior members. They ensured every legislator one important subcommittee assignment. They restricted elders from dominating the elite committees of the House or the Senate. They elected committee chairs and ranking minority members via grass roots caucuses. They increased congressional staff to keep members and committees better informed. They created the nonpartisan Congressional Budget Office (CBO) to enable Congress to make budgetary and growth estimates independent of the increasingly partisan executive branch Office of Management and Budget (OMB). They opened subcommittee and committee meetings, markup sessions, and conference committee negotiations to interested parties, including the press.

Reformers made many other undramatic but important alterations in "inside" politics in Washington. All these changes undermined the power of traditional congressional leaders and made Capitol Hill a more free-wheeling place than it had been in almost a century. Where once there were very few power centers, now there were very many.

Public interest advocates benefited from such changes. Business leaders did not. They had difficulty understanding how the rules of the political game in Congress were changing or how power began shifting from the White House to the Congress during the Vietnam War and the Watergate-plagued presidency of Richard Nixon. CEOs' lives were further complicated when adept reformers like Ralph Nader arrived with agendas detailing precisely what they wanted the more open and brawny Democratic Congress to do. They not only wanted (and got) panindustrial regulations, they also wanted (and got) federal agencies to enforce those regulations, and these were organized in ways that could keep the regulators from being captured, co-opted, or bought off by those they regulated.

Middle-class reformers like Nader believed that industry-specific regulatory agencies start off regulating their single industries vigorously, turn conciliatory in their middle age, and finally devolve into captured senility. James Q. Wilson calls this type of regulation "client" politics. In client politics, benefits are concentrated, but the social costs of providing them are widely distributed. A tariff favoring a specific industry is an example of client politics; so are most agricultural price supports. Client politics, activists believed, inevitably breed regulatory accommodations between corporate and government power, since the sprawling social costs are hard to measure or act upon, while the benefits are easy to compute and lobby for.

The regulatory activists of the sixties and seventies, therefore, replaced the politics of single-industry regulatory accommodation with the politics of panindustrial regulatory confrontation. They did this by replacing Wilson's client regulation with what Wilson calls "entrepreneurial" regulation. Entrepreneurial regulation utterly reverses the cost-benefit equations of client regulation. Instead of diffuse social costs and focused economic benefits for the regulated industry, there were widespread and identifiable social benefits and very concentrated industrial costs to provide those benefits. Nader's first successful campaign for auto safety and emission standards illustrates the principle. Almost everybody drove and absolutely everybody breathed, but Detroit's automakers paid the federally mandated expenses of safer and less polluting vehicles for the greater good of society as a whole.

Automakers, not surprisingly, didn't like this new regulatory logic one bit, but there was little that Detroit or any other single industry acting alone could do about the new standards that the new social reformers got passed into law. Most environmental and safety regulations, moreover, were only initially focused on specific industries; they were the forerunners of far broader efforts to regulate aspects of all industries. They were, in fact, "functional" regulations, which no one industry, however powerful, could oppose successfully. Given, too, that the benefits of cleaner air or safer products were so widespread, they could be opposed effectively only by broad alliances of industries. As we've seen, however, U.S. business wasn't well organized in a broad, multiindustry, fashion at this time.

Nader et al. outmaneuvered big business politically in other ways. They helped draft regulations with broad functional mandates, which specifically required agencies like the EPA to ignore industries' economic compliance costs when formulating or applying regulatory standards. Regulators were buffered from the regulated by locating the new federal regulatory agencies within the executive branch in order to protect them from industry counterattacks. In addition, judicial oversight restricted the administrative discretion of these regulatory bureaucracies. The reformers, borrowing a page from the corporate legal books, got legislation passed enabling public interest lawyers to bring class action lawsuits against errant regulators, thus restricting corporations from using technical statutes like the Administrative Procedures Act of 1946 to win back at the low-profile implementation stage what they had seemingly lost at the high-profile passage stage. Via these detailed legalisms, regulatory reformers constrained corporate monetary, lobbying, and legal powers in many ways.

Businessmen, as they gradually comprehended what was happening to them, reacted with a mixture of furor and disbelief and blamed the political messengers for bringing them progressively bad regulatory news. They assumed that Nader and his (mostly Democratic) political allies were the engines of the ship, not the bow of the ship. They believed that a conspiracy of willful radicals was driving events, rather than being driven by them. They ignored inconvenient evidence that the broad, new panindustrial regulatory mandates had wide popular support. The proliferation of equal rights organizations among occupationally disadvantaged groups seemed unimportant. Data showing the environment was becoming a primary political concern for millions were ignored. General Motors tried primitive intimidation instead: in 1965 it hired detectives to try to discredit Nader personally. The effort failed, and GM's chagrined CEO had to apologize publicly to Nader before Congress. But even though GM had to pay Nader hefty damages to settle the lawsuit, the regulatory campaign was still "of the same order as the hula hoop—a fad. Six months from now we'll probably be on another kick." So BC's chairman assured his fellow CEOs in May 1966. The fad, however, continued. By mid-1967, BC meetings echoed with complaints about agitators providing people with protections they didn't need.

Muddled corporate denial like this didn't work. Five important national environmental organizations came into being between 1967 and 1971. Membership in established environmental groups doubled and redoubled. The first edition of the *Whole Earth Catalogue* appeared in 1968. Earth Day, in April 1970, involved a tenth of the population. *Ms. Magazine*, the first strong Clean Air Act, the EPA, and OSHA all began in 1970. Not until 1971, however, were CEOs from big corporations like DuPont and GM admitting at BC meetings that new social regulations were no fluke, no conspiracy, no flash in the pan. And since frontal assaults on environmental and other panindustrial social regulations were in vain, new strategies and tactics were required.

By 1971, other ground had also shifted under CEOs' feet. The economy was mired in stagflation, and the country was about to experience the first and only nonwar wage and price controls in its history.

How wage and price controls came to America during Richard Nixon's presidency is a story of frustration, a saga that mixes politics and economics. Nixon had won office in 1968 in an election that pitted him against the Democrats and the Democrats against themselves. Without the partisan civil war symbolized by Governor George Corley Wallace's 10-million-vote independent presidential candidacy, Nixon, who won a mere 300,000-vote majority against his major Democratic opponent, Hubert Humphrey, in an election that brought 71.5 million people to the polls, never would have become president at all.

Once installed in the White House, Nixon wanted to lead as Kennedy had, on the global frontiers of freedom abroad. Domestically—and in particular, economically—Nixon delegated powers to subordinates. Those subordinates quickly discovered they had their work cut out for them. LBJ had left the Nixon administration to deal with the largest deficit since 1945 and an inflation rate of 5 percent a year. In standard conservative fashion, Republicans addressed both problems with a tighter monetary policy and an effort to cut back federal spending.

Neither policy worked. Interest rates rose to levels not seen since the Civil War, unemployment doubled, recession arrived—and inflation only edged higher, to 6 percent. Spending reductions, meanwhile, ran into trouble in Congress. Nixon was the first president in a hundred years to enter office without his party being a majority in either house. And Democratic congressional leaders weren't shy about controlling spending in ways that conservatives disliked nor about *not* controlling it in ways conservatives would have liked. Military spending, for instance, was cut, while social welfare spending was not only not—but instead rose by 60 percent during Nixon's terms. Furious conservatives, unable to successfully engineer either a credit crunch or spending controls, then had no choice but to raise taxes. Nixon did this by turning a "temporary" 10 percent Vietnam War tax surcharge that LBJ had passed in 1968 (with BC and big business support) into a permanent increase. None of this was popular in corporate circles. By the end of Nixon's first year in office, inflation, taxes, the national debt, and federal spending were all up. Inflation, in fact, was higher than it had been in twenty years.

It wasn't supposed to be that way. But "the rules of economics," as Nixon's chastened Federal Reserve Chairman Arthur Burns remarked, "are not working quite the way they used to." Indeed they weren't. Not only was inflation up, unemployment was too. Stagflation had arrived. In the summer of 1970, the largest corporate failure in U.S. history up to that time took place when the multibillion-dollar Penn Central Railroad went bankrupt. A few months later, Lockheed Aircraft was saved from an identical fate only by the last-minute infusion of federal loan guarantees totaling $2 billion. A global run on the U.S. dollar began. Fears of a 1930s-style depression were rife. Midterm congressional elections in November 1970 went badly for the GOP. Nixon had to figure out how to lead more effectively regarding the nation's economy, or the nation wasn't likely to reelect him in 1972.

A few days after the 1970 election results were in, Nixon and his political high command began to plan "bold action, positive action to show that the government was actually leading—controlling events." Nixon needed an economic czar for his administration, and in December he got one, in the person of John Connally of Texas, whom Nixon appointed as his new secretary of the treasury.

Recruiting Connally was a coup. Connally, a longtime LBJ protégé, brought Nixon bipartisan credibility with conservative Democrats in the West and South, who were already soured on liberalism by the Vietnam War protests and by social issues, including feminism, shifting sexual mores, and race relations. Nixon needed all of Connally's considerable skills: in January 1971, only one in four Americans approved of the job Nixon was doing as president. Powerful unions, despite high unemployment, were striking and gaining double-digit pay increases to protect their members from inflation. Half a dozen leading Democratic members of Congress were already organizing presidential campaigns to beat Nixon in 1972. The Democratic Congress these men led had just passed veto-proof blank check legislation allowing Nixon to freeze wages, prices, rents, and salaries and to impose wage and price controls. Nixon had repeatedly stated that he opposed wage-price controls; so this way, Democrats could crucify Nixon for his failure to be "bold and positive."

Connally understood what political positioning like this was all about, so he made haste to beat congressional liberals at their own game, secretly designing a controls program of his own. On August 15, 1971, when Congress was out of town on summer recess, President Nixon went on nationwide television to announce his administration's "New Economic Policy." Nixon had outmaneuvered liberal Democrats completely. He was replacing their hoped-for strong control program with his weaker conservative version. Nixon's part in the performance was to announce "phase one": a ninety-day freeze on wages, prices, rents, salaries, stock dividends, and interest rates—effective immediately. Nixon also called for two business tax cuts, which Congress gave him; levied a temporary 10 percent surtax on imports; and slowed the global run on the U.S. dollar by taking the United States finally and completely off the intergovernment gold standard, which was a key component of the post-1945 Bretton Woods international monetary system. Once the drama of phase one was concluded, Nixon, never particularly interested in or knowledgeable about economics, passed responsibility for running the remaining phases of the program to a shifting series of appointees under the initial oversight of Treasury Secretary Connally.

Big business couldn't have been happier. The times were definitely out of joint: profits were plummeting and fears of depression and strikes common. Unless corporate leaders supported Nixon, he'd almost surely lose his reelection bid, and then they would almost certainly be left to the mercies of a Democratic president and a Democratic Congress. As practical business managers, they understood that politics was often managerial and that the precise ways in which broad programs were organized, implemented, and administered were crucial. Business leaders in the BC believed that Nixon, and more particularly, Connally, could protect them by administering the controls their way. Accordingly, the BC and the CED joined the NAM and the USCC in supporting the first wage-price controls program in America since the Korean War. The logic here was, again, not to prevent government from meddling *in* business but to ensure that government acted *for* business. Once again, economic concern induced symbiotic arrangements.

The controls program, at first, worked well—or well enough—from the big business perspective. But, by the middle of 1972, four problems combined to hemorrhage Nixon's conservative, probusiness controls program: union opposition, congressional revolt, Nixon's political alienation of John Connally, and finally, Watergate.

1. *Union opposition.* Business, and big business, wanted unions completely excluded from the crucial details of controls policymaking. But

powerful unions had other ideas. AFL-CIO's George Meany threatened that his hitherto strong support for the Vietnam War could end unless Nixon gave labor a piece of the policy action. Nixon agreed. Union leaders, from their outlying posts in the administration's controls bureaucracy, fought to preserve union interests and paychecks. Unions wanted fringe benefits excluded from wage controls. They demanded that the large wage gains many had contracted for before the controls program began be allowed to stand, even though they exceeded controls limitations. Finally, unions wanted wage increases that exceeded those limits allowed if productivity had increased and if the wage hikes would not have an inflationary effect.

2. *Congressional revolt*. Congressional Democrats also attacked the controls program. Only temporary authority from Congress made controls possible in the first place. And congressional Democratic leaders were furious at being outmaneuvered by Nixon. Controls, for example, denied them the economic issue they had expected to be their ticket to victory in 1972. When the control legislation came before Congress for extension, Nixon's aides, including Connally, spent massive amounts of political capital fighting back legislative amendments, exemptions, clarifications, and requirements aimed at buying back the support of powerful interest groups—including unions—who believed that, while conservatives might be holding the controls gun to their heads, it was the Democrats who had loaded that gun and handed it to Richard Nixon. Worse, Democratic presidential contenders in Congress—denied a relatively safe dollars and cents, stagflation, issue—also made opposition to the Vietnam War (which most had hitherto supported) into a primary issue of the 1972 campaign.

3. *Nixon's political alienation of John Connally*. Connally resigned as treasury secretary in May 1972. One day earlier, George Wallace's second major independent presidential bid was ended when he was permanently crippled by an assassin's bullet in a Maryland shopping center. George Wallace's 10 million, mostly Democratic, supporters of 1968 were now up for grabs, and one way to grab them was for Nixon to select Connally as his vice presidential running mate. The incumbent vice president was Spiro Agnew, a cipher popular with only the Republican right wing. Replacing Agnew with Connally would likely gain Nixon millions of Wallace and LBJ Democratic votes, without losing him GOP votes. The previous January, Nixon had told Connally explicitly that Connally was his choice to be the next president after himself. What better way to help ensure this result than by placing Connally on a bipartisan conservative-unity ticket now?

It didn't happen that way. Nixon briefly investigated axing Agnew as the 1972 Republican convention approached but did not follow through.

Compliments to Connally increased. But such political talk was cheap. Connally continued his election efforts on Nixon's behalf, raising millions of dollars and establishing a national Democrats for Nixon organization. In September, Nixon officially opened his campaign at Connally's Texas ranch. But even after Nixon won reelection by a landslide, no favors for Connally were forthcoming. Nixon chose Henry Kissinger over Connally for his new secretary of state. Connally officially announced his conversion to the Republican party in May 1973; still nothing other than an ad hoc and pro forma special adviser post in the White House was tendered to him. One month later, Connally resigned his consolation prize position to return to Texas. "Obviously," he told reporters, "I'm not being fully utilized in an advisory capacity." He had no operational responsibilities—in other words, no real power. Richard Nixon, always fearful and jealous of aides he could not dominate, had just lost a man who, more than any other, might have allowed him to preserve his conservative, business-oriented, wage-price controls program or even to survive the Watergate scandals.

4. *Watergate*. Nixon began politically alienating John Connally just as Watergate surfaced with the arrest of burglars and buggers at the headquarters of the Democratic National Committee on June 17, 1972. Even before this year-long political sabotage and dirty tricks campaign against the Democrats became public, Nixon's ability to maintain momentum on wage-price controls was eroding. But after the judicial and political investigations of Watergate began in mid-1972, the president's ability to organize anything (especially anything economic) evaporated. Nixon won by a landslide in November, but given that that election in no way changed the balance of power in Congress, congressional Democratic leaders started gunning for him one day after the votes were counted.

Wage and price controls died, for all practical purposes, almost immediately. By January 1973, all mandatory and government-administered controls became "voluntary and self-administered." Prices, wages, and inflation rates took off into the stratosphere. As Arab OPEC oil embargoes and price hikes kicked in at the end of 1973, America was off on one of the worst inflationary binges in its history. The consumer price index doubled in ten years. Workers struggling to maintain their purchasing power seethed, and managers watching profits sag grumbled.

By the end of Nixon's first presidential term, big business leaders had learned some unwelcome lessons. A divided government headed (ever more insecurely) by a conservative president couldn't protect them from a wave of new social regulations. Panindustrial environmental and other statutes had only proliferated. Nor could a fatally wounded president save them from stagflation through a business-oriented program of wage and price controls. If conservative presidents couldn't protect business (and they couldn't), perhaps it was time for organized business to learn new ways to protect itself. Corporate politicians, plainly, had a lot to learn. Business leaders had lost their political effectiveness when their standard approaches to politics became outdated and when they misunderstood the structural and ideological changes taking place in society. Corporate America started to regain power and influence only as it learned new political techniques.

Organizational change came first. Businessmen needed better collective and panindustrial tools to effect change. Conservative, presidentially administered economic controls, single-industry regulatory accommodations, political protection money paid to power barons on congressional committees, ad hoc lobbying by single firms or industries, and the watering down of regulatory legislation through administrative law appeals were no longer successful strategies. "Virtually the entire American business community," David Vogel writes, "experienced a series of political setbacks without parallel in the postwar period." New panindustrial regulations administered most of this punishment. To halt the regulatory trend, big business had to reorganize itself politically.

Business had legitimate complaints. Laments were not only predictable shrieks of offended privilege. Some unions did cheat on wage-price controls. The ever changing environmental science and the regulations based on it led companies to be excoriated decades later for, say, disposing of chemical waste even in full compliance with the best-known safe procedures of the period. Ex post facto environmental cleanup and liability costs could bankrupt companies (e.g., asbestos manufacturers). Toxic effects tests developed by the EPA and other agencies used linear-assumption dosage-level risk-extrapolation techniques (degree of risk changing in direct and unchanging proportion to amount of exposure), which overpenalized industries producing substances with no significant health effects at all until some unknown critical mass of exposure was reached. These techniques underpenalized industries utilizing other compounds so potent that even a small amount of them posed grave health risks. Environmentalists too often ignored critical-mass-type public health dangers and often simplistically argued that there were no safe levels of exposure to any toxic substance.

True believers, hysterics, and scoundrels also inhabited portions of the diverse public interest movement, just as they inhabited government and corporations in the paranoiac era of Vietnam, Watergate, and stagflation. Consumer product safety hysteria, for example, emerged by the mid-1970s. Responsible regulators curbed products that failed or harmed people during normal, intelligent use. But some regulators whose missions outran their ethics began arguing that corporations were legally liable for damages suffered when people used their products even in abnormal or stupid ways. Ladder companies papered their stepladders with warnings so that dimwits who stood on top rungs or paint can platforms wouldn't be likely to win lawsuits. Manufacturers of electric hair dryers warned consumers that it wasn't rational to operate them while standing in the shower. An apex of sorts was reached in 1978 with an outcry against skateboards as unsafe for children. A Nader associate heading the Consumer Product Safety Commission responded that most parents were probably far more interested in banning thrill seeking ten-year-olds than they were in banning their skateboards.

These occasional obvious regulatory excesses intensified corporate desires for new political tools. Business was paying for much of what reformers wanted: regulatory costs further lowered profits for almost all large firms, including many in industries not previously regulated heavily by Washington. Status anxieties fueled corporate political activism. By 1970, Supreme Court Justice Lewis F. Powell had proclaimed that a financially and otherwise ruinous "attack on free enterprise" was under way. In 1971 *Newsweek* published an article titled "The American Corporation Under Fire." As economic laws stopped working, belief in business decreased. Polls showed steep declines in those expressing "a great deal of confidence" in the heads of large corporations, from 55 percent in 1966 to only 15 percent ten years later. Big business was losing—big.

Precisely how to go about mobilizing politically, however, wasn't obvious to corporate leaders. For those answers, CEOs sought advice from businessmen with wide, varied, and successful political experience: men like John Connally and Republican presidents' man of all work Bryce Harlow. Connally, the Texas oilman, and Harlow, longtime lobbyist for Procter and Gamble, were both members of Nixon's cabinet in 1972 and 1973. They were excellent choices as consultants for anxious CEOs.

Both men told it like it was. Big business had to protect itself. Nixon was no shield to hide behind. He wasn't interested in economics. He had no strong convictions about "domestic policies in general or government regulations in particular." He was the first president in a hundred years whose party controlled neither house of Congress. Nixon's forte was foreign policy, and he liked campaign money, legal and illegal, but he wasn't going to protect business from Congress if that interfered with his primary power concerns abroad. He was JFK in reverse. On regulations, taxes, and other matters, business was on its own. By 1973, mired in Watergate, Richard Nixon couldn't even protect himself.

Corporate self-help, Connally and Harlow contended, was essential.

Panindustrial challenges required panindustrial responses. Only corporate mass mobilization could counteract regulatory insurgency. The BC, as Harlow put it, must change from a business advisory council to presidents to a business action council with Congress. This meant more than cash at elections—CEOs had paid political access and protection money to presidents and congressional sachems for years. But now presidents (especially Watergate's Nixon) were hemorrhaging power, and congressional committees were increasingly powerful and independent. Corporations had to arrive early enough in committee deliberations to make a difference. To do this, permanent and expanded lobbying and intelligence gathering operations in Washington were necessary. CEOs had long orated about business confidence; now they had to rebuild their own confidence by creating dynamic alliances of interest beyond anything most large companies had ever attempted politically before.

Connally and Harlow's frank organizational advice befit the disordered political and economic environment of 1970s America. Nixon self-destructed politically. His successor Gerald Ford self-destructively granted Nixon a "full, free, and absolute" pardon before Nixon was tried for or convicted of anything. Recession and inflation occurred simultaneously. In the 1974 midterm elections, Republicans went down to their worst defeat since Goldwater. A decade of slow, conservative, congressional gains were wiped out. President Ford proved as unable as Nixon had been unwilling to protect corporations. Nor was Ford able to win election or help restore GOP congressional fortunes.

Republicans were so weak after Watergate that President Ford, though he used vetoes freely and threatened far more, barely hung on to enough support in the fractured Congress to eviscerate the only strong Democratic effort to enact full-employment legislation in thirty years—during the depths of the deep recession of 1974–76. The Humphrey-Hawkins bill originally required Washington to become the employer of last resort whenever jobless rates rose above 3 percent. Nothing remotely like this had gained a high profile in Washington since similar legislation had been amended into innocuousness in 1946. Socialism and social planning became of more concern to conservatives than they'd been since fears of a renewed depression rippled through America following World War II.

Full-employment public works jobs programs were defeated again. But political difficulties remained. Federal outlays rose: Washington spent twice as much in 1970 as it had in 1961, and it spent 40 percent more (in constant dollars) at the end of the inflationary 1970s than it did at the beginning. Worse, Congress limited spending that business liked and increased spending that business disliked. Military and R&D spending fell in real (inflation-adjusted) terms. Social Security entitlements, however, did not. Meanwhile, corporations and high-income individuals paid higher tax rates to finance federal spending after 1969 than they had during the balmy years of the JFK and LBJ tax cuts.

Taxes weren't the only higher cost items on corporate balance sheets. Wages and salaries stayed high too. During the eight years following 1965, America enjoyed the lowest unemployment rates since 1945. Vietnam War military spending boomed an already booming economy, and union workers and many professionals did very well—often too well. All fought hard to maintain the real values of their boom-induced paychecks after inflation and recession began in 1969. Pushing down wages and salaries as the economy faltered was a slow, grinding, strike-filled process, resembling repeated trips to the economic dentist. This, recall, is a major reason business wanted Nixon to do large parts of this job for them via wage-price controls. As corporations pushed to lower real labor costs once controls died in 1972–73, other costs rose. Panindustrial regulatory costs, of course, were major concerns.

So, alas, was energy. After 1973, postwar America's cheap energy decades abruptly ended as oil producing nations took control of the production and pricing of their resources, confiscated or bought out international oil combines like ARAMCO, and substituted cartel pricing by state oil authorities and OPEC for the shifting corporate arrangements that U.S. leaders had started midwifing into existence after World War II. As a result of the Arab OPEC oil embargo of 1973–74 and the panic following the Iranian revolution of 1978–79, the price of oil rose eight to twenty times. For an economy consuming 30 percent of the world's energy (for less than 5 percent of the world's people), the consequences were wrenching. Oil and natural gas provided 75 percent of America's energy. The frustrations of motorists queuing up in gas station lines were only the most visible parts of the story. Corporate frustration and vulnerability were often more profound. During the 1970s, foreign oil imports rose from one-eighth to just under half of the oil Americans used. U.S. oil and energy companies benefited from being free riders on OPEC cartel pricing, but other major industries—autos, most visibly—were poleaxed.

The combined effect of war, social welfare entitlements, dilatory taxation, stagflation, aborted wage-price controls, panindustrial regulations, and the revolution in global energy costs was predictable: inflation on a scale never before seen in America in peacetime. Price indexes doubled between 1970 and 1980. Inflation was over 10 percent a year. Growth, meanwhile, slumped. By the middle of the decade, stagflation brought an unwelcome mixture of decreases in workers' purchasing power (through inflation) and unemployment rates of 10 percent (through stagnation). It was the 1960s politics of growth in reverse: instead of dividing gains, the 1970s apportioned scarcity.

International competition was yet another reason for faltering economics and querulous politics. After twenty-five years of U.S. corporate dominance in global affairs, America's affluence ended. Japanese, Western European, and other competitors moved into the U.S. market at the very time that that market's growth slowed. In 1969, U.S. imports were only 5.7 percent of its GNP, a level essentially unchanged since 1929. Imported manufactured products were only 14 percent of the manufacturing sector's GNP. By 1979, however, imports almost doubled (to 11 percent of GNP) and manufactured imports tripled (to 38 percent of manufacturing GNP). For the first time in the twentieth century, American industry was forced to compete strongly at home, especially in steel, autos, textiles and electrical manufacturing. America's global corporate challenge of the 1950s and 1960s was replaced in the 1970s and 1980s by multilateral global competition. A rust belt of U.S. heavy industry ensued.

As competition increased, corporate profits declined. Hitherto comfortable oligopolistic firms were being hit by both rising costs and falling revenues at once. Follow-the-leader pricing no longer worked. Consumers no longer had to Buy American; they drove off in Toyotas, Hondas, VWs, Volvos, or Nissans or plugged in their Sonys. Corporate profits, which peaked at 9–10 percent in the late 1960s, headed downward for the next ten years, however they were measured. By the late 1970s, net after-tax rates of return for U.S. corporations averaged 5–6 percent, a decline of more than a third. Decline was not universal; firms like IBM and Xerox did much better than firms like Chrysler and US Steel. But overall trends were down, and they were what mattered most to big business–government relations. Growth politics was replaced by the politics of stasis and selective decline. Steep recessions in 1974–75 and 1978–80 underlined the difficulty: rapid growth was history.

Average Americans, too, gradually realized that very much had changed. In the almost thirty years between 1945 and 1973, the average family's purchasing power had doubled. The percentage of Americans in poverty dropped from one-third to one-seventh with only slight income redistribution. But after 1973, average family purchasing power grew not at all, poverty rates edged up, income inequalities between college-educated and non-college-educated and between minority and nonminority people worsened. American political economics developed decidedly surly tones.

By 1975, a genuine sense of crisis existed among the nation's leading CEOs. Elite gatherings resounded with statements that business leaders had to learn to operate by a whole new set of political rules in Washington. CEOs themselves, not old-style lobbyists, had to arrive early, propose consistently, defuse problems "before they get politically hot," and cease merely opposing policy initiatives they didn't like. Harlow's and Connally's earlier lessons about big business activity tailored to a new and more powerful Congress finally got assimilated. With further help from congressional Republicans and cooperative Democrats, including House Majority Leader (and, shortly, Speaker) Thomas P. ("Tip") O'Neill, CEOs at last went into battle directly. They maximized political returns by targeting legislators from districts in which their firms had large investments, facilities, retail networks, work forces, and payrolls.

The institutional embodiment of all this corporate political activity was the Business Roundtable. It became and remains (together with the BC, to which it is, in membership terms, closely related) the peak organization of big business political power in the United States. The Roundtable sought to combine the long-term policy development role of the CED with the short-term access, influence, and lobbying advantages of the BC.

The same CEOs prominent in the BC and the CED, unsurprisingly, were also those leading the Roundtable. After the Roundtable became prominent in Washington power circles after 1975, a few facts about its normally secretive operations became clear. The Roundtable's first four chairmen were the CEOs of ALCOA, GE, DuPont, and GM. The CEOs of nine of the top ten, thirty-seven of the top fifty, and sixty-three of the top hundred of America's industrial companies were members. Like the BC, on which it was loosely modeled, only CEOs were members. All 200 CEO members met together only rarely, however. The Roundtable functioned by committee. The forty-five-member Policy Committee oversaw approximately a dozen task forces, which formulated Roundtable policy in specialized areas, including taxation, labor relations, regulation, energy, environment, health insurance, and international trade and investment. The Policy Committee had the final say on task force decisions.

The overlap between the forty-nine individuals leading the Roundtable (one chairman, three cochairmen, and forty-five Policy Committee members) and the approximately one hundred active members of the BC was immense (75–82 percent in the Roundtable's first decade). During the same period, a third of the Policy Committee also served on the hundred-member board of directors of the CED. CEOs who chaired the Roundtable regularly chaired or cochaired the BC and the CED. The Roundtable, in short, *was* the BC, under another name.* It was also the forum for CED activists concerned about their failure to achieve corporate consensus on social and economic issues during the decade after 1965. Such Roundtable-BC-CED interlocks testified to enduring facts of life in corporate America: government was big and would remain so; and symbiosis between large corporations and the government was also inevitable. The precise terms for such collaboration were always debatable, but the necessity for it was not. As a result, CEOs of the same corporations that created the BC and the CED to meet the challenges of public sector growth during the Depression, World War II, and the cold war created the Business Roundtable to meet the challenges of the next major expansion of federal power.

The big business political mobilization that created the Business Round-table soon succeeded. Corporations that lost battles in 1965–75 fought most opponents to a standstill in 1975–78 and then began successful campaigns for reduced taxation, spending, regulation, and inflation during the presidencies of Jimmy Carter, Ronald Reagan, and George Bush.

---

*In 1991–92, 93 of the 100 active members of the BC were also members of the 211-member Roundtable. Sixty-one members of the BC were on the Roundtable's 83-member Policy Committee. Ten of the 19 members of the BC's Executive Committee were also Business Roundtable Policy Committee members.

8

CORPORATE RESURGENCE FROM CARTER TO REAGAN

When Jimmy Carter took office in January 1977, America was awash in pessimism and self-pity. Carter's dark-horse victory showed how disenchanted Americans were with corruption, crisis, and economic decline. Stagflation, guerilla war abroad, and guerilla government at home eroded affluence and optimism. Redistribution replaced growth as Americans fought for diminishing numbers of seats on the gravy train. More social welfare and more armaments and lower tax rates and no deficits became impossible economic combinations.

Politics, as well as economics, changed. By 1976, almost half the citizenry considered big government a threat, not a solution, especially those who believed that multiplying social rights were not complemented by greater social responsibilities. Democratic Carter, like Republican Gerald Ford, cast the 1976 election in terms of restoring moral values, limited government, smaller deficits, tight money, selective deregulation, and tax reform. Ford blamed major economic ills like 10 percent inflation and 9 percent unemployment on big-spender Democrats in Congress. Carter promised that his cooperation with a Democratic Congress would restore order more effectively than divided government and Ford's vetoes could. Only 54.25 percent of voters voted in the least-energized presidential contest since 1948.

What Carter would do after his election was anybody's guess. He had vaguely promised much to many. Carter the outsider and symbolic populist, ran against "the mess in Washington." But he carefully presented America's troubles as personal, not systemic; as matters of individual, not institutional, failure. Carter indicted the "political and economic elite," but *Fortune* magazine saw him as no threat whatever to the existing corporate order.

Fortune was right. Carter was the most economically conservative Democratic president since Woodrow Wilson sixty years before. He promised limited government and balanced budgets. The reforms Carter offered did not cost Washington money but emphasized cost effectiveness. He wanted no big new spending programs at all. Efficiency, not equity or anticommun-

ism, was the focus of his administration. Carter helped eviscerate Humphrey-Hawkins and other full-employment bills; he opposed expensive
national health insurance initiatives; he proposed cutting a too-sacrosanct
Social Security. Carter thus alienated liberals—like one disgruntled senator
who attacked his "small-town chamber of commerce" thinking.

Carter knew his hold on congressional affections was weak, so he sought,
like Kennedy, to marginalize liberal Democrats and conservative Republicans alike. Carter, like Kennedy, gave moderate Republicans and conserva-
tive-to-moderate Democrats bipartisan proposals to excite their interest.
Kennedy had used tax cuts; Carter used selective deregulation.

Carter's deregulation strategy was the most successful economic policy
initiative of his administration. He did not seek to deregulate business
generally or to roll back popular panindustrial regulations. Instead, he
cleverly deregulated only those industries regulated in traditional, single-
industry ways, the type of regulation that to critics like Nader was worse
than no regulation at all. By completing bipartisan initiatives begun under
Nixon and Ford, Carter and Congress between 1978 and 1980 deregulated
airlines, railroads, trucking, intercity buses, and cable television. They
also speeded up the deregulation of banks, securities transactions, and
telephone communication. Single-industry deregulation was most thorough
in transportation, in which symbiotic price-fixing and route allocation
arrangements ceased. Television (via greatly expedited cable TV franchises)
and banking (via decreases in FDIC and FSLIC regulatory market allocation
and price-fixing powers that helped produce Himalayan savings and loan
and bank bailouts in the Reagan-Bush era) were also heavily affected. As
distrust of the federal government became endemic, conservatives and
Naderites alike applauded cutting back single-industry regulations. Wilson's entrepreneurial politics were at work. The losses to industries reluctant to be deregulated were concentrated; the short-term economic benefits
from deregulation were far more widespread.

Carter strengthened enforcement of the newer panindustrial regulations,
thereby making liberals happy at very low cost to the government. Carter's
unhappy experience with energy (and specifically oil) policy had demonstrated to him how politically scorching panindustrial regulations could be.

The problem with oil deregulation was economic. Although transportation, communication, and financial deregulation promised lower prices to
consumers, the deregulation of oil brought only higher prices. After Carter
tried to phase out price controls on domestic oil that Congress had established immediately after the Arab OPEC embargo of 1973–74, the political
currents went against him. The benefits of deregulating oil prices were very

visibly concentrated in a single industry. But the costs were widespread, affecting every major economic interest group in the country.

Carter's early proposals for oil price decontrol, windfall profits taxes on domestic oil producers, higher federal gasoline taxes for consumers, and income tax rebates for less affluent people and industries were coherent and well considered, but they were repeatedly torn to pieces by conservative, corporate, liberal, and public interest proponents in Congress—conservative advocates of pure and simple price decontrol (who would allow U.S. oil producers to be free riders on OPEC prices without paying a penny for the privilege) and liberal supporters of no decontrol or deregulation at all (who pontificated that the end of a postwar era of cheap energy was a conspiracy hatched by multinational U.S. oil companies). The arguments were often reptilian: Republicans and conservative Democrats orated about free markets that had almost never been in the oil business (and which few oilmen had ever wanted), and liberal Democrats postured about breaking up big oil via antitrust laws, then ran for political cover. Ideological theatrics ruled, so nothing of practical legislative consequence resulted.

Congressional gridlock continued until a second round of Middle East oil price increases rippled through the world economy after the outbreak of the Iraq-Iran war in 1979. Then Carter, furious at bipartisan political obstructionism, threatened to use presidential emergency powers to decontrol domestic oil prices unilaterally and gradually—with or without Congress's permission. Forced to do something at last, and belatedly aware that the cheap energy era and the good old days of ARAMCO were over, congressional Democrats finally acted. They cobbled together legislation giving all major interests something. Conservatives and oilmen got domestic price decontrol; liberals got a temporary windfall profits tax and (short-lived) federal R&D programs for alternative energy sources and energy conservation; and opportunists got most of the several hundred billions of dollars in temporary windfall profits taxes reserved for corporate and middle-class (as opposed to lower class) tax cuts. Special interest tax exemptions abounded; for the state of Alaska, for Indian tribes, for smaller independent oilmen whose money had long financed many Democrats, and so on ad infinitum. Final compromises satisfied nobody; they mainly illustrated the querulous state of U.S. politics by the end of the economically frustrating 1970s.

As President Carter's own badly splintered party stymied him in Congress on oil deregulation and much else besides, corporate politicians took heart. Governing America wasn't getting any easier; opportunities for nullification and obstructionism were many. By 1978, Carter, plagued by rising inflation and unemployment rates, was so weak that all his key domestic policy initiatives could be assaulted with relative impunity. Two failed initiatives particularly demonstrate liberalism's reduced force: the legislative struggles to create the Consumer Protection Agency (CPA) and to pass labor law reform. Corporate politicians organized to defeat both of these efforts.

The CPA fight came first. Since 1973, Ralph Nader had tried to unite diverse consumer protection bodies into a single cabinet-level department, to protect nascent panindustrial regulatory programs. The CPA was to be another EPA: a power center for the people (read middle-class professionals) against the corporate interests. Corporate interests, however, had other ideas. In 1969 firms and trade associations organized a coalition against Nader called the Consumer Issues Working Group. From then until January 1977, GOP presidential veto threats kept a CPA bill from passing Congress. After Carter arrived, however, business lost its White House protection.

By then, however, corporations mobilized against Nader received powerful panindustrial reinforcements. The Business Roundtable was the key new power coalition for elite big business. Its rise wasn't unique. The USCC tripled its budget and doubled its membership (from 80,000 to 160,000) during the 1970s. Imitating the CEO-based lobbying tactics of the Roundtable, the USCC organized congressional action committees of "about 30 executives . . . personally acquainted with their representatives or senators." The USCC also expanded on the tactics pioneered by its public interest opponents. Central, here, were direct mail appeals and Biznet, a national cable TV network that mobilized grass roots business support for or against legislation. Such innovations allowed the USCC to generate as many as 12,000 phone calls in twenty-four hours to legislators' offices. The hitherto insignificant National Federation of Independent Business (NFIB), meanwhile, became an important new voice for very small businesses. It swelled from a few hundred to half a million members between 1970 and 1979.

All this new corporate political clout added up. David Vogel estimates that by 1978 corporations and trade associations spent "between $850 million and $900 million a year mobilizing their resources." Simultaneously, the CEOs of the top thousand manufacturing companies spent 40 percent of their time working on "public issues," double the percentages of only two years before. A panindustrial regulatory upsurge had produced an emphatic panindustrial corporate response. When, therefore, the CPA campaign peaked early in 1978, corporate counterattacks were widespread, well coordinated, and powerful. The CPA went down to unexpected defeat in February. "The age of justified outrage is over," one victorious wag remarked.

Soon it was organized labor's turn. Corporate America already knew how to form broad panindustrial coalitions to contain unions. Under Business Roundtable leadership, it did so again. At issue was an effort to strengthen the enforcement, access, and oversight provisions of the National Labor Relations Act to make it easier for unions to organize workers, especially in the open shop heartland of the West and South. Ending the decades-long legal evasions by southern textile companies like J. P. Stevens, creating much shorter time limits for holding representation elections, and enlarging (read liberalizing) NLRB's bureaucracy were all central aims of the legislation.

The responses of the NAM, the USCC, and the NFIB were predictable. They all opposed all reform, just as their small business membership had always done. The Business Roundtable's response, however, took longer to clarify. Most Roundtable corporations were unionized; they had made their cautious peace with the AFL-CIO decades ago. Support for open shop small firms had seldom been high on their agenda. Recession, falling profits, and increasing global competition, however, finally decided a majority of the Roundtable's Policy Committee in favor of a strong stand against labor law reform. The union status quo had become (barely) acceptable; any expansion of union powers in an unsettled economy was not.

Corporate collaboration now commenced in earnest. By May 1978, all important business groups began another effort to marginalize unions. If they could defeat a long-sought labor bill in a Democratic Congress during a Democratic presidential administration, big labor could go into political cold storage.

Clever choreography helped corporate efforts succeed. Few in Congress comprehended labor policy nuances, but suspicion about big business remained powerful on Capitol Hill. Roundtable member companies, therefore, kept low profiles. Instead, its CEOs' corporate jets provided free shuttle service to Washington for smaller business people whose legislators were weak or undecided about the bill. "I can't remember when we last experienced a lobby effort like this," an awed Senate aide remarked. "I don't think they missed a single possible opponent of the bill in our state." As down-home business people hammered on political doors, telephone calls, telegrams, and computer-generated mass mailings flowed in from Main Street, USA. Politics quickly became damage control. Last-minute efforts to engineer face-saving compromises failed. In June, badly shaken congressional Democrats voted labor law reform down to a resounding defeat. In Congress, union tides ebbed, as Naderite tides had earlier.

The year 1978 became a watershed in modern American politics. Corporate politicians, after winning defensive victories, moved on to win offensive ones. The phrase "tax revolt" entered the nation's political vocabulary; in June, just as labor law reform died, California voters passed by a vote of two to one grass roots initiative legislation pruning local property taxes and limiting their future expansion. Opposition from unions, politicians, and big business, fearful that higher state corporate taxes would be levied to make up for lower individual taxes, failed to stop the electoral bandwagon. California's booming economy posed unusually severe problems to lower and fixed-income homeowners whose real estate taxes had ballooned along with their property values. Proposition 13 set off nationwide shock waves. Distrust of government appeared endemic; middle-class and upper middle-class Americans seemed increasingly prone to believe that all levels of government were wasteful conspiracies to rip them off.

Few national politicians ignored such warnings. Just before California's tax revolt went national, Jimmy Carter introduced legislation to simultaneously perk up the economy via tax reductions and raise revenues and decrease the deficit by closing tax loopholes. Corporate carrots in the bill included increased investment tax credits; sticks included higher capital gains taxes and a tougher approach to business deductions for entertainment and lobbying expenses.

Carter failed dismally. "Never in the history of the income tax," John F. Witte writes, "were [reform] proposals so out of step with congressional intentions, and never were they so completely defeated." Just as 1978 was a Waterloo for public interest regulators and unions, so it was for Keynesian tax reformers. A Democratic Congress voided major corporate income tax increases, decreased capital gains taxes by 33 percent, opened new corporate, middle-income and upper-income loopholes, and replaced self-financing reforms with a collection of tax reductions that Carter hadn't asked for and didn't want.

It was the Kennedy tax cut of 1962 and the Kennedy-Johnson tax cuts of 1964 all over again—with a conservative twist. Cuts were general, not targeted, and there was little pretence of liberalism in the final version of the bill. Kennedy and Johnson had traded away a lot of tax reform to gain more tax reduction in balmy economic times, when deficits were relatively small. Carter, however, faced insurgency within his own party that substituted pre-Keynesian reductions for reform, made tax schedules less progressive, and did so in a stagflationary period where the deficit was large and growing. The Kennedy and Johnson reforms were compromised; Carter's reforms were repudiated.

Conservative Keynesianism was moribund, and old-fashioned trickle-down economics was back in style. Conservative Democrats who had never liked any kind of Keynes moved to the right. Eisenhower Democrats and Hoover and Eisenhower Republicans kept cuts in capital gains, in corporate income taxes, in individual income taxes, and in accelerated depreciation tax write-offs high on their policy agendas until the era of Ronald Reagan, when their efforts were supported by the Business Roundtable, the USCC, GE, and an influential new umbrella coalition called the American Council for Capital Formation, run by high-ranking treasury officials from the Nixon and Ford administrations.

The political fate of the 1978 tax bill sealed Carter's economic fate. Cautious as he was, the mainstream of the fractured Democratic Congress was now far more cautious. Carter's ability to lead declined with popular faith in active political management of the economy. What remained of Carter's presidency was mostly theater: the appearance of activity was substituted for the reality. With the exception of energy and international diplomacy (the Panama Canal Treaty and the Egyptian-Israeli Peace Accords of 1978), Carter's ability to maintain policy momentum withered.

Corporate political action, meanwhile, became more assertive. Late in 1978, with his tax initiative in ruins, Carter made one final doomed attempt to reassert control over the nation's economic agenda. Inflation and unemployment were rising again, middle-income taxpayer revolts were spreading, and businessmen and bankers were restless. To mollify the right, Carter crunched credit markets via higher Federal Reserve interest rates. To mollify liberals, he announced a voluntary wage-price control program.

Big businesses supported tight credit as thoroughly as more credit-strapped small businesses opposed it. But burned by an unhappy experience in 1971–74 of mandatory peacetime wage-price controls, with a Republican president unable to protect them from an argumentative Democratic Congress, big business had no desire to repeat controls with Carter and the fractious Democrats only four years later. It did not do, however, to say so—particularly not, when groups like the Business Roundtable utterly ignored the possibility that big business had any responsibility for price inflation. Instead of fighting Carter's wage-price controls, savvy corporate activists privately maneuvered, with much success, to limit their practical effects. Most businesses were happy to control wages using Carter's imprimatur; prices, however, they were not at all anxious to have controlled, pleading low profit margins, market forces, or other self-interested rationales.

The differences between the "yes, but" accommodationists of the BC and the Business Roundtable and the "no!" confrontationists of the NAM and the USCC regarding Carter's voluntary controls of 1978–80 once again prove instructive. The latter two opposed any controls, believing them to be Trojan horses for socialism. The BC and the Roundtable, however, played power, not ideology, agreeing to support voluntary wage-price controls *if* Carter kept interest rates high, reduced deficits, cut spending, sought additional corporate tax cuts, and backed legislation requiring cost-benefit analyses of the economic impact of all proposed new regulations, and ignored liberal demands for mandatory controls. While the NAM and the USCC sulked, the BC and the Roundtable engaged in quid pro quo.

Facing 9 percent inflation and 6.5 percent unemployment, Carter agreed to corporate accommodationists' conditions. No mandatory controls program was ever introduced by the White House, even after voluntary price controls did nothing to halt the economic staggers that produced 15 percent inflation and 7.5 percent unemployment by 1980. Controls stayed pro forma because of Roundtable lobbying. Price restraints were riddled with administrative exemptions. Charades made increases appear smaller than reality. The voluntary price increase guideline for auto companies, for instance, was 6 percent. But 10 percent price increases were allowed on 1980 car models reclassified as "completely new products" because of style changes. GM was allowed to pass the costs of complying with product safety and environmental laws along to consumers without counting them as price increases.

Charade or not, Carter's controls still irked aggressive defenders of free enterprise. *Wall Street Journal* editorials, for instance, lambasted the Business Roundtable for cooperating with the administration. Business opinion polarized by late 1978 and early 1979; in the most unsettled economy since the Great Depression, corporate moderates and conservatives got immoderate in their disagreements about how strongly to attack the decaying Democrats. By July 1979, the president was so discouraged he recast a national address on needed energy policy into a jeremiad on America's "crisis of the spirit." The nation was bogged down in paralysis, stagnation, and drift. So was Carter, who immediately sacked half his cabinet and whose popularity ratings dropped below those of Richard Nixon just before he resigned in 1974 to avoid impeachment. Carter retreated into foreign policy "crises" to improve his plummeting political fortunes.

With a presidency in free-fall and Congress in disarray, big business had its best opportunity since 1952 to reshape the nation's policy agenda. But although business was in agreement about what it wanted, it was divided about how it wanted it done. As Carter's presidency unraveled, six major corporate policy priorities existed:

—Tax cuts for business and upper-income individuals
—Regulatory reduction of panindustrial minimum standards

—Tighter monetary policy (higher interest rates) instead of higher taxes or wage-price controls, to control inflation

—Tighter spending controls, particularly outlays for Great Society entitlements

—Decreased federal deficits (what couldn't be paid for in taxes shouldn't be financed by IOUs)

—Faster economic growth (via the combined effects of the first five priorities).

Business also agreed on techniques necessary to achieve these priorities:

—grass roots organizing networks, often focused around single issues

—panindustrial corporate coalitions

—Washington-based lobbyists*

—the use of political money to gain access to and influence with elected politicians†

—the hiring of Washington lawyers skilled in the nuances of bureaucratic networks and regulatory law‡

—the increased use of media (especially television) to influence attitudes via the sponsorship of news programs, the cultivation of journalists, and "spin control" of public issues

—increased financial support for conservative public interest think tanks§

Broad agreement about agenda and techniques, however, masked many specific differences. Large corporations preferred a target rifle approach; smaller and medium-sized companies normally preferred shotguns. CEOs running big companies operating in many industries and markets talked about changing specifics at the margin; laissez-faire was a dreamworld to such men—undiscriminating dismantle-the-government approaches were

---

*Washington lobbyists increased from 365 in 1961 to 23,000 by the end of the 1980s.

† Political action committees (PACs) were the key new institutional tool here, as a result of 1974 federal campaign finance reform legislation. Federal court decisions, which later equated money with free speech, limited the applicability of these reforms to Congress, which only further fueled the growth of PACs to 1,700 by the end of the 1980s: 60 percent of the largest 500 industrial firms had PACs.

‡ The number of Washington lawyers increased from 1,500 in 1961 to 46,000 by the end of the 1980s.

§ The CED had performed this role since 1943. After the mid-1960s, it was joined by new or restructured policy research bodies: the American Enterprise Institute for Public Policy Research, the Hoover Institution, the CATO Foundation, the Center for Strategic and International Studies at Georgetown University, the Institute for Contemporary Studies, and the Heritage Foundation, all bankrolled by corporate dollars.

economically irrational. Small business people who knew only a single industry or a single domestic marketplace, however, found it easier to be ideological and undiscriminating; they were not vertically integrated, conglomerated, or active in foreign trade. They were often unaware of how Washington subsidized industries for social purposes and profited relatively little from government incentives. Minimalist conservatives ignored the many ways in which big business might suffer from generalized assaults on big government.

Accommodationist big businessmen knew better. The paradox was that government was supposed to do more and do it better but avoid becoming bigger. For fifty years, American leaders had resolved the paradox between traditional ideas about limited central government and untraditional desires to increase the scope and scale of government's missions by mixing federal money and private (and state and local) control. Power in America was shared between public and private sectors, in ways that were rare elsewhere. Webs of symbiotic association between big business and the state came from this shared power.

Business often accomplished public purposes—and profited by it. By the end of the 1970s, any large, diverse, high-tech corporation involved in foreign trade and investment had been affected by public policies in powerful ways. One-fifth of all federal spending went for the goods and services Washington buys from private corporations and (to a lesser degree) from nonprofit institutions like universities. Since 1940, defense-related spending has been the main area for such contracting: by the 1960s, 85 percent of federal purchasing of goods and services was defense related. In the 1990s, one in ten Americans in the labor force (including armed services personnel) is employed in a defense or defense-related job. The aerospace, shipbuilding, and electronics industries are exceedingly dependent upon federal military spending.

By the end of the 1960s, according to the National Science Foundation, Washington paid for 90 percent of R&D spending in aviation and space, 65 percent in electronics, 42 percent in scientific instruments, 31 percent in machinery, 28 percent in new metal alloys, 24 percent in automobiles, and 20 percent in chemicals. By the end of the 1970s, Washington was paying for fully half of total R&D spending.

In the 1960s two-thirds of federal R&D spending was defense or space related. By the 1970s, that percentage had fallen to just over half but rose to two-thirds again in the 1980s. Via such spending, the United States maintained the technological superiority necessary for remaining a world power.

Patent rights to new products developed by private companies working on federally funded projects were fully protected for (the mostly very large) companies by legislation passed in 1963, over the opposition of (mostly small) firms. Communications satellites are an excellent example of new technology created with federal R&D dollars, built with federal contracting monies and then effectively given away to wealthy individuals and large communications corporations, including AT&T, ITT, RCA, and Western Union, via the subsidized sale in 1962 of the private-public hybrid called the Communications Satellite Corporation.

After 1975, about 10 percent of federal spending went to state and local governments. These grants were tied to fulfilling goals in areas as diverse as education, mass transportation, housing, health, and welfare. This sharing of administrative and political responsibility allowed federal spending to keep growing without concomitant growth in the number of federal civilian employees—a response to the popular reaction against big government. Throughout 1955–85, federal spending grew 275 percent, while the number of federal civilian employees grew only 25 percent. This "dismantling" of Washington had powerful local and regional economic effects on industries as diverse as construction, transportation, and health care.

Business also benefits from the federal tax code via tax incentives, tax subsidies, tax loopholes, or tax expenditures. Government in this way seeks to get the private sector to accomplish public purposes. Tax-free industrial development bonds, oil depletion allowances, accelerated depreciation rules, tax credits, tax deductions for consumer credit, and many another favoritisms exemplify the phenomenon. At stake are billions of dollars in rewards.

For example, federal tax incentives since the 1950s created welfare capitalist retirement pension programs and health insurance programs covering a majority of workers in American industry, since employer contributions to these programs were not taxed. Small businesses that did not provide such programs did not benefit from this tax-subsidized welfare capitalism. By the 1970s tax subsidies and tax incentives for big business so honeycombed the federal tax code that *tax loophole* and *tax revolt* entered the populist political lexicon.

Federal loan guarantees and loan subsidies blossomed amid stagflation and tax revolt. Government was supposed to do more but not to spend more. A way to resolve this economic paradox was to keep federal activity "off budget." In other words, instead of spending its own (tax) money, Washington financially guaranteed private sector activities. Housing finance guarantees undertaken by the VA and the FHA exemplify the phenomenon. To entice private lenders, Washington guaranteed to pay off loans if private creditors defaulted.

By the 1970s, burgeoning student guaranteed loans were convenient off-budget substitutes for more federal aid to higher education. Creating the Pension Benefits Guaranty Corporation in 1974 was an off-budget way to underwrite welfare capitalist arrangements in faltering unionized industries, including steel and automobiles. In 1980, Congress increased federal FDIC and FSLIC guarantees from $40,000 to $100,000 per bank deposit (not, note, per individual bank depositor)—this at a time when 75 percent of U.S. households had not more than $10,000 in liquid assets. This action clearly favored wealthy bank depositors and the banks themselves. Banks and S&Ls, which were being deregulated at the time, were being subsidized to undertake riskier investments in a depressed economy. Again, the strategy was off budget: Washington would be good for all the debts S&Ls and banks couldn't repay their creditors.

Federal foreign investment and trade incentives were a boon to multinationals. Oil companies, as we've seen, received regulatory and tax incentives to make massive strategic investments abroad. After 1956, American corporations also paid lower U.S. tax rates on profits they repatriated from most underdeveloped nations outside of the communist bloc (so that business could spread the gospel of free enterprise). High-tech corporations also received the benefits of export subsidies via the Export-Import Bank, which made below-market loans to foreign buyers so they could buy U.S. aircraft, electrical machinery, nuclear reactors, and telecommunications equipment. By 1980, two-thirds of all Ex-Im subsidies went to assist foreign sales by only seven large firms: Boeing, GE, Westinghouse, McDonnell Douglas, Lockheed, Combustion Engineering, and AT&T. ITT, Motorola, GTE, and Rockwell International accounted for most of the rest.

Additional symbiotic arrangements include the Overseas Private Investment Corporation (OPIC), created to provide public investment guarantees for private companies in case their holdings or profits were confiscated by foreign governments; tie-in arrangements that require all recipients of U.S. foreign aid to spend the vast majority of that money for the purchase of American goods; and export promotion on behalf of high-tech corporations to erode foreign barriers to U.S. foreign trade. Large multinational firms like IBM and big business organizations like the CED, the BC, and the Business Roundtable have generally supported all such symbiotic arrangements as necessary tools to level the competitive playing fields with more overtly state-supported foreign competitors. Smaller companies active only in domestic markets and smaller business organizations like the NAM and the USCC have either ignored or opposed such incentives, which benefit their sprawling memberships comparatively little.

Corporations also benefit from various federal regulations. Struggles over panindustrial regulations mask regulatory arenas of big business and government accommodation. Assume, for simplicity, that public regulations governing private activities come in four major types: (1) quality standards, (2) price standards, (3) conditions of entry, and (4) number of practitioners or agents. Antitrust, thus, is a number-of-practitioners-or-agents type of regulation. Large firms have had continuing interest in the ways in which antitrust laws have—and have not—been enforced. In general, large firms have benefited from antitrust laws, which overwhelmingly focus on horizontal (same industry) anticompetitive practices, like mergers and price fixing and underplay vertical (control of sources of raw materials or the making and sale of finished products) mergers or conglomerate (multiindustry) mergers.

In America there is also no such thing as a national incorporation law. Instead, fifty different state laws govern how a firm goes about getting the entrepreneurial advantages of limited financial liability (just as there are fifty different state laws governing how motorists go about getting a driver's license). Fifty different state incorporation laws mean that big corporations can shop around to get the best legal deal, a process smaller, locally based, firms rarely undertake. It is a radical idea in America to centralize incorporation regulations in Washington.

The important thing to understand about all types of regulation is that they are America's substitute for government ownership. From public utilities to pure food and drug laws to leasing of public lands to import quotas, the story is the same—regulations impose costs on the private sector, and the private sector often does not like it. The obvious alternative, government ownership, has almost never been tried. Government usually owns only the losses; it rarely owns the gains. Profit is the prerogative of the private sector, not the public sector, and large corporations recognize the importance of this fact.

Free enterprise, then, might have been the gospel of commercial pygmies, but free enterprise would have cost the more accommodationist big businessmen plenty. Free enterprise translated into low tax rates or lenient labor laws was fine; free enterprise as a loss of federal export subsidies, investment guarantees, tax incentives, contracts, or R&D awards was not. The world was a more eclectic, ambiguous, and ad hoc place than Adam Smith or Barry Goldwater thought. Pure competition would be hell.

Large corporations also had political concerns about laissez-faire. Big business, because of the many corporate members of the 1,159 advisory committees, commissions, boards, and councils in official Washington in 1976, had more ways to access and pressure the nation's leaders than small business did. This knife, however, could cut both ways. Government also had more ways to pressure big business. And "government" in the 1970s usually meant Congress, a body that had been majority Democratic in both houses for thirty-six of the preceding forty years.

Given the ideology and interests of big business, Ronald Reagan was not its preferred candidate in the 1980 presidential election. As Democrats raged at one another, as U.S. hostages were seized in Teheran, and as gold prices, a traditional barometer of investor pessimism, soared from $300 an ounce to a stratospheric $835 in only six months during late 1979, corporate politicians backed one of their own: John Connally of Texas.

Connally had everything. He was an early and close LBJ intimate, oil lobbyist, entrepreneur, Texas governor, and victim of an assassin's bullet in Dallas during JFK's martyrdom. He had opposed Great Society spending programs and antiwar protests. He was an Eisenhower Republican in Democratic clothing who knew how to influence Democrats like him on Capitol Hill. He had been Nixon's secretary of the treasury from the end of 1970 to the middle of 1972 and a tough negotiator with European and Japanese competitors on international trade and exchange rate policies.

He was an activist conservative who knew that you *used* economic power, you didn't fritter it away in search of a laissez-faire dream. He was a Nixon loyalist who didn't leak delicate stories to reporters and who had labored hard to help realign presidential politics in 1972 by attracting non-Republicans to Nixon in droves. He was briefly Nixon's preferred presidential successor and Gerald Ford's preference for vice president when Spiro Agnew resigned in 1973. Nelson Rockefeller wanted Connally to replace him as vice president on a Ford ticket three years later.

John Connally was the most successful GOP fundraiser of the day; a Carter with charisma and self-confidence; a man whom Democratic National Committee Chairman Bob Strauss of Texas liked even after Connally changed his party affiliation. Twenty major corporations and banks had put Connally on their boards of directors. His politics came from being an entrepreneur and a political go-between, not from Reagan-style nostalgia for free enterprise. Connally was a hard-eyed, bottom-line, economic politician. He wanted America to stop subsidizing an expansionist Israel once the postwar era of cheap energy ended in 1973–74 and to use American economic muscle to force Israel (as George Bush later attempted) to cut land for peace deals with neighboring Arab states. Connally lent his considerable support only to campaigns he already believed in. He was a cynic, even unromantic, but also a man of faith in a corporate America that had given him his economic chance in life.

CEOs of America's top 200 companies understood and respected John Connally. They backed his 1980 presidential bid in droves. So did independent oilmen, high-rolling western bankers, and S&L operators whose financial support was increasingly important to both political parties. "To say that Connally was the darling of corporate America was an understatement," wrote his biographer. In fourteen months, Connally spent $11 million in the only completely privately financed presidential bid of the past twenty years.

John Connally's corporate money and supporters, however, lost to Ronald Reagan. Reagan had charisma too, and he had it without Connally's Texas big money elitism. Connally lectured Americans on how to use big government to change national circumstances. Reagan was different. While he was as strong as Connally on cold warrior political and military power, on questions of economic power Reagan's answer was simple: government power didn't have to be used, it had to be constrained—or abolished. Economic bigness was suspect to Reagan, and government was the problem, not the solution. Social Security should be made voluntary, taxes should be cut; subsidized capitalism should be replaced with unalloyed competition. America had been on the wrong track for decades. Symbiosis was socialism under another name. New realities did not need to be understood; the old ideological virtues were sufficient. Connally was, to Reagan, a closet liberal talking about what people should believe. Reagan, meanwhile, was a consummate politician, reflecting what tens of millions of Americans did believe.

Ronald Reagan understood the frustration-ridden politics of his time in ways that corporate CEOs and John Connally did not. Connally, after spending $11 million, ended up with one lone delegate to the Republican National Convention. Reagan, voicing the growing get-government-off-our-backs mood of 1970s America, won his party's nomination for president.

Big business CEOs, accordingly, abandoned Connally, the prince and savior of the rich and successful. To mollify accommodationist Eisenhower Republicans, they influenced Reagan to select George Bush as his vice-presidental running mate. Reagan, however, was no big business candidate. His bases of business support were the same, in fact, as Goldwater's: small, not large; low tech, not high tech; and domestic, not multinational. Reagan did not pattern himself after Ike, the reluctant manager of a mixed system of public and private economic power, but after Calvin Coolidge, who served before the New Deal, World War II, the cold war, and the mixed system that resulted from them all. Reagan was New Right, a self-made man from the West, and like Goldwater, out to protect the "sacred values of the frontier, individualism and opportunity, freedom." All this Reagan defined as freedom from, rather than freedom to.

Reagan, like his first chief policy adviser in the White House, libertarian economist Martin Anderson of Stanford University, believed that corporate leaders active in Washington for decades had a basic conceptual problem. They "knew deep down that Reagan meant what he said on free enterprise," intoned Anderson. These erring CEOs were "for free enterprise too," he continued, "but they don't necessarily know what it is." The implication was clear: during the Reagan administration, corporate reeducation in Adam Smith's economics was going to begin in earnest.

Corporate CEOs bit their tongues: most of them quietly despised lectures from academic economists. But they wanted certain things from Reagan, including freedom from taxes, regulations, and inflation and from higher federal spending and the middle-class entitlements that were its major component. They also wanted freedom from the growing federal deficit and the economic and political challenges it posed. Most of all they wanted freedom from the stagflation of the Nixon, Ford, and Carter presidencies. Whether or not a New Right growth bonanza would come along and solve America's economic problems—as Reagan and his closest advisers devoutly expected—was debatable, but meanwhile, billions rode on Reagan achieving his early agenda of minimal government.

Events made Reagan excellently situated to deliver on some major promises. For the Democrats, 1980 was a political disaster on a par with 1946. For only the second time in fifty years, not only did their presidential candidate lose but their party lost working political control of its historical congressional power base. Nine incumbent Democratic senators lost, enabling the GOP to secure control of the Senate for the first time in twenty-five years. The picture in the House wasn't much better. Democrats had had a two to one majority—143 votes more than the Republicans—when Jimmy Carter arrived in Washington; when he left, that lead was only 49. Thirty-three House Democratic seats went Republican in 1980, the GOP's second-best showing since 1946. "The reality," House Speaker Tip O'Neill later recalled, "was even worse than the numbers suggested, as the election was especially tough on the senior [Democratic] members . . . including several of the chairmen and leaders." One-eighth of House Democratic votes were gone; just over one-third of the 33 Senate seats up for grabs in 1980 were won by newly elected Republicans.

Democrats not only got beaten, they got scared. Fears of middle-class disenchantment had rocked Congress in 1978, when a majority of Democrats staged their own tax cut revolt against Jimmy Carter. Once Reagan defeated Carter, surviving Democrats assumed even more cautious, middle- and upper middle-class stances. Democrats' hearts might be on the left, but their votes were on the right. Liberals focused on economic growth, the economy, and entrepreneurship, not on new government spending programs, equity, or bureaucracies, as the focal points of social action.

This shift clarified when Reagan proposed the largest tax cut in United States history as the centerpiece of his new administration. Reagan tax policy began in a populist vein. The new president from California, birthplace of the 1970s tax revolt, had for years championed items like a 33 percent tax cut in individual income tax rates and the indexing of tax rates to inflation. Such goals especially benefited the country's smallest businesses, which filed individual, not corporate, tax returns. By January 1981, however, these populist supply-side policy proposals were wedded to others oriented to big business, including cuts in corporate tax rates, higher investment tax credits, and accelerated depreciation allowances. These items owed much to quiet but effective lobbying by the same corporate tax reduction coalition that earlier helped eviscerate Carter's 1978 tax reform bill.

This tax reduction coalition, as we've seen, was broad. It combined the forces of two major panindustrial lobbies, one representing small business and the other big business: the USCC and the Business Roundtable. The Roundtable leader most active in tax policy (Reginald Jones of GE) was in intimate contact with well-placed superlobbyists. Chief among these lobbyists was Charls Walker, a Texas Republican, a former treasury official, and a John Connally protégé who ran a think tank called the American Council for Capital Formation. Walker soon became even better situated as the head of President-elect Ronald Reagan's tax policy transition team to plan strategy and select personnel for the incoming administration.

Webs of insider corporate relations helped big business. Although Democrats were in disarray, a Democratic majority did still exist in the House. And Reagan had only won 50.7 percent of the popular vote, to Carter's 41 percent and independent John Anderson's 8 percent. Had the 1980 presidential election gone *against* Carter or *for* Reagan? Initially, Reagan's power to accomplish sweeping change was ambiguous; Reaganites clearly needed the cooperation of moderate Republicans and conservative Democrats in both the Senate and the House, people who were not committed to laissez-faire or frontal assaults on the symbiotic welfare state. Without these bipartisan swing votes, Reagan's tax bills simply couldn't pass Congress.

To create a bipartisan alliance, inside operators like Charls Walker were crucial. Walker not only worked temporarily for Reagan, he was also on permanent retainer, until 1987, to the Business Roundtable. This proved excellent for big business, ensuring that non-Reaganite conservatives focused on what big businessmen and their representatives told them about cutting taxes. Walker and others like him talked plenty about tax cuts during the formative months of the Reagan administration. What resulted was a tax bonanza for large corporations.

Democratic leaders soon realized that Walker was busy creating a bipartisan tax cutting coalition in Congress. They feared wholesale defection of conservative Democrats if they opposed it. So House Democratic barons played "yes, but." They countered Reagan's tax cut proposals with ones that just happened to "generally reflect" long-standing Business Roundtable policy recommendations. A bidding war resulted. Tax cut proposals came from Reaganites determined to lead and from Democrats trying to stop Reagan from leading by replacing his supply-side agenda with a more traditional, and more big business oriented, tax cutting agenda of their own.

It was all-gain, no-pain politics for congressional swing voters and their larger corporate allies in the middle. Reaganites offered, Democrats counteroffered, and Reaganites again raised the stakes. House Democratic leaders matched a full 80 percent of Reagan's cuts (corporate far more than individual) before finally being outbid on both. Tax cut proposals and benefits proliferated so fast that Reagan's own libertarian budget director, David Stockman, moaned that "the hogs were really feeding" and that "the greed level, the level of opportunism, just got out of control." Liberal Democrat David Obey of Wisconsin quipped that "it would probably be cheaper if we just gave everybody in the country three wishes." The hundreds of billions of dollars in tax reductions over the course of Reagan's first term was far greater than any conservative tax cutter had ever previously advocated. Business taxes alone were cut $150 billion over five years.

The varieties of bipartisan corporate tax reduction were awesome. Capital-intensive companies particularly benefited from bipartisan devotion to aiding America's slow-growth core industries via economic incentives, including investment tax credits and accelerated depreciation allowances. For six years, most of America's largest manufacturing companies went on a tax holiday—such a holiday that Reagan's first Secretary of the Treasury

Donald T. Regan complained to him at the end of 1983 that GE, Boeing, General Dynamics, and fifty-seven other large firms had paid not a penny in taxes during that year and that Reagan's personal secretary had paid more than all combined. Corporate tax breaks had gotten out of hand. A "near piratical" situation existed.

One short-lived reason why Regan fulminated about piracy was "safe harbor leasing," a bipartisan loophole added to the 1981 Reagan tax bill at the last minute. The idea was simple. Tax deductions like accelerated depreciation lowered taxes only for companies making any profits to tax. What about companies that, for various competitive or tax-sheltered reasons, were not reporting any taxable corporate income at all? Shouldn't something be done for profit-poor automakers and steel makers, for example?

Sure it should—and safe harbor leasing came to be. It allowed firms earning no profits and paying no federal tax to compute depreciation and other tax benefits they would have gotten if they had paid taxes. These benefits were then refunded to the companies in the form of credits against future federal taxes. These companies then sold their hundreds of millions of dollars of credits to profitable firms like GE and IBM for cash, at a discount. GE and IBM then used the credits they'd bought to buy their way out of *their* federal tax obligations. GE wiped out most of its 1981 taxes by buying tax credits from unprofitable companies like Chrysler and Ford and ended up with $110 million in future tax refunds to boot. "Greed Electric," GE's critics muttered.

The irony was that symbiosis, 1980s style, now involved Washington subsidizing successful large corporations to subsidize less successful ones: in a triumph of ideological minimalism, politicians of both parties effectively hired GE and IBM to help bail out Chrysler and Ford for them via the tax code—and called the results laissez-faire.

The conservative glow created by the Reagan tax bill of 1981 couldn't last, and it didn't. Lower taxes together with reduced regulations, lower federal spending, and reduced inflation rates were supposed to engender an immediate economic boom. They didn't. The tax bonanza of 1981 was followed in 1982 and 1983 by the worst economic downturn in America since the 1930s.

Lacking the growth miracle that supply-side economists had freely promised and that big business had freely cashed in on during the tax cut bidding war, the Reagan administration's ability to cut back panindustrial regulations and nonmilitary spending now faltered. Recession arrived, and inflation fell. But elsewhere, the Reagan administration and its corporate allies of convenience lost as many battles as they won. Panindustrial fiscal alliances frayed. Reaganites, more and more anxious to cut spending to decrease the increasing annual deficits they had promised would never be there to begin with, proposed more and more spending cuts to pay for some of the revenue reductions they had mandated. As Reaganites pushed harder on spending, however, they soon ran into big business resistance.

The fate of the Export-Import Bank clarifies what was at stake. The Ex-Im was created in the 1930s to subsidize farm exports. Following World War II, it went on to subsidize American exports of expensive capital goods like aircraft and computers, by making low-interest loans to foreign purchasers. By 1980 two-thirds of all Ex-Im loans subsidized the foreign sales of only seven large U.S. firms like Boeing and GE. These seven firms, and others like ITT that accounted for the rest of Ex-Im's annual budget, had no desire to see that budget reduced. The Ex-Im budget of $5.5 billion was peanuts in a $600-billion federal budget, but it was an important peanut.

Big business firms like Boeing, accordingly, fought hard for Ex-Im. Efforts by budget director David Stockman to drastically cut Ex-Im's annual spending to demonstrate a determination to do unto well-organized and powerful big business as he was then doing to ill-organized and politically marginal groups failed. Big corporations read Reaganites some lessons in capitalist reality: France, Japan, Taiwan, South Korea, and other nations had Ex-Im Banks, too; if the United States didn't give subsidized loans, they would. Exports, additionally, were twice as important to America's economy (as a percentage of GNP) than they had been only ten years before. Did Washington want to kill the corporate geese that laid the golden eggs?

No, Washington didn't. At least bipartisan majorities in Congress didn't. Cuts totaling 9 percent were finally mandated. Reaganites wrangled furiously about what to do about Ex-Im for the rest of Reagan's first term. Stockman and libertarians like him wanted Ex-Im's direct loans abolished. The Treasury, Commerce, and State Departments fought just as hard to continue—or even expand—the use of Ex-Im as a tool of national economic and diplomatic policy in a world not designed by Barry Goldwater. Ex-Im loan funding gradually decreased.

In 1986, Reaganites attacked again, requesting no money at all for the agency. Thereafter, Congress funded $1 billion anyway. Congress and the Reagan and Bush White Houses kept Ex-Im alive at slowly diminishing annual amounts. Trade deficits amounted to $100 billion a year. Export-oriented business, umbrella coalitions, and panindustrial groups like the NAM (publicly) and the Business Roundtable (privately) complained that conservative populists were shooting American capitalism in the foot in search of its laissez-faire dream.

White House adviser Martin Anderson had not been fibbing when he announced that Reagan meant what he said about minimal government. Anderson, like Stockman and other committed Reaganites, saw big business, big government, big labor, and panindustrial regulators as parts of an unholy alliance throttling America by knocking down the "line dividing state and society . . . like the walls of Jericho." Here was resurgent hard right conservatism of pre–New Deal and immediate post–World War II America with a vengeance. Except for the cold war (which hadn't been fought expensively enough or hard enough), everything Washington had tried (or been asked) to do was bad. "The sovereign state," Stockman wailed, was "an open bazaar, its fiscal and legal resources plundered by organized interest groups. . . . Government was no longer accountable to the people because the instruments of government had been seized, the better to serve the ends of society's modern-day guilds and syndicates: the trade associations, unions, professions, and other organized interests." Only a "frontal assault on the American welfare state" could resolve such problems, and return America to the golden era of a "minimalist government, a spare and stingy creature," which would abolish the "coast-to-coast patchwork of dependencies, shelters, protections, and redistributions that the nation's politicians had brokered over the [post-1930] decades."

It is no wonder, given such conservative conspiracy theories, that Ronald Reagan hung Calvin Coolidge's portrait in a place of honor in his White House. Nor is it any wonder that corporate politicians found themselves in their dealings with the Reagan administration like the allegorical lady riding the tiger. They'd gotten on the Reagan bandwagon; how were they going to get off without hurting themselves? As recession, slow growth, deficits, income and wealth polarization, and other problems complicated the recovery of the economy after the trough of 1982–83, corporations were forced to define which of their relations to the public sector were legitimate, which needed to expand, and which were either illegitimate or unnecessary.

Constrained by the ideological bonds of their minimalist past, Americans were backing yet again into the symbiotic realities of their present and their future.

9

THE REAGAN REVOLUTION
AND AFTERWARD

By 1982 beautiful economic visions had clouded. Reaganites and their corporate allies of convenience were succeeding too well on tax reductions, while not succeeding well enough on economic growth. Cuts in tax rates were supposed to produce a growth surge and a consequent increase in tax revenues. This was the root promise of Reaganism.

Growth didn't surge as hoped. First, the economy spun into deep recession. Seven years of slow recovery followed and then another long recession. Tax revenues sagged because of slow growth and massive tax cuts, the gap between federal spending and revenues grew, and the national debt tripled from $1 trillion to $3 trillion during Reagan's terms.

Single-answer supply-side tax cutters blamed single-answer tight credit monetarists, and they both blamed devious, frightened, or opportunistic Democrats who wouldn't cut excessive federal spending for their favored political clienteles. Military spending, meanwhile, sped upward from $200 billion to $300 billion in constant (1992) dollars. Spending to defend against the evil empire of the Soviet Union rarely seemed excessive to conservatives. Reagan, like Kennedy, warned that the red enemy was verily at the gates.

The military quarter of the budget became untouchable: to cut it was unpatriotic. That left the Social Security social insurance one-third of the budget: it was politically untouchable. To cut it, Democrats too often pontificated, was to reduce *all* elderly Americans to penury. Bipartisan political demagoguery ruled. The remaining 40 percent of the budget included everything else Washington did for everybody. This portion of spending was pruned, and pruned again. The problem was that "everything else" affected indignant political constituencies, including people frustrated by the end of a generation of affluence who thought they could recreate the good old days of regularly increasing real incomes by simply having their taxes cut. But these people did not like spending for their programs decreased or Social Security taxes to rise to pay for previously mandated increases in Social Security spending. Given that almost half of adult Americans couldn't define "economic recession," the fiscal dynamics of scarcity in the 1980s were electoral dynamite. Politicians accustomed to dividing the gains of economic growth via tax cuts and spending increases reluctantly faced the fact that boom times for American capitalism were over. Spending, accordingly, needed to be capped, reduced, and redistributed.

This was not what Ronald Reagan had bargained for or promised. Something was badly amiss. By 1982, Depression levels of unemployment and business bankruptcies arrived in the older manufacturing industry regions and the trade union heartland. Liberals suspected conservatives of planning it that way. The New Right had known all along, their argument went, that Reagan's growth economics was a farce. They knew the 1981 tax cuts would produce lower revenues and soaring deficits. Reagan was "Herbert Hoover with a smile" and had slashed tax rates only for the reactionary purpose of starving Washington to death by denying it funds. Their logic was wrong. It ignored that the tax cut bidding war of 1981 was thoroughly bipartisan. It ignored the fact that New Right tax cutters, although incorrect, were sincere. As the recession worsened, however, political opinion was often more angry than rational. Ronald Reagan had lied, and now he was going to pay for it.

The price Reagan must pay, a beleaguered congressional leadership believed, was to increase taxes. Congress would pare more nonmilitary spending, and Reagan would get almost everything he wanted to rearm America against communism; Reagan's part would be to support tax increases.

Reagan balked. He remained committed to his tax cutting program of 1981. He had started off championing cuts in individual tax rates. Big business lobbying had then committed him to huge cuts in corporate taxes, as well. To do as a restive Congress was demanding meant choosing between these two groups: which tax cuts must be maintained, which could be traded off? But Reagan refused to choose. He remained a fervent supply-sider, believing that a growth miracle was on its way and that America should stay the course. Congress, he thought, was full of faint political spirits. Reagan's optimism was costly economics but excellent politics: he avoided bringing bad news to anybody, leaving that to Congress's increasingly skeptical leaders of both parties, who couldn't afford to be so Panglossian or so opportunistic. They knew Reagan would never back down on income tax cuts for individuals, which left only one alternative: corporate tax cuts must be rolled back.

Once congressional leaders bit the bullet, political economics for corporate America got complicated. In 1981, everybody had won and nobody had lost. But now, some firms and industries were going to have to give back part of their tax cuts: one-fifth of the corporate tax largesse of 1981 was slated for termination in 1982, including politically disastrous programs like tax leasing. Corporate unities thereupon evaporated, and corporate cat fights commenced. Tax benefits worth $20 billion a year were at stake. A howling and uneven recession was on. Industries like auto and steel were mangled, while aerospace and computers boomed. Profit-squeezed heavy manufacturing firms that had benefited most from key 1981 tax reductions (like accelerated depreciation) screamed disloyalty. The NAM, the USCC, and the Business Roundtable all protested any and all corporate give backs; the Roundtable and the NAM subsequently muted their indignation to preserve their political capital, but not the USCC.

Profitable hi-tech firms and service industries meanwhile proved amenable to partial give backs, since most of them had gained relatively little from the 1981 tax cuts—having few buildings, machines, or transport to depreciate. Although computer and aerospace firms lost tasty extras like tax leasing, these losses only meant reduced profits in a "smart weapon" rearmament boom. They didn't mean, as they did for steel and autos, oceans more of red ink. The mostly corporate tax increase of 1982, then, pitted successful economic sectors like computers and aerospace firms against unsuccessful ones like steel and autos. It also signaled that the halcyon days of piggybacking Old Right big business tax cuts on New Right individual tax cuts might be over.

They were. Recession increased tensions between Reaganites and big business. As Reagan's first term ended, a growth miracle still hadn't happened, and deficits still grew. Reagan partisans seethed that big business had not led the markets out of recession to smite liberalism and the statists. Congress seethed about bringing voters even more bad news about spending cutbacks. Business taxes were raised again as the recession bottomed out, in a reluctant repeat of 1982. Scenting an issue for the 1984 presidential campaign, Democratic candidate Walter Mondale proposed even higher tax increases for business and upper-income individuals. Mondale died at the polls not primarily because he backed corporate tax hikes but because he supported individual ones, which were anathema to Reagan and to a fractious electorate. Mondale's fate was instructive. Increasing income tax rates on individuals, most of whose real incomes weren't rising, was suicidal.

Tax reform, however, might be another matter. Tax *reform*, as its bipartisan supporters conceived of it after the 1984 election, would raise nobody's tax *rates*. Instead, it would actually lower many corporate and all individual tax rates by abolishing expensive tax loopholes enjoyed by only a relative few. The reformers had a point. Tax loopholes had proliferated in the revenue code during the unsettling decade of 1973–83. The tax rate structures often meant little; what mattered were industry-specific and sectoral incentives, created by Democrats and Republicans alike. The mortgage interest deduction, for example, is a loophole that assists home owners and residential construction firms. The oil depletion allowance (which lowered all oil companies' taxes before 1975 but only the taxes of smaller independent oil companies after that) is offered to one industry so that it will locate and develop new petroleum resources.

As the 1980s progressed, a fragile alliance of conservative Republicans and liberal Democrats began to attack some of these loopholes. Conservative Republicans disliked big-business-oriented loopholes on both ideological and interest grounds: recession after 1981 and slow growth after 1984 were throttling the national political realignment that Reaganites had long hoped for, making free-enterprise user-unfriendly. Democrats regained a whopping hundred-seat majority in the House in 1982 and hung onto 70 percent of that majority even when Reagan smothered Mondale in 1984. Continued GOP control of the Senate might well swing on public perception of Republicans as something other than "the party of the rich and big business."

Liberal Democrats had their own reasons for disliking many corporate tax loopholes. After all, it had been conservative southern Democrats, not liberal northern ones, who had created most of them (vide, the oil depletion allowance). Reagan had talked about "freeing business." Two, however, could play the freeing business game. Big business had gotten tax cuts, deregulation, and other benefits while also enjoying ample public subsidies that very few people knew about. Now corporations, liberals decided, were going to pay for such opportunism. Free enterprise sure didn't mean that "Greed Electric" should be able to rake in billions of dollars in tax leases. To increasing numbers of younger liberals, free enterprise was epitomized by innovative entrepreneurs like those in California's Silicon Valley. To these neoliberal Democrats, tax rates should be cut for such newfangled smaller businesses, for the poor, and for the sacred middle class by forcing oldfangled, loophole-favored, big businesses to pay the bills.

When the frustrated conservative Republicans and neoliberal Democrats unexpectedly joined forces, it became every industry for itself. The complex 1984–86 tax reform struggle looked like the 1981 tax bidding war in reverse. Instead of well-organized business interest groups holding balkanized politicians hostage, now a bipartisan political tax reform alliance held corporations hostage, playing industry off against industry, since every dollar of tax cut for one would be a dollar taken from another's closed loophole.

In the final legislation, capital-intensive sectors, which had gained the most in 1982, lost the most in 1986. Non-capital-intensive firms and small business lobbies helped end tax privileges they didn't benefit from to gain lower rates they would benefit from. It was, again, the political economy of the bottom line. Special deals abounded. Oil, natural gas, timber, and hard-hit smokestack industries retained big tax advantages; but heavy manufacturing as a whole lost. Retailing, trucking, the apparel industry, electronics, and food distribution firms won. On the services side, real estate, construction, and insurance companies lost, as did banks—after enraging Reagan and Congress by their demagoguery regarding an earlier and unexceptionable reform proposal to levy a withholding tax on bank deposits.

Some industries or firms hung on to special tax deals, but a pattern of political change was evident. The Republican right was disengaging itself from big business interests, which it distrusted after Reagan's growth miracle failed to materialize, damning the party's populist image. A majority of Democrats affected populism too, voting to penalize favored—and often big—corporations. Business incentives like the investment tax credit were ended. Millions of poorer Americans were taken off the income tax rolls entirely. Democrats sought greater credibility in restive middle-class and upper middle-class circles by advocating cutting maximum individual rates in half, abandoning most of their remaining loyalty to the apparently radical principle of progressive income taxation.

The days of all gain, no pain for corporate America on taxes were over for the moment. In a slow growth, recession-ridden America still lacking the hearty economic growth rates Reagan had promised, and with most working Americans' annual incomes still stagnant compared to their 1973 levels, such days would not soon return.

But even though the slow growth (or no growth) political economy of the 1980s complicated big business–government relations, and even though Goldwater Republicans were in the White House and mutable Democrats in Congress, symbiosis remained inevitable. For big business, there were no permanent alliances in Washington any more, only permanent interests.

Regulation, particularly panindustrial regulation, was one of these permanent interests. It, however, was not a goal Reagan conservatives and big business leaders initially cooperated on effectively. Although both wanted deregulation, Reaganites were more Catholic than the Pope. Corporate America had learned, over a decade of expensive experience, that environmental and other regulations were best opposed incrementally. Minimal government Reaganites, however, had learned few such practical lessons and often attacked federal regulations everywhere and all at once.

The frontal assaults commenced in 1981 and soon failed. Reagan's first Secretary of the Interior James Watt symbolized the zealous attack approach to deregulation. Watt was from Wyoming, an arid state whose lands are half owned by the federal government. Washington owned almost as much or more of seven other western states. In all, 30 percent of the land area of the entire country is federally owned. Federal control of huge western water projects gave Washington a further, and necessarily symbiotic, concern with the pace and extent of economic development in thirsty lands.

Watt disliked it all. It reeked of socialism. He wanted federally owned western lands that his Interior Department controlled given to the states and advocated an immediate freeze on federal acquisition of new lands. He called Indian reservations "exercises in failed socialism." He wanted national forests and wilderness areas opened to private enterprise to a far greater extent than ever before. "We will mine more, drill more, cut more timber to use our resources," he vowed. Within three months, Watt became very controversial.

Watt was confrontational by design. He characterized himself as the Reagan administration's "lightning rod" and "high-risk player." He honored the same western entrepreneurs as Reagan did: people who understood "free market doctrine as autobiography." Watt believed Reagan's victory gave him as much power to change environmental regulations affecting the public lands as Reagan had to alter the income tax code. Watt, a classic western booster, began with a whoop and a holler.

A surer recipe for trouble with environmentalists didn't exist. Watt's deregulatory plans were so thorough that the controlled development, hunting- and fishing-oriented environmentalists (most of whom had voted for Reagan) joined forces with the pristine wilderness, no development environmentalists, with whom they normally had very little in common. Court suits proliferated. Federal judges ordered Watt to stop "flouting" the mining and oil drilling regulations that Interior administered. Congressional tempers got intemperate.

Watt's confrontational approach wasn't unique. Over at the Environmental Protection Agency, other deregulators began grand offensives of their own. Spending fell, bureaucratic cutbacks and reorganizations multiplied, environmental groups were frozen out of hearings, regulated industry groups were listened to, and scores of new personnel maintained illegal economic connections with private companies that their agency regulated. Such confrontational politics produced counterattacks in courtrooms and Congress. Six congressional investigations of the EPA were under way by late 1982, and EPA's "high-risk player" director was cited for contempt of Congress that December.

Little of this environmental brawl served big business well. Corporate America's power often was inversely proportional to popular awareness and concern about issues. By becoming lightning rods for dissent, Watt at Interior and his opposite numbers at EPA polarized policy and slowed down incremental compromises on long-standing issues like greater resource development on public lands, cost-benefit analyses of existing and proposed regulations, and financial incentives for pollution abatement. Watt and EPA called upon Americans to battle for the Lord, states' rights, and free enterprise and to expel liberals from the Garden. Activists in environmental organizations, meanwhile, thanked their lucky stars for zealotry. "If there hadn't been a James Watt," said the chief lobbyist for the fast-growing Sierra Club, "we would have had to invent one."

Disarray, congressional investigations, and front page stories about the "dismemberment" of environmental laws were not at all what large oil, chemical, and other corporations wanted. Gradual erosion of regulations via administrative decisions little noticed or understood by any but the most technically aware policy activists worked far better for big business. An ideological EPA awash in controversy didn't even formulate specific legislative proposals (as opposed to grand philosophical principles) when Congress amended a major environmental law—the Clean Air Act of 1970—which an umbrella coalition of large corporations had slated for four years for revision. Corporate amendment efforts, accordingly, failed. Meanwhile, rebellious state governments threatened large national firms with stronger environmental regulations than the federal ones Watt most opposed.

By mid-1982, it was clear to corporate activists such as those in the Business Roundtable that a far lower profile, less overtly confrontational, strategy on regulatory reform was required, and the emphasis shifted from overt frontal assaults popular among self-made entrepreneurs to covert flank attacks popular among larger industrialists. By late 1983, Watt and all of Reagan's initial appointees at the EPA were gone. Relative moderates like Vice President George Bush, head of the Reagan Task Force on Regulatory Relief, and new EPA head William Ruckelshaus joined hard-eyed economists in the Office of Management and Budget to take over primary responsibility for the administration's deregulation policy. Their key accomplishment was reducing the amounts of corporate data acquired, assessed, disseminated, and applied by regulators. Bush and Ruckelshaus played "yes, but" incremental politics, not "no!" ideological politics. No major piece of panindustrial regulation, environmental or other, was abolished during the Reagan years. Standoffs on funding and staffing levels at plagued agencies like EPA were negotiated with Congress. Deregulators stopped using meat-axes and started using target rifles.

Not all Reagan era regulatory reforms were equally popular. The chemical industry, for example, disliked paying billions of dollars to help finance the Superfund to clean up dangerous waste sites. It wanted Washington to foot the whole bill, and to protect them from angry state regulators as well; Washington did neither. But big business as a whole benefited because more deregulation occurred than during the Watt era. In energy development, pollution abatement control, worker health and safety, and compensatory hiring and employment, the later Reagan years saw important successes for business. Administrative hardball at OSHA, in particular, paid off. The gradual appointment of a new, more conservative, generation of federal court judges gave industry more weight in judicial confrontations about regulatory implementation. Upper middle-class reformers who cared deeply about new social issues like pristine wilderness or rain forests cared much less about less pristine matters like the reclaiming of strip mines in West Virginia or the spraying of insecticides on Mexican migrant workers in California orange groves.

After 1983, corporate America weakened certain panindustrial social regulations incrementally and slowed the growth of others. It also redirected general policy in important ways, particularly in gradually applying the principles of cost-benefit analysis to new and proposed regulations via economic impact statements. But big business leaders uprooted nothing; they knew they couldn't. Throughout the 1980s, public health, not economic growth, was the primary political criterion for resolving fundamental environmental issues. This infuriated ideologues, but no renewed assaults à la Watt occurred. Instead, the Reagan administration kept a low profile and let the courts and the OMB carry on the fight.

The Bush administration continued this low-profile approach. Bush created the Council on Competitiveness, which was led by Vice President Dan Quayle. Quayle's organization, a direct successor to the one George Bush ran (less aggressively) when he was vice president, made sure that "regulations fulfill[ed] the statute with a minimal amount of economic impact." Conservative cost-benefit ratios and private industry consultations became the Competitiveness Council's stock in trade. Big business, unsurprisingly, approved such quiet arrangements. However, simply easing "excessive" regulation was not the deregulation the hard core right wanted. Changes were taking place only at the margins: the speeding up of biotechnology development and pharmaceutical approval procedures, the decreasing of civil litigation appeals, the redefining of federally protected wetlands. These deregulatory struggles were technocratic; they did not, except rhetorically, promise to save free enterprise from the monster state.

Even civil rights showed the extent of New Right accommodation to regulatory symbiosis. In affirmative action, as nowhere else, laissez-faire rhetoric ruled. It was easy, it was cheap, and it cost demagogues like David Duke, Congressman Newt Gingrich, and Senator Jesse Helms nothing. It also, however, gained nothing for businesses facing practical legal problems: lawsuits from minorities claiming racial or sexual discrimination on the job or lawsuits from nonminorities claiming reverse job discrimination. Legal clarity about civil rights in their economic and occupational dimensions was essential. Tightened standards, not libertarian rhetoric, were necessary for orderly corporate planning.

Legal limitations, meanwhile, occurred at the margins of legislation, far from the public eye or understanding. While the hard core right shrilled, corporate politicians concentrated on what the courts decided. After 1981, as the makeup of the federal judiciary became more conservative, important legal changes occurred affecting affirmative action and the ways federal regulatory agencies like the EEOC enforced it. The burden of proof, for instance, shifted. Employers no longer had to prove that their hiring and promotion procedures were essential to business success, as opposed to being veiled instruments of prejudice; rather, employees had to prove that a specific discriminatory practice produced the unequal results they complained of. Class action lawsuits based on statistical disparities in a specific labor force became harder to wage or to win. Discrimination, increasingly, had to be proved specifically (regarding an individual), not in general (regarding a group). Obviously race-weighted practices like "race-norming" examination results were abolished. Corporations were able to avoid quota systems, which they had maintained as protection against lawsuits.

Such legal complexities served the purposes of corporate accommodationists like those in the Business Roundtable, who in 1990 began talking with civil rights groups and congressional leaders to help craft the implementation details of a bipartisan civil rights bill. Confrontationists, however, were angered, wanting grand assaults on all forms of affirmative action. Bush, meanwhile, flip-flopped, first casting a benign eye on big business accommodationists, then reversing himself, disavowing the Roundtable, and vetoing the civil rights bill (the first time in a hundred years a civil rights bill was vetoed). Finally, Bush reversed himself again, and signed a revised civil rights statute that kept the legal situation essentially unchanged.

The debate had been about whether, for instance, "business necessity" or a "legitimate business objective" could legalize employment practices that in effect screened out very many minorities or women. These debates had nothing to do with laissez-faire but concerned symbiotic legal accommodations between big business and public policy. Bush, fearful of New Right demagoguery, had embarrassed Roundtable CEOs by decrying their behind-the-scenes civil rights negotiations, but he did not change the practical results of these negotiations one iota. Much as ideologues despised it, incrementalism ruled regarding corporate conservatism in civil rights. Big business, as so often before, faced facts, not theories: it sought to narrow affirmative action, not lynch it. So, belatedly, did observant small business (which legislators of both parties had earlier and quietly protected with a cap of $150,000 in damages that could be sought from them). And even President Bush, who signed the minimally revised civil rights bill after months of needless delay, was won over.

While covert incremental tactics limited or eroded new panindustrial regulations, regarding the oldest panindustrial regulations of all, collective bargaining, big business was more overt and confrontational. When Reagan became president, almost all economic indicators were dreary for unions. National union members as a percentage of the labor force dropped to 20 percent (and falling) in 1977, the lowest level in almost forty years. Total numbers of union members were stuck at about 20 million. Only 70 percent of manufacturing workers belonged to unions, the lowest in twenty-five years. Union membership in core industrial states and large metropolitan areas was likewise falling. In 1975, unions began losing most of their attempts to organize nonunion plants. Only growth in public sector unions masked the twenty-year absolute decline of unions in the private sector.

AFL-CIO President George Meany, aged eighty-five when he retired in 1980, failed to anticipate or resolve these growing and grievous problems. America's economy was now markedly less self-sufficient in terms of markets and resources; oil shortages, increases in manufactured imports, and a doubling of the proportion of GNP generated by exports all showed that. Rising foreign industrial competition, accelerated foreign direct investment, and the export of manufacturing and assembly jobs to nations with lower labor costs did, too. The older manufacturing industries that had underpinned organized labor's strength bore the brunt of many of these structural changes. The computer revolution, meanwhile, produced a burst of automation that further eroded the membership bases of industrial unions. Unions were caught between the technological devil and the globally competitive deep blue sea.

In response, Meany and leaders like him sought corporate and government protection. Big labor was used to being a junior partner in the big-business–big-government détente based on rising affluence, low inflation, oligopoly pricing, weak foreign competition, complementary relations between welfare capitalism and the welfare state, Taft-Hartley restrictions limiting union organizing, and ad hoc federal intervention in major strikes affecting cold war national security. Since the 1950s, accommodation to this status quo maintained cocoons of union prosperity in America's industrial heartland.

After 1970, however, the economic dynamics changed: the customary corporate and government protections weren't forthcoming, and the status quo of the core industrial economy was threatened for the first time since the end of World War II. Corporate-government and union-management accommodations frayed. By June 1980, a special issue of *Business Week* entitled "The Reindustrialization of America" depicted a grim wartime Uncle Sam rolling up his sleeves to struggle to repair American manufacturing. "For the first time since the 1930s," David Vogel wrote, "the future of the large corporation could not be taken for granted." Big business and its employees, in David Halberstam's words, now lost their "sense of immunity from the world." Growing economic concerns shifted mass attitudes. "Big business was now disliked not because it was too powerful but because it was . . . too inefficient." High-roller entrepreneurs and innovative small business people not tied to the habits of mind (or collective bargaining contracts) of the past assumed mythic status, particularly within the new Reagan administration.

All this spelled trouble for unions, and it wasn't long in coming. In August 1981, after months of discord, 13,000 air traffic controllers working for the FAA at airports around the nation struck. Their leaders had backed Reagan in 1980 and now wanted a political payback. The controllers opted for a full-scale confrontation, not a less risky work slowdown. They also were violating employment agreements and court orders prohibiting them from striking. They rued the day.

The new president was riding a wave of popularity—after having survived an assassin's bullets only four months before. He quickly sacked all the striking controllers, replaced them with substitutes from the military services and elsewhere, supported FAA's refusal to rehire any striker for any reason, and peppered the reeling controller's union with lawsuits that quickly bankrupted and destroyed it. Public opinion polls showed a two to one support for Reagan's stand. Divided AFL-CIO leaders complained to reporters but did nothing to prolong the contest. A relatively strong and affluent public sector crafts union had overreached itself in a supremely public way. Reagan, thank you, was CEO of the federal government.

The disastrous air traffic controllers' strike isolated unions politically and promoted broader attacks on them, in both the public and the private sector. In Washington, Reagan regulators of the National Labor Relations Board began a bureaucratic work slowdown. Delays in hearing union appeals about unfair employer labor practices became chronic. Administrative hardball changed the policy the NLRB had followed for forty years. For instance, it began allowing employers to sack workers for complaining to state officials about unsafe working conditions or for swearing at nonstrikers from picket lines. Unions won only a quarter of their NLRB appeals by the end of Reagan's first term, compared with half under Carter and two-thirds under Ford.

The union reversals at the NLRB were mimicked at OSHA, where Reagan appointees decreased job safety inspections, cut hazardous citations in half, and decreased fines by two-thirds. OSHA budget and staff cutbacks stopped only in 1983, when Congress forced out James Watt and Reagan's original EPA leadership. The quiet erosion of labor standards however, continued, via Reagan-appointed federal judges. Courts allowed firms to evade unions by contracting out work to nonunion subcontractors, to void union contracts by moving corporate facilities, to create two-tier union contracts, in which newer workers received significantly lower wages and benefits than older workers did, and even (temporarily) to void union contracts by pro forma bankruptcy proceedings. Politics was, again, very often in the details—and on many a regulatory and legal detail, unions lost and kept losing. Winning, for unions, increasingly meant only gradual erosion, rather than fast decline. When in 1983–84 America started moving out of the worst economic slump since the 1930s, a lower percentage of private sector workers were unionized than at any time since Pearl Harbor.

These low-profile legal struggles served large corporations well—and had since late in the Carter administration, when the relatively accommodationist firms of the Business Roundtable had begun quietly cooperating on labor issues with firms in the smaller, overtly confrontational NAM and USCC. Higher profile union busting, scabs, and lockouts threatened a return to the bad old days of corporate labor relations during the 1930s.

Too direct threats could energize labor to unite to defend itself, as environmentalists had against James Watt; and they could lead to fence-mending
between unions and middle-class liberals, who though often suspicious of
unions as just one more self-serving special interest were not interested in
recreating the good old days of the open shop 1920s. Arcane legal debates
about common situs picketing, Chapter 11 bankruptcy proceedings, and
the increasingly lengthy appeals processes of the NLRB threatened little
of that. Unions suffered from a reputation for being inflexible and old-
fashioned, and labor conflicts were mostly unreported in the popular news
media (especially television). Their strength eroded only gradually, which
satisfied big business just fine.

The Reagan presidency produced a dealignment in American politics
but no thorough party realignment. Conservatives cut income tax rates and
inflation, abated a panindustrial regulatory upsurge, pared the one-third of
federal spending not involved with either the military or social insurance
programs, and got Washington out of the economic redistribution business
to a significant extent. By the still-depressed year of 1983, however, the
initial energy of the Reagan Revolution was spent. America now merely
drifted rightward. New Right libertarians like Martin Anderson, James
Watt, and David Stockman departed Washington in droves. Watt and others
had assumed that most Americans wanted a significantly reduced federal
government: Stockman's "spare and stingy creature."

They were wrong. "The American people," pollster Everett Carl Ladd
wrote in *Fortune* just after the start of the rightward surge in Washington
that began with the passage of California's Proposition 13, "have not become
more conservative in their attitudes toward government. . . . The heart of
the indictment is a call not for *less* government but for *better* government."
Eisenhower, not Coolidge, was America's leadership model. America's
sprawling symbiotic system was wasteful and disorganized; it needed to be
made more efficient and cost effective, but it shouldn't be dismantled. Let-
'er-rip free enterprise was risky. The decade since 1970 had been one of
fading expectations and fragile affluence. The last thing Americans wanted
was more risks. "Giveaways" for the undeserving (because unemployed)
poor was one thing; "incentives" for the upstanding (and employed) middle
class was quite another. Americans still wanted a mixed system of public
and private power; they just didn't want to pay so much for it.

Pay, however, they did. Reagan reforms didn't come free. State and local
spending—the "new federalism"—made up for some federal spending cuts
and eviscerated programs, and regressive state and local taxes replaced

progressive federal taxes. More regressive levies to keep Social Security social insurance solvent followed in 1983. By the end of the 1980s, the overall tax burden on individuals (federal, state, local, and Social Security) was such that rich, poor, and in-between in America all now gave about the same proportion of their income to tax collectors.

This was not what millions who voted for Reagan had had in mind. But Reagan and his followers were captives of their initial all-gain, no-pain tax cutting theology. They had overpromised concerning the growth and income effects of tax cuts, both individual and corporate. When trickle-down Coolidge-style economics did not work as overadvertised, the rich (the top fifth of households) got very much better off, the poor (the bottom fifth) got slightly worse off, and everybody else ended up right about where they'd started, once taxes, inflation, and periods of recessionary and other unemployment were factored in.

"Stay the course," Reagan advised, and a majority of that half of the adult population composing the electorate did so. Reagan might be economically buoyant beyond the bounds of good sense, but at least people knew what he believed in—and besides, he wasn't going to raise *their* (personal income) taxes. Through the worst economic downturn since the 1930s and during the slow real growth rate period thereafter, Reagan remained personally popular. Personal popularity did not add up to partisan popularity, however. Republicans lost control of the Senate in 1986 and fell further, thereafter. By 1982, Republican House strength had decreased to within eight votes of its pre-Reagan level. It recovered briefly, and then, by 1990, left the GOP in a minority of five of them to every eight Democrats.

Basically, Americans were hedging their bets in the 1980s, just as they had done under Eisenhower in the 1950s. Distrusting laissez-faire, Americans had created a public sector. Distrusting, in turn, a powerful state, Americans had made sure that America's public sector very often subsidized, guaranteed, or regulated the private sector so that it could accomplish varied social goals, instead of attempting to do the job itself. In this sense, the policy ambiguities of divided government at the close of the Reagan presidency precisely reflected the ideological ambiguities inherent in a symbiotic system of interconnections between big business and government. Trusting neither, Americans opted for an economic order run by both. Businessmen remained politicians—and politicians, businessmen—out of practical and enduring organizational necessity.

POSTSCRIPT: NEW YEAR'S DAY 1992

New Year's Day 1992 was a rare opportunity to take stock and sum up. Putting things in perspective was especially necessary this year. Retirement loomed for a sixty-five-year-old CEO of a major American corporation relaxing in the den of his suburban home near Chicago. His business career, begun after college and military service just as Dwight David Eisenhower was elected president in 1952, was now closing after a dozen years as head of his company during the Reagan and Bush presidencies.

It had been a curious time to be a corporate leader. The decade of the 1980s mixed boom and gloom. Speculative buy-out or takeover binges had rivaled the worst financial excesses of the Roaring Twenties. Yet simultaneously, waves of productive innovation in computers and robotics impressed anyone who remembered, as he did, an earlier world in which electronic data processing hadn't existed at all.

Perhaps his years as CEO between 1980 and 1992 encompassed both the best and the worst in America. The fervid 1960s were mostly irrelevant now. He'd disliked those years heartily—extremists had turned economic growth into a dirty word, affluence was taken for granted, claims to persecuted minority status proliferated, and big business was cast as the villain in radical morality plays. It was a more sensible, if challenging, world now and had been since 1973. America's global power and prosperity were both limited after OPEC, Watergate, and Vietnam. As a major result, big business might not be more liked, but it was more needed, which kept liberals in line and conservatives in both parties in the White House. The days of America as a self-contained affluent society were over. Most employees were more concerned about maintaining their living standards than about expanding them. Unions were weaker, and so productivity increases were easier to enforce. Politicos had to specify in advance where new revenues would come from to pay for proposed new public programs. Not that there weren't problems: mandates—federally enforced minimum standards—allowed the cost of things like child care, family leave, disabled access and hiring, and national health insurance to be paid for by the private sector.

National health insurance, however, was not necessarily a bad idea. Our CEO's corporation had provided health care to its employees since the 1950s, but now medical costs were ballooning out of control, and something had to be done. Even the NAM, the USCC, and the NFIB admitted that companies couldn't control costs by themselves and that business and government should cooperate to reform health insurance.

As always, however, the politics and the economics of the issue were all in the details. Some aging and ailing auto and steel corporations with aging and ailing work forces were happy to abandon welfare capitalism and shift the growing costs to the taxpayers. Healthier firms like GE were interested in leveling the competitive playing field by forcing all employers to pay for workers' health care costs. The first approach risked nationalizing the private health insurance industry, the other infuriated smaller businesses, which argued that they simply couldn't afford the benefits provided by large firms.

How to resolve such disagreements? A coalition of the Business Roundtable, several major unions, insurance organizations, and the huge American Association of Retired Persons was on the right track: it went beyond airy vagaries; it arrived early and proposed consistently; and it isolated those liberals and union leaders who wanted a government-as-single-payer national health insurance system. Instead, the coalition wanted government to pay for only the working and nonworking poor via an expansion of Medicaid and sought to maintain a traditional, welfare capitalist, employer-based system for everyone else. It opposed federal or state governments mandating the exact coverage, to reassure small business. It also proposed tax credits and insurance pools for small employers, to shift part of the cost (indirectly) to the taxpayer and part to the private insurance industry and, through them, to physicians. It proceeded gradually, saying "yes, but," instead of "no!" Expanded national health insurance in America was coming. The practical task was to ensure that the system eventually decided upon was one where the state didn't replace the private sector but created more incentives for it to accomplish desired social purposes.

So far, the logic had worked. Democratic congressional leaders supported a corporation-based play-or-pay approach, in which government would insure only those whom private industry didn't. AFL-CIO leaders were split on the crucial question of government-only versus government-mandated programs. Moderate Republicans backed the Roundtable's modified welfare capitalist approach. The conservative Republicans in the Bush White House made no proposals at all until forced to in an election year—and then they only dithered and postured. Careful Democrats like Governor

Bill Clinton of Arkansas supported most of the Roundtable-AARP-union coalition's policy recommendations.

Meanwhile, more than 35 million Americans had no health protection at all, partly because cost cutting state and federal officials had restricted eligibility for Medicaid until it covered only 40 percent of those living below the federal poverty line. Conservatism like Bush's was self-defeating. You couldn't replace something with nothing. A succession of vetoes was not a domestic policy, as even Bush himself too belatedly discovered. Unless Reaganite conservatives realized that tax cuts alone couldn't solve social problems, they risked losing control of the political agenda.

That agenda was important. There were things on it that big firms wanted from government. Although small business lobbyists often saw politics as a series of negatives, big firms were affected every day by scores of federal regulations, and some of these regulations provided important commercial protection. Did our CEO's firm want the federal government to limit states' ability to pass product liability and environmental laws? Yes, it did. Did his company support efforts by the chemical industry to have most companies (as opposed to chemical companies alone) finance the corporate portion of the Superfund, EPA's toxic waste clean-up effort? No, it didn't.

What about hostile takeovers? Did he want oil companies swimming in cash or vulture capitalists financed by junk bonds to gobble up *his* company? No, of course not. Too many of the mergers of the 1970s and 1980s were leveraged buy-outs—debt-for-equity swaps that swelled stock prices before hostile suitors gained majority control. A major way that the vastly indebted takeover artists then met their loan payments was by breaking up the firms they had acquired and selling off the most profitable chunks. Managers like himself often had to defend their corporations against buccaneering takeover efforts by sacrificing longer-term to shorter-term profits, by boosting dividend and stock prices to make takeover bids prohibitively expensive; by paying financial blackmail to junk bonders to buy out their company holdings at inflated prices, or by calling on regulatory officials to tighten rules to make it harder to undertake unfriendly takeovers.

The CEO was among those who had implored federal and state governments to curb the takeover mania, and some state governments and the Securities and Exchange Commission had finally started paying attention. But until investment firms like Drexel Burnham Lambert and their speculative houses of cards had started falling apart shortly after Reagan left the White House, government hadn't done enough to regulate trade to trade's advantage. His corporation was in the market for government, as it was in the market for other services in a modern economy: sometimes in cooperation with other firms, sometimes opposed to them.

This reality was becoming increasingly important as world trade occupied his company's corporate strategy making and as the country's economic growth became more export dependent. Few CEOs, anyway, had ever believed in the universe according to Daniel Boone, Adam Smith, or the Reagan wing of the GOP. Certainly, Western European and Asian competitors rarely had. In Japan, South Korea, France, Germany, and other major capitalist nations, corporate relations with the state were very often symbiotic. (Only in Britain was there anything resembling the minimalist ideology of traditional U.S. conservatives.) It did not do to ignore such a reality, as global competition moved from low-tech to high-tech markets. It was one thing to lose important segments of toy, textile, shoe, auto, and steel markets to Japan, Inc., and others; it was quite another to lose the competitive technological edge that America had maintained for all of the past half century in fields like electronics, computers, and aerospace. "Sunset" industries were the past, where dominance couldn't easily be regained; "sunrise" industries were the future.

Our CEO had tried to get that message across in Washington for years. It was one thing to support freer world trade and to apply pressure in the GATT and elsewhere to prune thickets of nontariff barriers that excluded U.S. goods from other countries' home markets without appearing to. Japan's continuing refusal to import lower cost foreign rice in any but tiny amounts was only the clearest in a very long list of exclusions, prohibitions, and regulatory barriers conveniently rationalized on cultural, environmental, product safety, or national security grounds.

Abroad, however, national security often had very different political connotations than in America. Abroad, national security was primarily economic. But America was the cornerstone of military security and had been since 1945. In America, therefore, leaders perceived of security in military, far more than economic, terms. This was shortsighted. Worse, as military confrontations with the U.S.S.R. steadily decreased after 1985, it was self-defeating. None of this meant that an America, Inc. would soon contend with Japan, with the emergent European Community, or with other rising state-oriented or state-orchestrated capitalisms: America was too individualistic and market oriented for that, and its government was too multifaceted, polycentristic, and permeable. New forms of global competition did mean, however, that regulations like the antitrust laws, formulated when America was a self-sufficient and highly tariff-protected economy, were badly outdated.

Slowly, conservative and other leaders were getting the message. Under Reagan and Bush, antitrust was a dead letter. Legalistic overkill like that which banned the U.S. Big Three automakers from sharing fuel-economy

research or technology in the 1970s—because monopoly might result—
was becoming rare. Old liberal proposals for industrial policies to provide
employment and investment subsidies to sunset industries such as steel
and auto were giving way to conservative proposals for competitiveness
policies to provide government regulatory and tax relief to sunrise industries
so that foreign countries' economic supports for their industries didn't place
U.S. corporations at competitive disadvantage. Analysts as diverse as
Democratic presidential candidates Paul Tsongas and Bill Clinton and
Republican policy guru Kevin Phillips chorused that the time had come to
admit to public-private symbioses and to organize them more coherently.
The fast developing biotechnology industry, for instance, had had thirty
years of federal R&D support for biomedical and agricultural research.
Now deliberate efforts had to be made to create other new multibillion-
dollar industries. In the science-based future, the boundaries between pure
and applied science and between government and industry needed to
become less ad hoc, not as a matter of ideology, but as a matter of interest.

Organizing the ad hoc was, again, all in the details, not in the broad
principles. Too many conservatives in America perceived of high technology
in military terms alone. They saw it as computers used only to ensure that
Stealth fighter bombers could accurately aim Smart bombs at Iraqi targets
during the Gulf War. Such long-standing military fixations delayed awareness that by the late 1970s R&D in areas like superconductivity, semicon-
ductors, high-definition television, microelectronics, optical electronics,
and superexact machine tools was becoming too expensive for any single
company, however large, to undertake.

R&D consortia—among corporations and between business and government—were now part of the prescription to avoid further relative economic
decline. In 1984, the National Cooperative Research Act recognized this
by opening legal doors for coordinated research among firms, allowing risks
and costs to be shared. Enthusiasm for broader industry-led government
research partnerships also blossomed. In 1987 Democratic House Majority
Leader Richard Gephardt and Reagan and Bush Commerce and Defense
Department officials cooperated with Silicon Valley entrepreneurs to create
SEMATECH, a joint public-private consortium to develop manufacturing
and production processes for computer memory chips, an engine of the
information revolution. SEMATECH was only the most prominent of a
hundred research consortia formed in the first seven years after the 1984
act. Its goal was to subsidize R&D in order to leapfrog over the (mostly
Japanese) competition in semiconductor technology by giving U.S. companies a menu of innovations to choose from.

Industry-led (and industry-initiated) symbiosis in high-tech R&D like this could be rationalized in military terms. More ambitious government-sponsored and government-subsidized joint manufacturing and marketing deals, however, quickly ran into free-market theology. Joint R&D like SEMATECH helped companies equally against state-supported foreign competitors, but it did not decrease domestic competition. Government-sponsored consortia to make or sell things, however, got government involved in picking winners: selecting which of various newly developed technologies should be built, a prospect that led Reagan and Bush economists to fear creeping socialism.

Our CEO found ideological distinctions like these hard to keep straight. Conservative economists seemed to accept passive government incentives: tax cuts and regulatory reductions, for example, were fine, because fewer federal revenues or bureaucrats were involved. Then conservative ideological tradition began to stretch to encompass acceptance of the drift to global and domestic cartels. After all, in the late 1970s and the 1980s, U.S. firms had initiated vast numbers of joint manufacturing and marketing deals with foreign firms. So in 1989 American laissez-faire enthusiasts, concerned about foreign control of key U.S. industries, started lauding domestic joint manufacturing ventures, especially in hard-hit industries like autos. As a result, in 1990 Chrysler and GM merged parts of their component and transmission manufacturing organizations. And even though U.S. Memories, an attempted merger of U.S. computer chip production, failed that same year, consortia to preserve the high-tech future were still acceptable, even when federal dollars were involved (so long, it seemed, as government officials had no too overt official say in determining future technological directions). The creation of the U.S. Advanced Battery Consortium to create improved electric car batteries, half of whose $262 million in seed money was federal, demonstrates the proprieties here. It seemed that Washington should support most of America's basic research, as it had for fifty years via agencies like the National Science Foundation and the National Institutes of Health, but that it should not support even generic premarket technology unless it had a clear impact on the military.

Ideological boundaries between public and private, however, were fluid. What didn't have an impact on the military these days? Improved batteries? Possibly. Computer memory chips? Clearly. Supercomputers? Absolutely. The government bought almost half of all supercomputers for everything from weapon design to code breaking. Military and spy supercomputers had to be U.S. made. And private sector buyers also bought American to assist Cray, the producer of two-thirds of all such systems now existent in the world. Years of government nurture and millions of dollars in federal subsidies to allow a Control Data subsidiary to begin competing with Cray and foreign producers failed in 1989, when the new company went bankrupt. But new symbiotic arrangements were afoot, via DARPA, for instance, which had been established under Eisenhower. And in computer research, business and government were as dynamically fused as they were in Japan. The nuclear energy industry was the same, as were vast reaches of aerospace and key segments of telecommunications, including satellite technology.

National security, however, still did not make all state subsidies and supports acceptable. A public-private R&D consortium to speed the development of high-definition television technology collapsed in 1989 when the American Electronics Association too publicly proposed that Washington supply $1.35 billion in grants, loans, and loan guarantees to support that effort. In 1990, it was DARPA's turn. A Democratic majority Congress expanded that agency's mandate in 1990 to enable it to provide venture capital to firms close to developing products that would strengthen America's high-tech industrial base and also have short-term military applications. Instead of only encouraging contract winners to set up companies or giving companies crucial early seed money to help attract private investors and corporate partners, DARPA could now own shares in high-tech companies closely related to the military, get a share of their profits, and sit on their boards of directors.

This was too much for the Bush administration. High-tech venture capitalism by a Pentagon agency was wicked. Soon after DARPA's director purchased partial ownership of a small Silicon Valley chip maker in April 1990, he was demoted. The White House then tried to chop DARPA's over $1-billion-a-year budget—but failed after loud industry and congressional opposition. Debates over free versus planned high-tech industrial development roiled on. What, our CEO wondered, should the limits be? Maybe what America needed to do was more of what America had already done, as it created its peculiar symbiotic system over the course of the preceding half century: federal money, but not federal control. R&D dollars, fine, but no say in how the R&D dollars were spent or what was developed with them. Washington as a passive financier but not an active regulator and certainly not a co-owner of anything.

OK, this was a sensible conservative start. But it still ignored the fact that Washington bought an immense amount of things like supercomputers and high-tech aviation. The customer was supposed to be sovereign: what the customer wanted most, the market would provide. If cost-plus and other federal purchases didn't affect markets, nothing did: one-third of all U.S. engineers weren't working in military fields by accident.

Or take the savings and loan and bank bailouts. Did our CEO like the results of federal money without federal control there? No, he didn't. Reagan-era banking policy had mixed thorough industry deregulation with large increases in federal liabilities for bad debts run up by inept or unlucky banks. Deregulated loans got riskier; bankers too often gambled badly; and when they did, it was left to Washington (i.e., the taxpayers) to pay off what became, after the failure of the huge Continental Illinois Bank in 1985, all of their bad debts.

Crashes in oil, property, and other highly speculative markets shortly thereafter produced plenty of other cases like Continental Illinois. More S&L and bank defaults occurred each year in the late 1980s than during any year since the 1930s. Free-enterprise regulators were placed in the supremely ironic position of being reluctant statists, as Washington took over the assets of hundreds of failed financial institutions. After 1989, the federal government became the world's largest property owner with no fewer than 36,000 loan-defaulted properties. Strong banks, meanwhile, successfully resisted being taxed more to replenish the FDIC and FSLIC insurance funds to pay the debts of their failed brethren. Government was left to solve problems that a mix of Reaganomics, regulatory denial, and ineffective industry self-regulation had not. A $500-billion tax bailout scheduled over thirty years resulted. A too-passive public sector had given the American economy the worst of both worlds: wild-blue-yonder laissez-faire underwritten by taxpayers like himself and his company.

"Socialism," the *Economist* of London wryly commented in 1991, had come to America at last. But the expensive and temporary difficulties of a portion of U.S. banking were no argument for genuine socialism to any American CEO worthy of the name. They were, however, an argument for making America's symbiotic system more consistent. Laissez-faire was, in many ways, a legend people lived in, a glorious mythology, a way individuals cloaked themselves in a rosy-hued past in which life was uncomplicated and (above all) individually successful. It was often no more relevant to modern realities than the fading dogmas of Marx or Lenin.

Take the mind-sets of many small business people, for example. They often sneered at CEOs of large companies like himself as entrepreneurial dinosaurs or worse. They were absurd, really, these small business people. They spoke in Daniel Boone and John Wayne idioms. Yet, in the service sectors, where small businesses were most numerous and powerful, and where trends toward bigness and concentration were fewest, franchising was all the rage. In real estate, restaurants, retailing, and so on, franchised small business was not really independent any more. It was a middle ground between individual capital and creativity and big business control of advertising, product line, servicing, site selection, and marketing. For instance, the instruction manual for McDonald's hamburger franchises, provided by the corporation's central office, totaled 385 pages. And McDonald's was only one of the chains that accounted for half a million of the most successful of the 13 million small businesses in the United States in 1980.

Coherent—that was the word he was looking for—*coherent*. It had been easy to afford symbiotic sprawl in the decades immediately after World War II. Now the nation had to tighten up its economy, which meant more than reiterating those general principles that business leaders could almost always agree on: tax cuts, regulatory reduction, and tougher labor laws, for example. Those principles assumed that government was inept at regulating any markets except those that business dearly wanted it to regulate. Such overtly self-interested selectivity hadn't worked well in the past, and it wouldn't work well in the future. Political fashions come and go—conservative one decade, liberal the next, and so it would continue. The rhetoric varied: "social compact," "business-government partnership."

The fact was that fragmented and factional policies couldn't much longer be afforded. The struggles America faced now were no longer predominantly military but predominantly economic and technological. And as foreign countries were increasingly involved and multinational corporate networks and competition increasingly the norm, government had an important role to play in helping build that economic and technological future—whether ideologues found it congenial or not. If Marx was indeed dead, perhaps it was time for less of Adam Smith, too.

Yachting, of all things, made the point. It was our CEO's favorite recreation, sailing on the Great Lakes, leaving the cares of the land behind. In the laissez-faire 1980s, increasingly skilled and innovative foreign challengers from Australia contended to capture the America's Cup for the first time ever. American yachtsmen defending the cup, meanwhile, competed furiously against one another just as they always had, in technology and organization, in strategy, and in design. Times, however, had changed. Technology was moving faster now. Computers and much else besides were applied to racing yachts. In 1983, pioneering Australian challengers abruptly ended a century of U.S. monopoly over sailing's most prestigious trophy.

And the Australians weren't alone. Sweden, Japan, and others were lining up to accomplish what British yachtsmen had never been able to achieve: to make the America's Cup distinctly non-American.

How was one to regain superiority in this tougher and more competitive world? Simply—or so it seemed in retrospect—Americans had to work together. To win back the America's Cup, they formed PACT, the Partnership for America's Cup Technology. PACT organizers required every group of U.S. yachtsmen who wished to compete for the honor of regaining the cup to pay $100,000 to help finance PACT. PACT then attracted IBM and other corporate sponsors with the bait of applied computer applications to ship design. PACT did not produce specific yacht designs, but provided, instead, computer simulations and models that all competing yachtsmen and yacht designers could use. It worked closely with the aerospace industry to adapt to yachts the computer software systems they had developed through federal contracts. Final yacht design decisions were left to each group of competitors. The building of impressive new designs began in 1987, and the America's Cup was recaptured that same year and defended successfully soon thereafter.

PACT's combined national forces mixed cooperation and competition, centralizing and organizing innovation in one of the most traditionally individualistic sports around. It wasn't America, Inc.: there was no private design or production combine yet, no state ministry providing seed capital or full funding to private organizations, à la Japan, Inc. But neither was there Daniel Boone competition in the old, and now self-defeating, style. Symbiosis, it appeared, had come to America to stay. Its terms would always be debatable; the fact of its dynamic evolution would not.

ABBREVIATIONS

AARP	American Association of Retired Persons
AEC	Atomic Energy Commission
AFL	American Federation of Labor
ALCOA	Aluminum Corporation of America
ARAMCO	Arabian American Oil Company
ATT	American Telephone and Telegraph
BC	Business Council
BCTR	Business Committee for Tax Reduction
CAP	Community Action Program
CBO	Congressional Budget Office
CBS	Columbia Broadcasting System
CED	Committee for Economic Development
CEO	chief executive officer
CIO	Congress of Industrial Organizations
CPA	Consumer Protection Agency
CPSC	Consumer Product Safety Commission
DARPA	Defense Advanced Research Projects Agency
ECA	Economic Cooperation Administration
EEOC	Equal Employment Opportunity Commission
EPA	Environmental Protection Agency
Ex-Im	Export-Import Bank
FAA	Federal Aviation Administration
Fannie Mae	Federal National Mortgage Association
FDIC	Federal Deposit Insurance Corporation
FDR	Franklin Delano Roosevelt
FHA	Federal Housing Administration
FICA	Federal Insurance Contribution Act (Social Security payroll tax deductions)
FLSA	Fair Labor Standards Act
Freddie Mac	Federal Home Loan Mortgage Corporation
FSLIC	Federal Savings and Loan Insurance Corporation
GATT	General Agreement on Tariffs and Trade
GE	General Electric
GM	General Motors
GNP	gross national product

GOP	Republican party (Grand Old Party)
GTE	General Telephone and Electronics
HEW	Department of Health, Education, and Welfare
HHS	Department of Health and Human Services
HOLC	Home Owners Loan Corporation
IBM	International Business Machines
IMF	International Monetary Fund
IRS	Internal Revenue Service
ITT	International Telephone and Telegraph
JFK	John Fitzgerald Kennedy
LBJ	Lyndon Baines Johnson
MIT	Massachusetts Institute of Technology
NAM	National Association of Manufacturers
NASA	National Aeronautics and Space Agency
NFIB	National Federation of Independent Business
NIRA	National Industrial Recovery Act
NLRB	National Labor Relations Board
NPC	National Petroleum Council
OEO	Office of Economic Opportunity
OMB	Office of Management and Budget
OPEC	Organization of Petroleum Exporting Companies
OPIC	Overseas Private Investment Corporation
OSHA	Occupational Safety and Health Administration
PAC	political action committee
PACT	Partnership for America's Cup Technology
PIWC	Petroleum Industry War Council
RCA	Radio Corporation of America
R&D	research and development
RFC	Reconstruction Finance Corporation
S&L	savings and loan bank
T-group	sensitivity training session
TVA	Tennessee Valley Authority
UAW	United Auto Workers
UMW	United Mine Workers
UNRRA	United Nations Relief and Rehabilitation Agency
USCC	United States Chamber of Commerce
U.S.S.R.	Union of Soviet Socialist Republics
VA	Veterans Administration

BIBLIOGRAPHICAL ESSAY

GENERAL ACCOUNTS

Surveys of big-business–big-government affairs in the United States after 1945 are of several types. A handful of historians have written broad surveys attempting to grasp the topic whole. Many more historians have preferred carefully limited topical studies or, more frequently, analyses of specific industries or firms. Political scientists of varying persuasions have generally focused on interest groups and have debated whether—and to what extent—power elites operate in America. Economists have weighed in with analyses of the ways in which commercial and other interests interact with politics in the process of economic policymaking. Political scientists and economists, like historians, offer far more specialized studies than broad synthetic works.

Louis Galambos and Joseph Pratt, *The Rise of the Corporate Commonwealth: U.S. Business and Public Policy in the Twentieth Century* (New York, 1988), provides the broadest overview. It's refreshingly well written and is cogent on matters of regulation and international trade. Kim McQuaid, *Big Business and Presidential Power: From FDR to Reagan* (New York, 1982), provides a rare inside view of political economics as perceived and acted upon by leaders of the nation's largest corporations. David Vogel, *Fluctuating Fortunes: The Political Power of Business in America* (New York, 1989), looks at both "center" and "periphery" corporate lobbies from the Kennedy era onward, focusing on labor, taxation, energy, and health and safety policies. The book is based on the too-often unutilized work of reporters for publications like the *Congressional Quarterly* and the *National Journal* and prunes the thickets of political science case studies into a coherent narrative.

A good solid introductory text on business-government relations and very much else is Mansel G. Blackford and K. Austin Kerr, *Business Enterprise in American History*, 2d ed. (Boston, 1990). Charles E. Lindblom, *Politics and Markets: The World's Political-Economic Systems* (New York, 1977); Graham K. Wilson, *Interest Groups in the United States* (New York, 1981); and Wilson, *Business and Politics: A Comparative Introduction* (London, 1985), put corporate efforts in context, both domestically and internationally. The last of the three is the best single introduction. Louis Galambos, *The Public Image of Big Business in America, 1880–1940* (Baltimore, 1975), charts early patterns of middle-class accommodation to big business. Francis X. Sutton, Seymour E. Harris, and Karl Kaysen, *The American Business*

Creed (New York, 1962), analyzes early patterns of business accommodation to the uncomfortable realities of larger government. Grant McConnell, *Private Power and American Democracy* (New York, 1966), is an old classic, as is Adolf A. Berle, Jr., *The Twentieth Century Capitalist Revolution* (New York, 1954).

Murray L. Weidenbaum, *Business, Government, and the Public*, 2d ed. (Englewood Cliffs, N.J., 1981); Theodore J. Lowi, *The End of Liberalism: The Second Republic of the United States*, 2d ed. (New York, 1979); Arnold W. Rose, *The Power Structure: Political Processes in American Society* (New York, 1967); Suzanne Keller, *Beyond the Ruling Class: Strategic Elites in Modern Society* (New York, 1963); C. Wright Mills, *The Power Elite* (New York, 1956); Michael Useem, *The Inner Circle: Large Corporations and the Rise of Business Political Activity in the U.S. and U.K.* (New York, 1984); G. William Domhoff, *Who Rules America Now: A View of the '80s* (Englewood Cliffs, N.J., 1983); Philip H. Burch, Jr., *Elites in American History: The New Deal to the Carter Administration* (New York, 1980); and Beth Mintz and Michael Schwartz, *The Power Structure of American Business* (Chicago, 1985), provide a spectrum of views, from the right to the left, of corporate-government relations in the political science literature.

Among economists, Herbert Stein, *The Fiscal Revolution in America* (Chicago, 1969); Stein, *Presidential Economics: The Making of Economic Policy, Roosevelt to Reagan and Beyond*, 2d ed. (Washington, D.C., 1988); John Kenneth Galbraith, *American Capitalism: The Concept of Countervailing Power*, 2d rev. ed. (Boston, 1956); and Galbraith, *The New Industrial State*, 3d rev. ed. (Boston, 1979), are far and away the most readable equivalents. Robert T. Averitt, *The Dual Economy: Dynamics of American Industrial Structure* (New York, 1968), is an analysis of oligopoly that has influenced most subsequent work, including Galbraith's. Robert M. Collins, *The Business Response to Keynes, 1929–1964* (New York, 1981); and Karl Schriftgeisser, *Business and Public Policy: The Role of the Committee for Economic Development, 1942–1967* (Englewood Cliffs, N.J., 1967), are necessary antidotes to the tendency of economists to confuse academic theory with political (or any other) reality.

PROLOGUE: AUGUST 1945

Historical literature for the Industrial Revolution, the Depression, and World War II abounds. For the managerial and social effects of the rise of big business, Alfred D. Chandler, Jr., *The Visible Hand: The Managerial Revolution in American Business* (Cambridge, 1977); and Daniel Nelson, *Managers and Workers: Origins of the New Factory System in the United States, 1880–1920* (Madison, 1975), should be used together—the former for a top-down perspective, the latter for a bottom-up view. Jonathan R. T. Hughes, *The Vital Few: The Entrepreneur and American Economic Progress*, expanded ed. (New York, 1986), shines with narrative energy. Sidney Fine, *Laissez Faire and the General Welfare State* (Ann Arbor, 1966); and Reinhard Bendix, *Work and Authority in Industry: Ideologies of Management in the*

Course of Industrialization (New York, 1956), are the sturdy, standard, accounts. Stuart D. Brandes, *American Welfare Capitalism, 1880–1940* (Chicago, 1976); and Thomas K. McCraw, *Prophets of Regulation* (Cambridge, 1984), cover early corporate and government efforts at social control and equity.

Edward D. Berkowitz and Kim McQuaid, *Creating the Welfare State: The Political Economy of Twentieth Century Reform*, rev. ed. (Lawrence, Kan., 1992), shows how private efforts affected public efforts, and vice versa. Irving Bernstein, *The Lean Years: A History of the American Worker, 1920–1933* (Boston, 1966); and Bernstein, *The Turbulent Years: A History of the American Worker, 1933–1941* (Boston, 1971), cover labor organizing with verve. Harry A. Millis and Emily C. Brown, *From the Wagner Act to Taft-Hartley: A Study of National Labor Policy and Labor Relations* (Chicago, 1950), covers the less stirring but equally important patterns of labor law.

General treatments of the Depression and the economic, industrial, and institutional changes wrought by it are surprisingly rare. Most efforts are oriented toward presidents and intellectuals, mostly because of the easy availability of public records in presidential and other research libraries. Two recent efforts aimed at redressing this imbalance are John A. Garraty, *The Great Depression* (New York, 1987), which provides a welcome and rare international dimension to American events, and Michael A. Bernstein, *The Great Depression: Delayed Recovery and Economic Change in America, 1929–1939* (New York, 1989), which gets serious about turning industrial statistics into clear testable hypotheses.

Two old favorites of mine are Theodore Rosenhof, *Dogma, Depression, and the New Deal: The Debate of Political Leaders over Economic Recovery* (Port Washington, N.Y., 1975), which demonstrates that economic downturns come and go while partisan rationalizations for them remain largely the same; and Broadus Mitchell, *Depression Decade: From the New Era Through the New Deal, 1929–1941* (New York, 1969). If all historians knew as much about the details of New Deal political economics as Mitchell did when he wrote his book in 1947, perhaps the fog banks of academic debate would be less thick than they are regarding a seminal event of the twentieth century. William E. Leuchtenburg, *Franklin D. Roosevelt and the New Deal* (New York, 1963); and Ellis W. Hawley, *The New Deal and the Problem of Monopoly* (Princeton, 1966), are enduring, valuable accounts. Harold G. Vatter, *The U.S. Economy in World War II* (New York, 1985), also deserves enduring status, if only because Vatter had the wit to examine changes that most of his peers treat in once-over-very-lightly fashion.

1 DEFINING POSTWAR NORMALCY: THE FIGHT OVER LABOR LAW

Collins, *The Business Response to Keynes*, is a fine introduction to business thinking on crucial economic variables during war and immediate postwar. Howell J. Harris, *The Right to Manage: Industrial Relations Policies of American Business in the 1940s* (Madison, 1982), also deserves more attention than it's yet received.

His book is a model of how to write contested history well, without vacillation or chameleonlike phrasing. Joel Seidman, *American Labor from Defense to Reconversion* (Chicago, 1953), covers an extensive ground clearly and concisely and without mind-dulling technocratese. Seidman is a very useful complement to Millis and Brown, *From the Wagner Act to Taft-Hartley*, the standard, but too often dull, account. Another useful complement is James A. Gross, *The Reshaping of the National Labor Relations Board: National Labor Policy in Transition, 1937–1947* (Albany, 1981). Arthur F. McClure, *The Truman Administration and the Problems of Post-War Labor, 1945–1948* (Rutherford, N.J., 1969), is a cogent introduction to the Taft-Hartley Act and goes light on the jargon. R. Alton Lee, *Truman and Taft-Hartley: A Question of Mandate* (Lexington, Ky., 1966), is, by comparison, stolid and workmanlike.

James Caldwell Foster, *The Union Politic: The CIO Political Action Committee* (Columbia, Mo., 1975), shows that labor's postwar leadership was not generally bright with creative political ideas. Relevant chapters in recent biographies, including Roger Morris, *Richard Nixon: The Rise of an American Politician* (New York, 1990); and Robert A. Caro, *The Years of Lyndon Johnson: Means of Ascent* (New York, 1990), demonstrate just how carefully ambitious young politicians avoided close postwar union affiliations. The fact that both Caro and Morris are marinated in skepticism about their subjects, in the post-Vietnam/post-Watergate style, does not, in this case, detract from the accuracy of their observations. McQuaid, *Big Business and Presidential Power*, shows how large corporate CEOs massaged congressional and executive branch opinion about crucial fine points of the Taft-Hartley legislation. Neil W. Chamberlain, *The Union Challenge to Management Control* (New York, 1948); and Herbert R. Northrup, *Boulwarism: The Labor Relations Policies of the General Electric Company* (Ann Arbor, Mich., 1964), are good for contemporary corporate labor relations activity.

Understanding the passage of the Taft-Hartley Act is impossible without understanding the social contexts in which it took form. For three quiet classics regarding wartime industrial mobilization and economic policies, see Bruce Catton, *The War Lords of Washington* (New York, 1948); Eliot Janeway, *The Struggle for Survival: A Chronicle of Economic Mobilization in World War II* (New Haven, 1951); and Gerald T. White, *Billions for Defense: Government Financing by the Defense Plant Corporation during World War II* (University, Ala., 1980). An official history is R. Elberton Smith, *The United States Army in World War II: The Army and Economic Mobilization* (Washington, D.C., 1959). Donald M. Nelson, *Arsenal of Democracy* (New York, 1946), is also useful.

For wartime social, political, and economic changes and for the immediate postwar reconversion, see John Morton Blum, *V was for Victory: Politics and American Culture during World War II* (New York, 1976); and Richard W. Polenberg, *War and Society: The United States, 1941–1945* (Philadelphia, 1972). Both are standards—and will remain so. Neither, however, can compare to Geoffrey Perrett, *Days of Sadness, Years of Triumph: The American People, 1939–1945* (New

York, 1973); David Brinkley, *Washington Goes to War* (New York, 1988); or William Manchester, *The Glory and the Dream: A Narrative History of America, 1932–1972* (Boston, 1974), for sheer verve and vividness.

For the Truman presidency, Robert J. Donovan, *Conflict and Crisis: The Presidency of Harry S. Truman, 1945–1948* (New York, 1977); and Donovan, *Tumultuous Years: The Presidency of Harry S. Truman, 1949–1953* (New York, 1982), should be used on conjunction with Bert Cochran, *Harry Truman and the Crisis Presidency* (New York, 1973); and Eric F. Goldman, *The Crucial Decade and After: America, 1945–1960* (New York, 1976). Robert H. Zieger, *American Workers, American Unions, 1920–1985* (Baltimore, 1986), provides a well-written and cogently argued view from within the unions looking out.

2   THE PATH TO THE MARSHALL PLAN

The Marshall Plan is an exceedingly hard subject to write about. Myriad vital details of international political and economic relations are involved. Students can too easily assume that the authors involved are writing around and around and around the subject, when in fact they're trying to introduce it in a rigorous enough way to make both diplomatic and commercial sense of a multifaceted foreign aid program that affected many countries in many ways. Robert A. Pollard, *Economic Security and the Origins of the Cold War, 1945–1950* (New York, 1985), is a well-written and concise overview of the major domestic and foreign elements of U.S. international policymaking from Bretton Woods to the Truman Doctrine and the Marshall Plan. It covers not only Western Europe but also American economic diplomacy in Asia. In a field that is sometimes necessarily polysyllabic and involuted, Pollard is a breath of fresh air.

Another major starting point should be Walter Isaacson and Evan Thomas, *The Wise Men: Six Friends and the World They Made* (New York, 1986). This is a sympathetic collective biography of Dean Acheson, Charles Bohlen, Averell Harriman, George F. Kennan, Robert J. Lovett, and John J. McCloy by two authors who were then *Time* magazine staffers. The book also contains background data on Paul Nitze, James Forrestal, and Robert Ball. This corporate lawyer gentry, which did so much to make U.S. foreign policy in the immediate postwar period, end up looking great vis-à-vis the quasi-isolationist left and right. The book is overtly elitist, which makes the prose and the arguments refreshingly clear. It also reflects the European orientation of all of its major subjects. Just as Pollard, *Economic Security*, is fine for the policy dimension, Isaacson and Thomas's book is fine for the human dimension and the internal domestic political struggles within official Washington.

Other biographies of major postwar foreign policy players with corporate antecedents are, in general, disappointing. Two new books, however, which appeared after this volume was completed, look like exceptions to this general rule. These are Townsend Hoopes and Douglas Brinkley, *Driven Patriot: The Life and Times of*

James Forrestal (New York, 1992); and Kai Bird, *The Chairman: John J. McCloy and the Making of the American Establishment* (New York, 1992). Another new book, Rudy Abramson, *Spanning the Century: The Life of W. Averell Harriman, 1891–1986* (New York, 1992), benefits from access to Harriman's private papers and a felicitous writing style. I found it especially good for the nuances of how Harriman helped ram the Marshall Plan through Congress. Finally, Jeffrey M. Dorwart, *Eberstadt and Forrestal: A National Security Partnership, 1909–1949* (College Station, Tex., 1991), charts one of the most important of the many investment broker interlocks in the World War II mobilization effort.

   Michel J. Hogan, *The Marshall Plan: America, Britain and the Reconstruction of Western Europe, 1947–1952* (New York, 1987), is important, detailed, but sometimes dense. This is partly because Hogan is concerned about explaining the precise political and economic terms via which both Washington and London aspired to buttress international capitalism and the ways in which they disagreed with one another. David Eakins' unfortunately unpublished Ph.D. dissertation, "The Development of Corporate Liberal Policy Research in the United States, 1885–1965" (University of Wisconsin, 1966), puts the businesslike procedures of the postwar policy planners in perspective. So does Hadley Arkes, *Bureaucracy, the Marshall Plan, and the National Interest* (Princeton, N.J., 1972). John Gimbel, *The Origins of the Marshall Plan* (Stanford, 1976), emphasizes the German economic reconstruction aspects of the Marshall Plan and argues that anti-U.S.S.R. rhetoric by business political activists like Will Clayton was merely a political device to get the legislation passed in Congress.

   Alan S. Milward, *The Reconstruction of Western Europe, 1945–1951* (Berkeley, 1984), weighs in for the Europeans, arguing that America was a lot less economically important to creating or administering European postwar recovery than its leaders supposed. Joseph M. Jones, *The Fifteen Weeks: February 21–June 5, 1947* (New York, 1955), provides a spirited account by a participant. Charles L. Mee, Jr., *The Marshall Plan: The Launching of the Pax Americana* (New York, 1984), has a title that makes its argument obvious. Robert E. Summers, ed., *Economic Aid to Europe: The Marshall Plan* (New York, 1948), provides a convenient spectrum of contemporary political reactions. Walter A. Millis and E. S. Duffield, eds., *The Forrestal Diaries* (New York, 1951), provides the gossip of power from within.

   David A. Baldwin, *Economic Development and American Foreign Policy* (Chicago, 1966), shows how businessmen legitimized and administered foreign aid programs throughout the postwar period. So does Burton I. Kaufman, *Trade and Aid: Eisenhower's Foreign Economic Policy* (Baltimore, 1982). Ralph J. Levering, *The Public and American Foreign Policy, 1918–1978* (New York, 1978), illuminates the isolationist-interventionist shifts. Mira Wilkins, *The Maturing of Multi-National Enterprise: American Business Abroad from 1914 to 1970* (Cambridge, 1974), is a magisterial overview of how corporations responded to postwar global opportunities. Joan Hoff Wilson, *American Business and Foreign Policy, 1920–1933* (Lexington, Ky., 1971); Lloyd C. Gardner, *Economic Aspects of New Deal Diplomacy* (Madison,

1964); and William H. Becker, *The Dynamics of Business-Government Relations: Industry and Exports, 1893–1921* (Chicago, 1982), clarify changes in post-1945 views, as compared with pre-1945 varieties.

Raymond A. Bauer, Ithiel De Sola Pool, and Lewis A. Dexter, *American Business and Public Policy: The Politics of Foreign Trade*, 2d ed. (Chicago, 1974); and Bruce M. Russett and Elizabeth C. Hanson, *Interest and Ideology: The Foreign Policy Beliefs of American Businessmen* (San Francisco, 1975), discuss splits and unities regarding the trade-offs between freer trade and world policeman status. Thomas Ferguson and Joel Rogers, *Right Turn: The Decline of the Democrats and the Future of American Politics* (New York, 1986); and Thomas Ferguson and Joel Rogers, ed., *The Hidden Election: Politics and Economics in the 1980 Presidential Campaign* (New York, 1981), accent disputes between multinational firms and domestically based, protectionist firms from the 1930s on. Their argument outruns their evidence at times, partly because they read the 1970s and 1980s back into the 1940s and 1950s.

Finally, general histories that help put Marshall Plan events in perspective include Stephen E. Ambrose, *Rise to Globalism: American Foreign Policy since 1938*, 6th rev. ed. (Baltimore, 1991), which is far and away the best one-volume introduction. See also John Lewis Gaddis, *The United States and the Origins of the Cold War, 1941–1947* (New York, 1972); Daniel Yergin, *Shattered Peace: The Origins of the Cold War and the National Security State* (Boston, 1977); Seyom Brown, *The Faces of Power: Constancy and Change in United States Foreign Policy from Truman to Reagan* (New York, 1983); Ronald Steel; *Walter Lippmann and the American Century* (Boston, 1980); Lawrence S. Wittner, *American Intervention in Greece, 1943–1949* (New York, 1982); Michael S. Sherry, *Preparing for the Next War: American Plans for Postwar Defense, 1941–1945* (New Haven, 1977); and Lawrence H. Shoup and William Minter, *Imperial Brain Trust: The Council on Foreign Relations and United States Foreign Policy* (New York, 1977). Together, these provide a basic sampling of a vast literature.

3   OIL: COLD WAR SYMBIOSIS AT AN APEX

Daniel Yergin, *The Prize: The Epic Quest for Oil, Money, and Power* (New York, 1991), is the broadest and most thorough source. It is especially full of vivid anecdote and economic background for the Middle Eastern side of the equation. Robert Lacey, *The Kingdom: Arabia and the House of Sa'ud* (New York, 1981), makes the Saudis and other oil producers a lot less enigmatic and a lot more economically and otherwise rational. Irvine H. Anderson, *ARAMCO, the United States, and Saudi Arabia: A Study in the Dynamics of Foreign Oil Policy, 1933–1950* (Princeton, 1981), is jargon-free and readable regarding the corporate, military, and diplomatic interweave that characterizes global oil politics in an energy age. So is Stephen D. Krasner, *Defending the National Interest: Raw Materials Investments and U.S. Foreign Policy* (Princeton, 1978).

David S. Painter, *Oil and the American Century: The Political Economy of U.S. Oil Policy, 1941–1954* (Baltimore, 1986), is especially good regarding the ironies involved in U.S. antitrust policy as (very unsuccessfully) applied to the global American oil producers as the cold war really got rolling in places like Korea and Iran. Five volumes that rake the global oil combines over the coals for price-fixing and hosts of other cartelized sins are John M. Blair, *The Control of Oil* (New York, 1977); Michael Tanzer, *The Energy Crisis: World Struggle for Power and Wealth* (New York, 1974); Anthony Sampson, *The Seven Sisters: The Great Oil Companies and the World They Created*, rev. ed. (London, 1988); Robert Engler, *The Brotherhood of Oil: Energy Policy and the Public Interest* (Chicago, 1976); and Robert Engler, *The Politics of Oil: A Study of Private Power and Democratic Directions* (Chicago, 1961 and 1976). The latter volume is best for 1940s and 1950s developments, particularly in terms of domestic U.S. politics.

Another necessary source for the ways in which U.S. domestic politics and domestic oil production related to global U.S. diplomacy and oil operations is Richard H. K. Vietor, *Energy Policy in America Since 1945: A Study of Business-Government Relations* (New York, 1984). Vietor is particularly nice for splits within the oil industry and for political leaders' hesitancy to involve themselves in resolving them. Gerald D. Nash, *United States Oil Policy, 1890–1964: Business and Government in Twentieth Century America* (Pittsburgh, 1968), is also a useful account. It was completed before the oil embargo of 1973–74 threw most political accommodations and diplomatic predispositions into a cocked hat.

How the oil shortages of the 1970s and the subsequent price rises for petroleum and other energy sources soured and balkanized American politics is covered in Craufurd D. Goodwin, ed., *Energy Policy in Perspective: Today's Problems, Yesterday's Solutions* (Washington, D.C., 1981); James Everett Katz, *Congress and National Energy Policy* (New Brunswick, N.J., 1984); Dorothy S. Zinberg, ed., *Uncertain Power: The Struggle for a National Energy Policy* (New York, 1983); Martin Greenberger et al., *Caught Unawares: The Energy Decade in Retrospect* (Cambridge, 1983); Aaron Wildavsky and Ellen Tenebaum, *The Politics of Mistrust: Estimating Oil and Gas Resources* (Beverly Hills, Calif., 1981). The titles above all speak of Americans' unease over the end of their energy dominance and their reluctance to recognize alternate realities. Vogel, *Fluctuating Fortunes*, conveniently summarizes the process of reacclimation by corporate CEOs. The best single overview by far, however, is and will likely remain David Halberstam, *The Reckoning* (New York, 1986). It is hard not to gush over this book, for it makes business history live and breathe. If you read anything on the domestic effects of the energy crisis of the 1970s, read this.

4   KOREA, COMMUNISM, AND CORRUPTION: THE PATH TO EISENHOWER

American businessmen, like Americans generally, had so many domestic and international challenges to contend with during the later stages of Truman's presidency that few were neutral about much that happened. Sympathetic treatments of the era include Cabell Phillips, *The Truman Presidency: The History of a Triumphant Succession* (New York, 1966); and Alonzo L. Hamby, *Beyond the New Deal: Harry S. Truman and American Liberalism* (New York, 1973). McQuaid, *Big Business and Presidential Power*; and Collins, *Business Response to Keynes*, show how peak national business organizations responded after 1948 to the debate within the Democratic leadership on major domestic issues.

Otis L. Graham, Jr., *Toward a Planned Society: From Roosevelt to Nixon* (New York, 1976), essays an ambitious synthesis of postwar domestic policymaking as a whole. James D. Savage, *Balanced Budgets and American Politics* (Ithaca, 1988), covers the symbolic politics of deficit spending and shakes his head over the hesitant devotion (at best) that conservative Democrats showed toward wild-eyed Keynesian economics. Stephen Bailey, *Congress Makes a Law: The Study Behind the Employment Act of 1946* (New York, 1950); Gary Mucciaroni, *The Political Failure of Employment Policy, 1945–1982* (Pittsburgh, 1990); and Margaret Weir, *Politics and Jobs: The Boundaries of Employment Policy in the United States* (Princeton, 1992), show just how unradical most American liberals of the postwar era were and just how successful corporate bodies like the CED were in avoiding social democracy. Thomas K. McCraw, *Prophets of Regulation: Charles Francis Adams, Louis D. Brandeis, James M. Landis, Alfred E. Kahn* (Cambridge, 1984), shows how partial to industry self-regulation many New Deal and Fair Deal regulators were.

John F. Witte, *The Politics and Development of the Federal Income Tax* (Madison, 1985), is good on the bemusement of congressional Democrats over fiscal policy and on how comparatively easy it was to keep money in well-heeled pockets by arranging the details of tax bills. Monte Poen, "The Truman Administration and National Health Insurance" (Ph.D. diss., University of Missouri, 1967); and Berkowitz and McQuaid, *Creating the Welfare State*, discuss other Fair Deal reforms that did not manage to happen. Robert H. Ferrell, ed., *Off the Record: The Private Papers of Harry S. Truman* (New York, 1980), portrays Truman's more-than-occasional frustration at the bipartisan opposition he faced. John Morton Blum, ed., *The Price of Vision: The Diaries of Henry A. Wallace* (Boston, 1973), shows how Truman's frustrations were more than amply returned by the left.

The Korean War mobilization is covered in Hamby, *Beyond the New Deal*. See also Burton I. Kaufman, *The Korean War* (Philadelphia, 1986); Jonathan R. T. Hughes, *The Governmental Habit: Economic Controls from Colonial Times to the Present* (New York, 1977); McConnell, *Private Power and American Democracy*; Edward R. Flash, Jr., *Economic Advice and Presidential Leadership: The Council of Economic Advisers* (New York, 1965); and most of all, Harold G. Vatter, *The U.S. Economy in the 1950s* (New York, 1963). Vatter's is a marvellous book, one too rarely used by historians. It's thorough, workmanlike, and crammed with data, and it's written by an economist of the old school—who can write well. For the diplomatic and military dramatics of the war itself,

Joseph C. Goulden's *Korea: The Untold Story of the War* (New York, 1982), is a good place to start.

Collins, *Business Response to Keynes*; and Vatter, *The U.S. Economy in the 1950s*, have convenient summaries of the 1951 Fed-Treasury accord and show how and why business leaders supported it; Schriftgeisser, *Business and Public Policy*, unfortunately, fails on both counts. A very cogent historical survey of the Fed is William Greider, *Secrets of the Temple: How the Federal Reserve Runs the Country* (New York, 1987). David Jones, *Fed Watching* (New York, 1986); Donald F. Kettl, *Leadership at the Fed* (New Haven, 1986); Thaibaut de Sainte Phalle, *The Federal Reserve: An Intentional Mystery* (New York, 1985); and Maxwell Newton, *The Fed: Inside the Federal Reserve* (New York, 1983), are also good for the consciously elitist orientation of monetary policy. Most of the paper trail on business activities regarding monetary policymaking and war mobilization is buried in file folders in archives.

The volumes on the rise of McCarthy and the red scare too rarely include business people as participants. For the great free-enterprise and anticommunist NAM and USCC campaigns between the end of World War II and the start of the Korean War, see Harris, *The Right to Manage*; the chapter by Peter Irons entitled "American Business and the Origins of McCarthyism: The Cold War Crusade of the United States Chamber of Commerce," in Robert E. Griffith and Athan Theoharis, eds., *The Specter: Original Essays on the Cold War and the Origins of McCarthyism* (New York, 1974); Morris, *Richard Nixon* (for the Nixon-USCC connection); Hobart Rowen, "America's Most Powerful Private Club," *Harper's*, September 1960 (for BC opposition to McCarthy); and Charles J. V. Murphy, "McCarthy and the Businessman," *Fortune*, April 1954 (for impressionistic evidence taken from a national survey). The May 1954 *Fortune* has a follow-up article on McCarthy and Texas businessmen.

David M. Oshinsky, *A Conspiracy So Immense: The World of Joe McCarthy* (New York, 1983); James T. Patterson, *Mr. Republican: A Biography of Robert A. Taft* (New York, 1972); and Herbert S. Parmet, *Richard Nixon and His America* (Boston, 1990), elaborate anticommunist thinking among the major conservative players. Richard M. Fried, *Men Against McCarthy* (New York, 1967), is good on McCarthy's congressional opponents. Michael Paul Rogin, *The Intellectuals and McCarthy: The Radical Specter* (Cambridge, 1967), well argues that McCarthyism was a more affluent and learned phenomenon than the affluent and learned like now to believe. Hubert Humphrey, *The Education of a Public Man: My Life in Politics* (Garden City, N.Y., 1976), is good for the political illogic spawned by the Korean War. David Halberstam, *The Powers That Be* (New York, 1979), treats key print and television CEOs of the period as the political and economic entrepreneurs they were.

The 1952 steel seizure case is treated in Maeva Marcus, *Truman and the Steel Seizure* (New York, 1977); and Alan F. Westin, *The Anatomy of a Constitutional Law Case: Youngstown Sheet and Tube Co. v. Sawyer; The Steel Seizure Decision* (New York, 1958). Clarence B. Randall, *Over My Shoulder* (Boston, 1956), provides a contemporary industry reaction.

5 EISENHOWER AND THE AMERICAN CORPORATE DREAM

John Patrick Diggins, *The Proud Decades: American in War and Peace, 1941–1960* (New York, 1988), and Geoffrey Perrett, *A Dream of Greatness: The American People, 1945–1963* (New York, 1979), are two general histories that put the post–Korean War conservative resurgence in perspective without assuming that conservative leaders were comfortable with the mixed economic system they inherited. Galambos and Pratt, *The Rise of the Corporate Commonwealth;* Stein, *The Fiscal Revolution in America;* Vatter, *The U.S. Economy in the 1950s,* Goldman, *The Crucial Decade and After;* and Zieger, *American Workers, American Unions,* are all good for the political effects of affluence.

Arthur Larson, *Eisenhower: The President Nobody Knew* (New York, 1968); Edwin L. Dale, Jr., *Conservatives in Power: A Study in Frustration* (Garden City, N.Y., 1960); and Robert H. Ferrell, ed., *The Eisenhower Diaries* (New York, 1981), detail Eisenhower's frustrations about being unable to wage the cold war cheaply. Walter A. McDougall, *The Heavens and the Earth: A Political History of the Space Age* (New York, 1985), presents a grim image of war technocracy triumphant. But, as he shares the same cold warrior assumptions of his hero, Ike, he is caught in the same conservative conundrum that led Eisenhower to bewail the existence and growth of a bipartisan military-industrial complex but do nothing practical about it.

Daniel Guttman and Barry Wilner, *The Shadow Government* (New York, 1976); and H. L. Nieburg, *In the Name of Science* (Chicago, 1966), provide mixed-system critiques from the left. John Newhouse, *War and Peace in the Nuclear Age* (New York, 1989); Michael D. Reagan, *Science and the Federal Patron* (New York, 1969); and Homer E. Newell, *Beyond the Atmosphere: The Early Years of Space Science* (Washington, D.C., 1980), provide specifics regarding thickets of military and civilian programs involving corporations. Michael D. Reagan, "The Business and Defense Services Administration, 1953–1957," *Western Political Quarterly* 14 (June 1961): 570–81; and U.S. Congress, House of Representatives, Judiciary Committee Antitrust Subcommittee, *Interim Report on WOCs and Government Advisory Groups,* 84th Congress, 2d sess. (Washington, D.C., 1956), provide rare glimpses of the corporate participants in the mixed-system advisory equation.

Herman Kroos, *Executive Opinion: What Business Leaders Said and Thought . . . 1920–1960* (Garden City, N.Y., 1971), is a quiet classic that shows how hard it was for many business spokesmen and their speech writers to relate ideology to changing realities. Pollard, *Economic Security and the Origins of the Cold War,* identifies Korea as the watershed that shifted corporate opinion toward the necessity of large peacetime military spending. Robert Griffith, "Dwight D. Eisenhower and the Corporate Commonwealth," *American Historical Review* 87 (February 1982): 87–122, synthesizes a whole out of Eisenhower's scattered thinking on the political economy of his day.

Ned Eichler, *The Merchant Builders* (Cambridge, 1982); and Eichler, *The Thrift Debacle* (Berkeley, 1989), provide cogent overviews of U.S. housing policy. See also

Marc A. Weiss, "Marketing and Financing Home Ownership: Mortgage Lending and Public Policy in the United States, 1918–1989," *Business and Economic History*, 2d ser. 18 (1989): 109–17; Anthony Downs, *The Revolution in Real Estate Finance* (Washington, D.C. 1981); Miles E. Colean, *A Backward Glance: The Growth of Government Housing Policy in the United States* (Washington, D.C., 1975); and J. Paul Mitchell, ed., *Federal Housing Policy and Programs: Past and Present* (New Brunswick, N.J., 1985). The postwar pension upsurge is covered in Peter F. Drucker, *The Unseen Revolution: How Pension Fund Socialism Came to America* (New York, 1976); and John Brooks, *The Great Leap* (New York, 1966). Gerald Zahavi, *Workers, Managers, and Welfare Capitalism: The Shoeworkers and Tanners of Endicott Johnson, 1890–1950* (Urbana, Ill., 1988), is a too-rare postwar welfare capitalist case study.

The corporate struggles over Social Security in the 1950s are thoroughly treated in Martha Derthick, *Policymaking for Social Security* (Washington, D.C., 1979); Edward D. Berkowitz, *America's Welfare State: From Roosevelt to Reagan* (Baltimore, 1991); and Berkowitz and McQuaid, *Creating the Welfare State*. Berkowitz, *America's Welfare State*, nicely analyzes the dynamics of both politics and policy. Arthur J. Altmeyer, *The Formative Years of Social Security* (Madison, 1963), is a very valuable record by a bureaucratic participant. Sanford J. Jacoby's unpublished "Employers and the Welfare State: The Role of Marion B. Folsom" is a sound and original effort to show that welfare capitalism and the welfare state are not separate universes, and never have been. The same is true of Jill Quadagno, *The Transformation of Old Age Security: Class and Politics in the American Welfare State* (Chicago, 1988).

For the organizational innovators of managerial capitalism, the classic is Alfred D. Chandler, Jr., *Strategy and Structure: Chapters in the History of the American Industrial Enterprise* (Cambridge, 1962). See also Chandler, "The Structure of American Industry in the Twentieth Century: A Historical Overview," *Business History Review* 43 (Autumn 1969): 255–98; and C. Northcote Parkinson, *Big Business* (London, 1974). Sutton, Harris, and Kaysen, *The American Business Creed*, differentiates managerial and classical business thinking. So does Earl F. Cheit, ed., *The Business Establishment* (New York, 1964); and Edward S. Mason, ed., *The Corporation in Modern Society* (Cambridge, 1960). Burton R. Fisher and Stephen B. Withey, *Big Business as the People See It: A Study of a Socio-Economic Institution* (Ann Arbor, 1951), illustrates shifts in postwar public opinion. Loren Baritz, *The Servants of Power: A History of the Use of Social Science in American Industry* (Middletown, Conn., 1960), covers postwar human engineering. So does Harris, *The Right to Manage*; Louis Hacker, ed., *The Corporate Takeover* (New York, 1964); and R. Alan Lawson, *The Failure of Independent Liberalism, 1930–1941* (New York, 1972).

For organized labor's troubles during the 1950s, see Alan K. McAdams, *Power and Politics in Labor Legislation* (New York, 1964); Joseph Goulden, *Meany* (New York, 1972); and Christopher L. Tomlins, *The State and the Unions: Labor Relations,*

Law, and the Organized Labor Movement in America, 1880–1960 (New York, 1985). For unions' subsequent troubles, see Thomas B. Edsall, *The New Politics of Inequality* (New York, 1984); Bennett Harrison and Barry Bluestone, *The Great U-Turn: Corporate Restructuring and the Polarizing of America* (New York, 1988); Vogel, *Fluctuating Fortunes;* and John P. Hoerr, *And the Wolf Finally Came: The Decline of the American Steel Industry* (Pittsburgh, 1988). Thomas Geoghegan, *Which Side Are You On: Trying to Be for Labor When It's Flat on Its Back* (New York, 1991), is stark, spare, and eloquent.

6 CORPORATIONS ON THE NEW FRONTIER

The flood of literature on the Kennedy era highlights the drama of foreign policy and civil rights. Two valuable exceptions to this general rule are Hobart Rowen, *The Free Enterprisers: Kennedy, Johnson, and the Business Establishment* (Philadelphia, 1964); and Jim F. Heath, *John F. Kennedy and the Business Community* (Chicago, 1969). A third general survey, Bernard Nossiter, *The Mythmakers: An Essay on Power and Wealth* (Boston, 1964), is disappointing, perhaps because Nossiter believes that Kennedy was a thwarted planner in many industrial and economic matters, an opinion Heath and Rowen do not share. The big-business–big-government accommodationism Kennedy exemplifies is illustrated by contemporary works like Galbraith, *American Capitalism;* David Lilienthal, *Big Business: A New Era* (New York, 1953); and Berle, *The Twentieth Century Capitalist Revolution.*

Other liberal accommodationist statements differentiating the (good) CED big businessmen from the (bad) USCC-style businessmen include Carl Kaysen, "Big Business and the Liberals, Then and Now," *New Republic,* Nov. 22, 1954; and Norton Long, "American Business and American Liberals: Slogans or Responsibility?" *Political Quarterly* 29 (April–June 1958): 166–77. The close similarities between JFK's and Eisenhower's cabinet selection procedures are covered in David Halberstam, *The Best and the Brightest* (New York, 1972); and Jean Edward Smith, *Lucius D. Clay: An American Life* (New York, 1990). David T. Stanley, Dean E. Mann, and Jameson W. Doig, *Men Who Govern: A Biographical Profile of Federal Political Executives* (Washington, D.C., 1967), gives data on comparative corporate appointments.

The antitrust background of the quarrel between the Kennedy administration and the BC started during Eisenhower's presidency. Theodore Kovaleff, *Business and Government During the Eisenhower Administration: A Study of the Antitrust Policy of the Antitrust Division of the Justice Department* (Athens, Oh., 1980), provides a pedestrian overview. John Herling, *The Great Price Conspiracy: The Story of the Antitrust Violations in the Electrical Industry* (Washington, D.C., 1962), makes a portion of the same history come alive. Heath, *John F. Kennedy and the Business Community;* Rowen, *The Free Enterprisers;* Collins, *The Business Response to Keynes;* and McQuaid, *Big Business and Presidential Power,* give the inside story from the corporate perspective. Theodore Sorensen, *Kennedy* (New York, 1965);

and Bruce Miroff, *Pragmatic Illusions: The Presidential Politics of John F. Kennedy* (New York, 1976), are, respectively, a sympathetic and a critical effort to put in perspective what Kennedy ended up doing with the big business BC. Godfrey Hodgson, *America in Our Time* (New York, 1976), is a relatively disinterested foreign view, from which I learned much.

The steel price hike of 1962 was by far the most dramatic corporate confrontation of Kennedy's presidency. Grant McConnell, *Steel and the Presidency—1962* (New York, 1963), is the best account. See also Roy Hoopes, *The Steel Crisis* (New York, 1963); and the relevant chapters of Walt Whitman Rostow, *The Diffusion of Power, 1957–1972* (New York, 1972). George J. McManus, *The Inside Story of Steel Wages and Prices, 1959–1967* (New York, 1967), is good for the federal pressures to which businessmen strongly objected. Roger M. Blough, *The Washington Embrace of Business* (New York, 1975), gives the views of this CEO of US Steel. Paul A. Tiffany, *The Decline of American Steel: How Management, Labor, and Government Went Wrong* (New York, 1988), makes blame universal. Craufurd D. Goodwin, ed., *Exhortation and Controls: The Search for a Wage-Price Policy, 1945–1972* (Washington, D.C., 1975), puts the hesitant "guidelines" approaches of Kennedy and the more powerful "moral suasion" of Johnson in broader economic contexts.

The logic behind the Kennedy-Johnson Keynesian tax cuts is explained in Walter W. Heller, *New Dimensions in Political Economy* (Cambridge, 1966). For one view of why that logic produced some negative dimensions, see Robert Lekachman, *Economists at Bay: Why the Experts Will Never Solve Your Problems* (New York, 1976). For congressional caution regarding Keynes, see E. Terence Jones, "Congressional Voting on Keynesian Legislation, 1945–1964," *Western Political Quarterly* 21 (June 1968): 240–51; and Savage, *Balanced Budgets and American Politics*.

7   THE TIME OF TROUBLES BEGINS: FROM LYNDON JOHNSON TO GERALD FORD

Sources for the weakness of corporate lobbying in the 1950s and 1960s include Bauer, Pool, and Dexter, *American Business and Public Policy*; Lester W. Milbraith, *The Washington Lobbyists* (Chicago, 1963); Karl Schriftgeisser, *The Lobbyists: The Art and Business of Influencing Lawmakers* (Boston, 1951); Wilson, *Interest Groups in the United States*; Philip R. Burch, Jr., "The NAM as An Interest Group," *Politics and Society* (Fall 1973): 97–130. Collins, *The Business Response to Keynes*; and McQuaid, *Big Business and Presidential Power*, report on archival and journalistic data regarding the CED and the BC. For updates on the story in the wake of the corporate reorganizations of the 1970s, see Paul J. Quirk, *Industry Influence in Federal Regulatory Agencies* (Princeton, 1981); and Evan Thomas, *The Man to See: Edward Bennett Williams, Ultimate Insider, Legendary Trial Lawyer* (New York, 1991).

For the Goldwater saga, see Theodore H. White, *The Making of the President, 1964* (New York, 1965); and especially Barry M. Goldwater, with Jack Casserly, *Goldwater* (Garden City, N.Y., 1988). For the war on poverty and war on the home front, William L. O'Neill, *Coming Apart: An Informal History of America in the*

1960s (New York, 1971); and Allen J. Matusow, *The Unravelling of America: A History of Liberalism in the 1960s* (New York, 1984), set the scene. Norman Macrae, *The Neurotic Trillionaire* (New York, 1970), is a judicious British view. Daniel P. Moynihan, *Maximum Feasible Misunderstanding* (New York, 1970), chronicles the community action programs. Nicholas Lemann's two-part essay, "The Unfinished War," *Atlantic Monthly*, December 1988 and January 1989, is a worthy early effort focusing on the shift from a jobs to an income-support strategy.

For other important parts of the broad picture, see Marshall Kaplan and Peggy Cucuti, eds., *The Great Society and Its Legacy: Twenty-five Years of U.S. Social Policy* (Durham, N.C., 1986); Henry J. Aaron, *Politics and the Professors: The Great Society in Perspective* (Washington, D.C., 1978); Jeffrey L. Pressman and Aaron Wildavsky, *Implementation: How Great Expectations in Washington Are Dashed in Oakland* (Berkeley, 1973); Martha Derthick, *Uncontrollable Spending for Social Services Grants* (Washington, D.C., 1975); Sar A. Levitan and Robert Taggart, *The Promise of Greatness* (Cambridge, 1976); John E. Schwarz, *America's Hidden Success: A Reassessment of Public Policy from Kennedy to Reagan*, rev. ed. (New York, 1988); and Margaret Weir, Ann Shola Orloff, and Theda Skocpol, eds., *The Politics of Social Policy in the United States* (Princeton, 1988).

Murray L. Weidenbaum, *Business, Government, and the Public*, 2d ed. (Englewood Cliffs, N.J., 1981); and Vogel, *Fluctuating Fortunes*, are very good for the corporate impacts of the new social regulations. James Q. Wilson, *The Politics of Regulation* (New York, 1980), is an outstanding effort to put corporate weakness at fighting off such regulation in economic and political perspective. Edwin M. Epstein, *The Corporation in American Politics* (Englewood Cliffs, N.J., 1969); and Daniel Patrick Moynihan, *The Politics of a Guaranteed Income: The Nixon Administration and the Family Assistance Plan* (New York, 1973), provide anecdotal evidence of business-government policy relations. Judith Fox, "Corporate Liberalism and the Concept of Public-Private Partnership in 20th Century Social and Economic Policy," honors thesis, Radcliffe College, 1981, is also a very worthy effort indeed.

Various CED publications, including its *The National Economy and the Vietnam War* (New York, 1968), also demonstrate how corporate political activists were alienated by the guns and butter approach by the time LBJ announced his retirement from presidential politics. Graham Wilson, *The Politics of Safety and Health* (Oxford, U.K., 1985); Mark V. Nadel, *The Politics of Consumer Protection* (Indianapolis, 1971); Charles Noble, *Liberalism at Work: The Rise and Fall of O.S.H.A.* (Philadelphia, 1986); Peter P. Pashigan, *The Political Economy of the Clean Air Act: Regional Self-Interest in Environmental Legislation* (St. Louis, 1982); Martha Derthick and Paul J. Quirk, *The Politics of Deregulation* (Washington, D.C., 1983); Steve Coll, *The Deal of the Century: The Breakup of AT&T* (New York, 1986); and Karen Orren, *Corporate Power and Social Change: The Politics of the Life Insurance Industry* (Baltimore, 1974), treat the post-1965 aspects of the regulatory offensives and business counteroffenses.

Johnson's growing troubles with business activists are detailed in Theodore J.

Levitt's two articles, "The Johnson Treatment," *Harvard Business Review* 45 (January–February 1967); and "Why Business Always Loses," *Harvard Business Review* 46 (March–April, 1968). Leonard Silk, *Nixonomics: How the Dismal Science of Free Enterprise Became the Black Art of Controls* (New York, 1972); Arnold R. Weber, *In Pursuit of Price Stability: The Wage-Price Freeze of 1971* (Washington, D.C., 1973); and Edward R. Tufte, *Political Control of the Economy* (Princeton, 1978), elaborate on how Nixon and the sometimes reluctant leadership of the Democratic Congress tried to buy their corporate credibility back. Two of the better known surveys of Watergate, Stanley I. Kutler, *The Wars of Watergate* (New York, 1990); and Kim McQuaid, *The Anxious Years: America in the Vietnam-Watergate Era* (New York, 1989), do not deal with the political protection racket the Nixon White House ran with major American corporations. Jonathan Schell, *The Time of Illusion* (New York, 1975), is a fine source. A nice monograph by one disapproving corporate participant is Thomas Burns, *Tales of I.T.T.: An Insider's Report* (Boston, 1974). For the defense of Nixon's commerce secretary and major business fundraiser, see Maurice H. Stans, *The Terrors of Justice: The Untold Story of Watergate* (New York, 1978).

For the effects of the energy crisis, see the texts cited in the bibliography to chapter 3; for the Humphrey-Hawkins full-employment initiative, see Mucciaroni, *The Political Failure of Employment Policy*; and Weir, *Politics and Jobs*. Business concern with the directions of American politics by the early 1970s is best detailed in Leonard Silk and David Vogel, *Ethics and Profits, The Crisis of Confidence in American Business* (New York, 1976). Sections of Jules Cohn, *The Conscience of the Corporations: Business and Urban Affairs, 1967–1970* (Baltimore, 1971); Irving S. Shapiro and Carl B. Kaufmann, *America's Third Revolution: Public Interest and the Private Role* (New York, 1984); Isadore Barmash, *The Chief Executives* (Philadelphia, 1978); Thornton Bradshaw and David Vogel, eds., *Corporations and Their Critics* (New York, 1981); Raymond Vernon, *Storm over the Multinationals* (Cambridge, 1977); and Ralph Nader and William Taylor, *The Big Boys: Power and Position in American Business* (New York, 1986), are also useful. The Silk and Vogel data were gathered from anonymous sources, but the Shapiro, Barmash, and Nader and Taylor volumes all detail the views of BC and Business Roundtable activists.

For the formation of the Business Roundtable itself, see journalistic treatments, including Barry M. Hager, "Business Roundtable: New Lobbying Force," *Congressional Quarterly*, September 17, 1977; and James W. Singer, "Business and Government: A New Quasi-Public Role," *National Journal*, April 15, 1978. Sustained treatments include Kim McQuaid, "The Roundtable: Getting Results in Washington," *Harvard Business Review* 59 (May–June 1981): 114–23; and McQuaid, "Big Business and Public Policy in Post–New Deal America: From Depression to Détente," *Antitrust Law and Economics Review* 11 (1979): 41–72.

James Reston, Jr., *The Lone Star: The Life of John Connally* (New York, 1989), illustrates why Connally was so popular with major businessmen. Robert L.

Hartmann, *Palace Politics: An Inside Account of the Ford Years* (New York, 1980), is good on the hapless political condition of Nixon's successor. John W. Sloan, "The Ford Presidency: A Conservative Approach to Economic Management," *Presidential Studies Quarterly* 14 (Fall 1984): 526–47; and Stein, *Presidential Economics*, detail Ford's efforts to lead on, regardless.

8 CORPORATE RESURGENCE FROM CARTER TO REAGAN

E. J. Dionne, Jr., *Why Americans Hate Politics* (New York, 1991), is a no-nonsense survey of the Carter and Reagan political era that gets beyond the usual rationalizations. Carter details his own policy troubles in his *Keeping Faith: Memoirs of a President* (New York, 1982). Betty Glad, *Jimmy Carter: In Search of the Great White House* (New York, 1980), details his background and economic assumptions. Joseph A. Califano, Jr., *Governing America: An Insider's Report from the White House* (New York, 1981), concludes that America was ungovernable, particularly under Carter's leadership. Laurence H. Shoup, *The Carter Presidency and Beyond: Power and Politics in the 1980s* (Palo Alto, Calif., 1980), treats Carter as a far from inept creature of the establishment. Tip O'Neill, with William Novak, *Man of the House* (New York, 1987), talks about Carter's ill-starred relations with Congress but avoids elaborating on the House's own internal incoherence under O'Neill's leadership.

Leroy N. Reisenbach, *Congressional Reform* (Washington, D.C., 1986); and Walter J. Oleszek, *Congressional Procedures and the Policy Process*, 3d ed. (Washington, D.C., 1989), provide convenient summaries of the post-Vietnam and post-Watergate changes in the ways Congress is organized and operates and how legislative visibility can aid lobbyists. Bernard Asbell, *The Senate Nobody Knows* (Garden City, N.Y., 1978); Elizabeth Drew, *Senator* (New York, 1979); Donald Riegle, *O Congress* (Garden City, N.Y., 1972); Eric Redman, *The Dance of Legislation* (New York, 1973); Robert Cwiklik, *House Rules* (New York, 1991); Michael J. Malbin, *Unelected Representatives: Congressional Staff and the Future of Representative Government* (New York, 1980); Harrison W. Fox, Jr., and Susan Webb Hammond, *Congressional Staffs: The Invisible Force in American Lawmaking* (New York, 1977); and Morris P. Fiorina, *Congress: Keystone of the Washington Establishment* (New Haven, 1977), are lively and informative regarding the powershift from the executive to the legislative branch.

Hedrick Smith, *The Power Game: How Washington Works* (New York, 1988), is the best written and most informative single overview of recent political changes in America that exists. John M. Barry, *The Ambition and the Power* (New York, 1989), chronicles the fall of Tip O'Neill's successor, Jim Wright, and analyzes the ethical, legal, and power considerations that have balkanized Congress in recent years. Brooks Jackson, *Honest Graft: Big Money and the American Political Process* (New York, 1988; Washington, D.C., 1990), fleshes out Smith's and Barry's accounts and helps put Carter's congressional failures in perspective.

Theodore J. Eismeier and Philip H. Pollock, *Business, Money, and the Rise of Corporate PACs in American Politics* (New York, 1988), is the best single source on recent patterns and strategies of corporate campaign cash. See also Thomas Byrne Edsall, *Power and Money: Writings About Politics, 1971–1987* (New York, 1988); Elizabeth Drew, *Politics and Money* (New York, 1983); George Thayer, *Who Shakes the Money Tree? American Campaign Practices from 1789 to the Present* (New York, 1973); Ann B. Matasar, *Corporate PACs and Federal Campaign Financing Laws: Use or Abuse of Power?* (New York, 1986); Edward Handler and John L. Mulkern, *Business in Politics: Campaign Strategies of Corporate Political Action Committees* (Lexington, Mass., 1982); Michael J. Malbin, ed., *Money and Politics in the United States* (Chatham, N.J., 1984); Michael J. Malbin, ed., *Parties, Interest Groups, and Campaign Finance Laws* (Washington, D.C., 1980); and Larry J. Sabato, *PAC Power: Inside the World of Political Action Committees* (New York, 1984).

Business money and corporate PACs have been a major focus—in fact, the major focus—for political science research in business-government relations for over a decade—in large part because the federal campaign financing laws of the 1970s provide data about dollars and organizations. This is unfortunate, for corporate coalitions matter more than cash does—cash contributions can often cancel each other out, while broad coalitions reinforce the power of specific corporations or industries. Coalitions, including panindustrial lobbies like the Business Roundtable, are therefore largely unreported by academics. For two valuable exceptions to this rule, see Sar A. Levitan and Martha R. Cooper, *Business Lobbies: The Public Good and the Bottom Line* (Baltimore, 1984); and Mark Green and Andrew Buchsbaum, *The Corporate Lobbies: Political Profiles of the Business Roundtable and the Chamber of Commerce* (Washington, D.C., 1980), which treat the corporate counterattack against panindustrial regulations that began in the late 1970s.

The big business victories of the Carter era and beyond would have been impossible without broader unrest about stagflation and taxation. For stagflation and its many effects, see Alan S. Blinder, *Economic Policy and the Great Stagflation* (New York, 1979); Irving S. Friedman, *Inflation: A World-Wide Disaster,* new ed. (Boston, 1980); Anthony S. Campagna, *U.S. National Economic Policy, 1917–1985* (New York, 1987); Martin Mayer, *The Fate of the Dollar* (New York, 1980); David P. Calleo, *The Imperious Economy* (Cambridge, 1982); George P. Shultz and Kenneth W. Dam, *Economic Policy Behind the Headlines* (New York, 1977); Darrell Delamaide, *Debt Shock: The Full Story of the World Credit Crisis* (Garden City, N.Y., 1984); and William R. Neikirk, *Volcker: Portrait of the Money Man* (New York, 1987).

J. Patrick Wright, *On a Clear Day You Can See General Motors* (Grosse Pointe, Mich., 1979); and Robert B. Reich and John D. Donahue, *The Chrysler Revival and the American System* (New York, 1985), are good on the shock waves sent out to the automobile industry. Hoerr, *And the Wolf Finally Came,* covers steel. Robert Kuttner, *Revolt of the Haves: Tax Rebellions and Hard Times* (New York, 1980), presciently analyzes the post-1978 tax revolts. Kuttner is also a source for the fate of Carter's tax bill; as is Witte, *Politics and Development of the Federal Income Tax*. Thomas A. Kochan, Harry C. Katz, and Robert B. McKersie, *The Transformation of American Industrial Relations* (New York, 1986), details the worsening state of the unions; as does Michael Goldfield, *The Decline of Organized Labor in the United States* (Chicago, 1987). The political shifts caused by stagflation and more assertive conservative (and corporate) lobbying are summarized in Peter Steinfels, *The Neo-Conservatives: The Men Who Are Changing America's Politics* (New York, 1979); and Randall Rothenberg, *The Neo-Liberals: Creating the New American Politics* (New York, 1984).

9 THE REAGAN REVOLUTION AND AFTERWARD

The short unhappy life of the "megaboom" created by the 1981 tax cuts is covered in David A. Stockman, *The Triumph of Politics* (New York, 1986); William Greider, *The Education of David Stockman and Other Americans* (New York, 1982); Donald T. Regan, *For the Record: From Wall Street to Washington* (San Diego, 1988); and John L. Palmer and Isabel V. Sawhill, eds., *The Reagan Record* (Cambridge, 1984). The business press, particularly the *Wall Street Journal*, *Fortune*, *Business Week*, and *Dun's Business Monthly*, are essential for the tax cut lobbying activities between 1979 and 1981 of individual industries and of corporate coalitions like the Carlton Group. The best portrait of corporate lobbyist Charls Walker is Elizabeth Drew's "Charlie." It is reprinted in Allan J. Cigler and Burdett A. Loomis, eds., *Interest Group Politics* (Washington, D.C., 1983).

Jeffrey H. Birnbaum and Alan S. Murray, *Showdown at Gucci Gulch: Lawmakers, Lobbyists, and the Unlikely Triumph of Tax Reform* (New York, 1987), shows how corporate coalitions quickly splintered once New Right economic revolution failed. It should be read in conjunction with the more detailed study, Timothy J. Conlan, Margaret T. Wrightson, and David R. Beam, *Taxing Choices: The Politics of Tax Reform* (Washington, D.C., 1990). Kevin B. Phillips, *Staying on Top: The Business Case for a National Industrial Policy* (New York, 1984); and Phillips, *The Politics of Rich and Poor: Wealth and the American Electorate in the Reagan Aftermath* (New York, 1990), illustrate some conservatives' concerns that slow growth and economic polarization was politically dangerous.

Lou Cannon, *Reagan* (New York, 1982); and Cannon, *President Reagan: The Role of a Lifetime* (New York, 1991), demonstrate the consistency of Reagan's small business orientation. Reston, *John Connally* (1989), discusses how unpopular Reagan was among larger corporate CEOs in the 1980 election, compared with Connally and, later, George Bush. Samuel P. Hays, *Beauty, Health, and Permanence: Environmental Politics in the United States, 1955–1985* (New York, 1987), treats the hard right deregulatory failures early in Reagan's first term. Two surveys very relevant to Reagan era regulatory policy are Michael E. Reagan, *Regulation: the Politics of Policy* (Boston, 1987); and Gary C. Bryner, *Bureaucratic Discretion: Law and Policy in Federal Regulatory Agencies* (New York, 1987).

Martin Mayer, *The Greatest-Ever Bank Robbery: The Collapse of the Savings and*

Loan Industry (New York, 1990); James Ring Adams, *The Big Fix: Inside the S&L Scandal* (New York, 1989); Steven Pizzo, Mary Fricker, and Paul Muolo, *Inside Job* (New York, 1989); James Pierce, *The Future of Banking* (New Haven, 1991); and Lowell Bryan, *Bankrupt* (New York, 1981), cover the expensive excesses of financial deregulation. Ron Chernow, *The House of Morgan: An American Banking Dynasty and the Rise of Modern Finance* (New York, 1990); Chris Welles, *The Last Days of the Club* (New York, 1975); Connie Bruck, *The Predator's Ball: The Junk Bond Raiders and the Man Who Staked Them* (New York, 1988); and Ken Auletta, *Greed and Glory on Wall Street: The Fall of the House of Lehman* (New York, 1986), survey the takeover binge of the late 1970s and beyond.

A new book published after this volume was completed is George Anders, *Merchants of Debt* (New York, 1992). Anders covers the leveraged buyout firm of Kohlberg, Kravis, and Roberts with a sadly relevant amount of bile. Jack W. Germond and Jules Witcover, *Blue Smoke and Mirrors* (New York, 1981); Germond and Witcover, *Wake Us When It's Over* (New York, 1985); and Germond and Witcover, *Whose Broad Stripes and Bright Stars?* (New York, 1989), are good for the technocratic approach to politics that allows inconvenient issues like the S&L scandals to be avoided, on the thoroughly bipartisan assumption that the vast majority of voting age adults are too stupid to understand them anyway. Germond and Witcover, be it noted, do not discuss them either.

POSTSCRIPT: NEW YEAR'S DAY 1992

Convenient sources for the sorts of symbiotic corporate-government arrangements common in the United States and other developed industrial nations include Sylvia Ostry, *Governments and Corporations in a Shrinking World: Trade and Innovation Politics in the United States, Europe, and Japan* (New York, 1990); Robert Kuttner, *The End of Laissez Faire: National Purpose and the Global Economy After the Cold War* (New York, 1991); Donald F. Kettl, *Government by Proxy: (Mis?)Managing Federal Programs* (Washington, D.C., 1988); Ira C. Magaziner and Robert B. Reich, *Minding America's Business: The Decline and Rise of the American Economy* (New York, 1983); George C. Lodge, *Perestroika for America: Restructuring Business-Government Relations for World Competitiveness* (Boston, 1990); Peter Navarro, *The Policy Game: How Special Interests and Ideologues Are Stealing America* (Lexington, Mass., 1984); Robert A. Pastor, *Congress and the Politics of U.S. Foreign Economic Policy, 1929–1976* (Berkeley, 1982); and William L. Long, *U.S. Export Control Policy: Executive Autonomy Versus Congressional Reform* (New York, 1989). The story of the Partnership for America's Cup Technology (PACT) comes from *Yachting* magazine, June 1991.

INDEX

Acheson, Dean, 38, 42–44, 69, 107
AEC (Atomic Energy Commission), 77
Affirmative action, 180
AFL. *See* American Federation of Labor
AFL-CIO, 98–100
Agnew, Spiro, 142
Air traffic controller strike, 182–83
ALCOA (Aluminum Corporation of America), 14
Allis Chalmers, 108–9
Altmeyer, Arthur, 89
Aluminum Corporation of America (ALCOA), 14
American Council for Capital Formation, 157, 167
American Federation of Labor (AFL), 4–5, 18, 22; communism and, 33, 67; merger with CIO, 98; origins, 4; Taft-Hartley Act and, 30, 32–33
American Petroleum Institute (API), 126
Anderson, Martin, 166, 171
Anderson, Robert, 106
API (American Petroleum Institute), 126
Arabian-American Oil Company (ARAMCO), 50–51, 53, 55–56, 147; Saudi-Arabian ownership of, 57
Atomic Energy Commission (AEC), 77
Automation, 96–97

Balance of trade, oil, 48–49, 53–54, 147
BC. *See* Business Council
BCTR (Business Committee for Tax Reduction), 122–23
Benton, William, 70
Berle, Adolf, 103
Bicks, Robert, 109
Blough, Roger, 109–10, 114–16

Boulware, Lemuel, 95–96
Braun, Wernher von, 78
Bretton Woods, 39, 47
Brownell, Herbert, 105–6, 109
Bundy, McGeorge, 110–11
Burns, Arthur, 140
Bush, George, 165, 178–79; civil rights and, 180–81; deregulation and, 179–80
Business Committee for Tax Reduction (BCTR), 122–23
Business Council (BC), 19–23, 25, 28–30; Business Roundtable and, 149; Carter wage-price controls and, 157–58; communism and, 69–71; Cordiner and, 109; Eisenhower and, 106; Federal Reserve Board and, 66; Hodges and, 108–10; Johnson and, 131; Kennedy and, 108–11; Korean War and, 59–62; Landrum-Griffin Act and, 100–101; lobbying and, 126–27; Marshall Plan and, 45–46; NAM and, 19–22, 157–58; National Labor-Management Conference and, 26, 29; Social Security and, 86; Taft-Hartley Act and, 30, 32
Business Roundtable, 154–55, 167, 174; BC and, 149; Carter wage-price controls and, 157–58; CED and, 149–50; civil rights and, 180–81; NAM and, 157–58; NLRB and, 155; Reagan and, 168; USCC and, 157–58

CAP (Community Action Program), 132–33
Carson, Rachel, 135
Carter, Jimmy: attitude toward big business, 151–52; CPA and, 154; deregulation and, 152–53; NLRB and, 155; oil

Library of Congress Cataloging-in-Publication Data

McQuaid, Kim.
   Uneasy partners : big business in American politics, 1945–1990 / Kim McQuaid.
       p.   cm. — (The American moment)
   Includes bibliographical references and index.
   ISBN 0-8018-4651-X (acid-free paper). — ISBN 0-8018-4652-8 (pbk. : acid-free paper)
   1. Industry and state—United States—History—20th century.   2. Business and politics—United States—History—20th century.   3. International economic relations—History—20th century.   I. Title.   II. Series.
HD3616.U46M383   1994
322'.3'0973—dc20   93-17520